STUDIES IN MEDIAEVAL HISTORY

Edited by GEOFFREY BARRACLOUGH

VOL. X

THE ROYAL POLICY OF RICHARD II:

ABSOLUTISM IN THE LATER MIDDLE AGES

THE ROYAL POLICY
OF RICHARD II:
ABSOLUTISM
IN THE
LATER MIDDLE AGES

RICHARD H. JONES

*Richard F. Scholz Professor of History,
Reed College, Portland, Oregon*

OXFORD
BASIL BLACKWELL
MCMLXVIII

631 10470 4

PRINTED IN GREAT BRITAIN
BY A. T. BROOME AND SON, 18 ST. CLEMENT'S, OXFORD
AND BOUND BY THE KEMP HALL BINDERY, OXFORD

FOREWORD

This study is an attempt to explain Richard II in terms that would have been meaningful to his contemporaries and remain significant to modern students. His reign has been known as a decisive point in the growth of the special powers of the commons and as a period of innovation in legal institutions. It was in fact both; my own attention was drawn to it thirty years ago because of its importance to parliamentary and legal history. But Richard's subjects and their descendants for several generations would hardly have thought in those terms at all. They were likely to be concerned primarily with the virtue or the wickedness of men who determined the shape of affairs; when they looked beyond the surface of dramatic political controversy they might discern an impersonal substantive conflict between the crown and the other powers of the realm. Bound up in the struggle were the competing claims of abundant governance and order as against rights and franchises, and the competing fears of despotism as against civil disorder. These concepts were endowed with specific relevance for everyone in the fourteenth and fifteenth centuries who participated in the conduct of the business of the realm or its lesser communities. None of them could have comprehended what later historians have meant by a parliamentary constitution. I have tried to show that Richard II and those who surrounded him were acutely aware of the problems which beset monarchy in his day even though they had little insight into their complex causes. Their programme, therefore, was designed to check the decline of prerogative power. Their failure and the reasons for it are more crucial to the later development of the English constitution than the spectacular precedents recited in the records of parliament in 1386, 1388 and 1399.

My principal obligations are three: to the many scholars who have enriched the study of the English fourteenth century and to whom I trust my debt will be obvious though I have not acknowledged it page by page; to a generation of students in my classes at Reed College who have often continued to discuss the problems of English history with me long after graduation and among whom I am particularly grateful to Professor Wallace MacCaffrey of Haverford College and Professor Thayron Sandquist of the University of Toronto for probing attention to the thesis of this book; and above all to Geoffrey Barraclough for helpful criticisms and suggestions which encouraged a substantial revision of the entire manuscript.

I have received much other help. My colleague Marvin Levich of the Reed philosophy department reviewed with me the problems of intellectual history relevant to the three final chapters and cited useful bibliography. Elizabeth Kimball was generous with her specific knowledge of the administration of justice in the late Middle Ages. Jane Ruby made available to me her unpublished research on Giles of Rome. The late Ernst Kantorowicz on more than one occasion took time to discuss at length his views on ritual and symbolic art as related to Richard II. Grants from the American Philosophical Society and the American Council of Learned Societies have been crucial to keeping my research active at various times. Librarians in many places have extended courtesy and assistance.

Reed College, 1966

TABLE OF CONTENTS

PAGE

Foreword v

Abbreviations... viii

CHAPTER

I Introduction 1

II The Formative Years 9

III The Challenge of 1386 28

IV The Failure of the Royalist Strategy 36

V The Appellant Triumph 47

VI The Prerogative Restored 64

VII Ricardian Absolutism 88

VIII The King Unkinged 100

IX Richard II and the Historians 113

X The Architects and Servants of Prerogative Absolutism 125

XI Absolutism and the Common Good 147

XII The Figure of God's Majesty 164

XIII Conclusion 176

Appendix A 187

Appendix B 191

ABBREVIATIONS

A.H.R.	*American Historical Review*
Ann. Ric.	*Annales Ricardi Secundi* (Ed. H. T. Riley, R.S., 1866)
B.I.H.R.	*Bulletin of the Institute of Historical Research*
Bull. J.R.Lib.	*Bulletin of the John Rylands Library*
Cal. Fine Rolls	*Calendar of Fine Rolls*
C.C.R.	*Calendar of Close Rolls*
C.Ch.R.	*Calendar of Charter Rolls*
C.P.R.	*Calendar of Patent Rolls*
Cont. Eul. Hist.	*Eulogium Historiarum* (Ed. F. S. Haydon, R.S., 1858–63)
Creton, History	Jehan Creton *Histoire du Roy d'Angleterre Richard* (Ed. J. Webb, 1819)
D.N.B.	*Dictionary of National Biography*
E.H.R.	*English Historical Review*
Econ. Hist. Rev.	*Economic History Review*
Foedera	T. Rymer, *Foedera, Etc.* (1704–35)
Froissart, Chroniques	*Chroniques* (Ed. Kervyn de Lettenhove, 1866–77)
Hardyng Chronicle	*The Chronicle of John Hardyng* (Ed. Ellis, 1812)
Hist. Ang.	*Historia Anglicana* (Ed. H. T. Riley, R.S., 1963–4)
J.E.H.	*Journal of Ecclesiastical History*
L.Q.R.	*Law Quarterly Review*
Leyces. Chron.	*Chronicon Henrici Knigton* (Ed. J. R. Lumby, R.S., 1889)
Perroy, Schisme	E. Perroy, *L'Angleterre et le grand schisme d'occident*
Rot. Parl.	*Rotuli Parliamentorum* (1767)
Statutes	*Statutes of the Realm* (1810–28)
Tout, Chapters	T. F. Tout, *Chapters in Medieval Administrative History*
T.R.H.S.	*Transactions of the Royal Historical Society*
Traison et Mort	*Chronique de la traison et mort de Richard II* (Ed. B. Williams, 1846)
Vita Ricardi	*Historia Vitae et Regni Ricardi Secundi* (Ed. T. Hearne, 1729)

CHAPTER I

INTRODUCTION

IN September of 1399 King Richard II was formally deposed. His cousin, Henry of Lancaster, had already assumed the power to rule at least two months earlier. The event was unusual, but by no means unprecedented. The forcible change of kings had much of the appearance of a palace revolution. Yet it involved a good deal more than either mere dynastic conspiracy or justifiable punishment of a wilful, temperamentally unbalanced sovereign. Although the official contemporary record suggested the contrary, it was policy, not caprice, which impelled the king along the career that led from the throne to mysterious oblivion in the dungeons of Pontefract; and in combining to destroy Richard the English community made a momentous decision concerning the nature of its relationship to the crown.

The initiative had been taken by the king. It was his behaviour which had forced the decision. The action of his opponents was always in reaction to his designs. So much and no more is clear, except in the terms of the official version of events which presents the spectacle of a king turned tyrant, a threat to the rights and liberties of all in his realm. The insufficiency of so simple an explanation, however, becomes immediately apparent if the events of the reign are examined in their European context. For in a general sense the embroilment of Richard and his powerful subjects was only an expression of the unrest and social disequilibrium common to West European kingdoms in the later fourteenth century. The relatively constant tension between monarchy and feudality, or indeed that between king and church, in an earlier period should not obscure their essential mutual interdependence, an interdependence which was no mere matter of custom, law, or attitude, but was on the contrary fundamental to the existence of any degree of order or organization in society. By 1400, for reasons which may be left to the scrutiny of historians of economic and social change, custom and reality no longer coincided. Kings were forced either to attempt to impose their will on particularist elements in despite of usage, or to witness impotently the distintegration of central authority. Of the rulers like Richard II, Pedro I of Castille, and Joao I of Portugal who determined to take action, only the Portuguese was successful. Circumstances or disposition left others like Charles VI of France helpless in the face of rampant aristocratic self-interest.

In these general terms kings and their antagonists may have been participants in struggles whose real sources they perceived very dimly if at all. But most men knew precisely why they supported or opposed the crown, and their conduct in specific circumstances, together with their actual or purported motives, profoundly affected the constitutional development of their respective kingdoms. The English dynastic revolution of 1399 must, therefore, be understood not only as one manifestation of a conflict of basic interest between late medieval monarchy and fourteenth century feudal society but also as an insular event of great significance.

Initially the relationship between the closing events of the reign of Edward III and the conflicts of Richard with his subjects must be considered. It has been customary to treat the final quarter of the century as a unified epoch in which the same basic issues produced in three successive stages a final decisive contest. The first of these stages would encompass the last parliaments of Edward's reign. The things which transpired in the highly publicized 'Good Parliament' of 1376 together with their immediate antecedents and their aftermath do shed a great deal of light upon the nature of social organization and the distribution of political responsibility in late medieval England. They also unquestionably furnished precedents which were utilized and enlarged upon in 1386–88 and again in 1397–99. There is much formal similarity among the three episodes. Each centred around attacks in parliament upon some of the most prominent person- ages of the realm. They terminated in an assault, in what must have seemed at least to be something very like a parliament, upon the most important personage himself. For the history of legal procedure a comparative chronological analysis is most fruitful. But to the constitutional historian, as to the participants in the conflicts themselves, the basic issues with which the two later crises were concerned were vastly different from those of the earlier one. It is this difference which conclusively stamps the reign of Richard II as a time of decision.

In 1376 a series of charges were brought against a group of servants of the crown. The charges dealt with specific evidences of individual dishonesty, and extended to the exercise of corrupt influence in the making of policy decisions. They were, according to contemporary accounts, initiated among the commons and laid before the lords for action. The king can hardly be said to have been concerned, except in the most indirect fashion. If the accusations were true, as some of them were satisfactorily shown to be, the aging Edward was guilty at least of gross neglect or cynical indifference to the good governance of his realm. Yet even the most partisan reporters attributed no real responsibility to him, nor was he aroused in any way to the defense of the accused who claimed to have been his friends and servants even when the name of his mistress was added to their number. If one of his sons, John of Gaunt, Duke of Lancaster, was thought by many to have been the real though unnamed object of the whole movement, the heir to the throne, quite without reason, was credited in some quarters with having been its sponsor.

Whatever their origin, the proceedings which made this parliament so noteworthy were by no means anti-royalist. They were not directed against either the king or the crown. They apparently had their source in a widespread dissatisfaction with military failures, and in a well-founded but exaggerated suspicion that corruption and incompetence were the real reasons for the financial difficulties which the government faced. There is no evidence of fear that the king and a group of courtiers were intending to establish a narrow exclusive control over government such, for example, as the Despensers had attempted under Edward II more than a half century earlier. No doubt there were many among the lords who disliked and feared John of Gaunt. Some of them very probably believed that his influence in public affairs might threaten their own private interests or limit their opportunities for self-advancement. Others, both lords and commons, may have looked upon the duke and his associates as constituting a serious menace to the welfare of the realm. The leaders of the estates in parliament had much in common. Motives among all of them were unquestionably mixed, but there is no reason to be sceptical of a sincere conviction on the part of many of the reformers that the king had been a passive victim of evil ministers. Thus instead of returning a favourable response to the royal plea for funds, the commons after extensive deliberation requested the collaboration of the lords in the punishment of those who had taken criminal advantage of the king's inertia. The joint action of the session culminated in the erection of a mechanism designed to prevent similar mishaps in the immediate future. Nothing more was intended than reform in its most narrow sense; that is, that an administration should be purged of its corrupt elements and that the offenders should be brought to book. It is for this reason that the proceedings, exciting and in many ways unprecedented as they were, stirred none of the ghosts which as the legacy of his father's reign had disquieted the kingdom in the years of Edward's youth.

In 1386, in 1388, and in 1399, on the other hand, those disturbing spirits were revived in all their awesomeness; for in those years the conflict was patently a struggle for power between the king and certain of his subjects. The complaint was not that monarchy was lax or indifferent, but that it was vigorously misdirected; not that it was weak, but that it threatened to become much too strong. The parliament of 1386 brought explicit attention to bear on issues which had been permitted to remain dormant for nearly sixty years. Only the most weighty reasons could have induced the aristocracy to risk the consequences of direct interference with the unquestioned agents of the crown in such a way as to invoke the precedents of the reign of Edward II. Yet that is precisely what they did, and there can be little doubt that whatever assistance they received from the commons it was a group among the magnates who supplied the initiative. As in 1376, there was collaboration between the estates. In 1386, however, the issues were incomparably more important than those of the earlier decade, and the overt leadership came from the great houses rather than from knights and career bishops.

The conflict, then, between the king and certain of his subjects which was engendered by the impeachment of the chancellor in 1386 opened a new era in the history of the English monarchy. Everyone who was in any way associated with the event was likely to have realized that the controversy was an unusually grave one, but no one, perhaps, could have guessed that a full century and a quarter would elapse before the throne would recover the stability it had enjoyed in the days of Edward III.

The explosion of 1386 was so devastating because despite their recognition of the potential consequences of action, the aristocratic leaders were willing to engineer an assault on the crown itself. Personal feeling and individual recklessness might account for the behaviour of a few, but near unanimity in so hazardous a business demanded more serious provocation. The royal policy posed a threat to baronial self-interest which made the risk worth taking.

The policy had begun with the new reign itself. In 1377, for the first time since the Conquest, a hereditary minor had succeeded to an uncontested throne. The fact symbolizes the ultimate subordination of the feudal quality of English monarchy to its dynastic aspect. There was no hint in any quarter of a proposal to invoke the old Norman and Angevin precedent of setting aside the direct heir by primogeniture in favour of an immediate member of the royal family who would be more competent at once to assume a real position of leadership. Expressions of misgiving are confined to lamentations over the unkind fortune which doomed the land to a minority at so inauspicious a time, and to warnings against the possible conspiracies of over-ambitious men placed too near to the throne.

Yet from the outset the minority was not to be a formless government. There is evidence that from the time of the coronation a consistent programme was in the process of development. Bound together by allegiance to the young king and to clear-cut theoretical principles, his intimate advisers aimed at nothing less than the establishment of a more unfettered and more powerful monarchy than England had known. Hampered by lack of authority and checked by powerful influences unsympathetic to their programme, they nonetheless pursued their objective throughout the early years of the new reign. The gravity of the crises of 1386–88 is the measure of their success. In the meantime, Richard himself was prepared, when the occasion might offer, to attempt to fulfill their most extravagant ambitions. The baronial reaction was inevitable.

The English monarchy which Edward III transmitted to his grandson was in a real sense much less powerful than it had been three quarters of a century earlier. The great offices of the realm no longer responded so readily or obediently to the king's command. Councils of every description had shown from time to time unmistakable signs of independence or of indifference to the royal will. The peers had gained in position at the expense of the crown in many ways, and they could, if they chose to do so, look back upon a series of precedents for vigorous opposition which included even the enforced abdication of a reigning king.

On the other hand, the king was by no means humbled, nor was there any sentiment that his estate should be reduced. The Avignonese captivity had irreparably undermined the strength of a powerful institutional rival. The expansion of the official bureaucracy furnished an instrumentality which might be seized upon as the agency for the achievement of royal independence. The extension of the abuse of local privilege cried out for correction. The slow but steady rise of a spirit of national consciousness contributed to the strength of any movement in behalf of centralized monarchy. The essence of a theory of regal absolutism was in the air. It lurked barely concealed in the treatises of the civil lawyers. It had been articulated bit by bit in the disputations of the papal-imperial controversy. It revealed its traces in the judgments of the English courts; and in the polemics of Wyclyf it had approached precise formulation. The tools and the ideas from which it appeared that a supreme, unchallenged power might be fashioned awaited only the organizing hand and the imaginative mind. If the appearance proved to be illusory, the existence of the chimera could not be denied.

'No sovereign,' said a modern historian, 'was ever more entirely the author of his own destruction than Richard II.'[1] In a sense, this is true, but not in that which its author intended. Richard perished, not because he wilfully refused to remain a 'constitutional' king, but because he dedicated himself persistently to a programme of reform, the ultimate aim of which was to establish a régime of royal absolutism. The distinction is far less subtle than it appears to be. As he conceived it, Richard's programme would have restored monarchy in England to its rightful

[1] C. W. C. Oman, *Political History of England* (1906), IV, p. 151.

place; it would have brought the traditional and natural tendencies of regal development to their divinely inspired maturity. This was quite another thing than headstrong tampering with an accepted constitution. He and his mentors may be accused of having misinterpreted both the history and the spirit of the preceding centuries, but in any event their emphasis was on continuity with the past. Any relaxation of royal power or any interference with the independence of the king's prerogative, in their opinion, marked a step in a novel and a false direction. Richard's reign was a tragedy, not because he was fitful and capricious, but because the problems which beset him demanded a solution of far more radical proportions than any he could visualize. What he proposed to do was to perfect the strength of medieval kingship by the employment of ideals and devices which preserved a strict inheritance from the old intellectual and social structure. In so doing, he aggravated the problems faced by a central governing authority rather than solving them. The final effect of his whole effort and the reaction to it was to deal the royal power a staggering blow from which it would not recover for a hundred years.

The Ricardian programme was intrinsically and fatally paradoxical. For all its theory of divine royalty, strained to ultimate comprehensible limits, it must still be derived from the laws of God. For all the permanence of the following by which this royal power was to be sustained, its supporters would necessarily be men who thought and acted in terms of social distinctions and basic property rights which reached back over the centuries into the past. Richard's policy, ironically enough, was so medieval that it could find no adequate solution to certain very practical late medieval problems. How could the king, for example, insist on the untouchable sanctity of his own inherent rights and not, at the same time adhere to the obligation to respect, indeed to defend, the unquestioned inherent rights of others? How could the fountainhead of justice itself flagrantly violate the most cherished and widely recognized principles of justice without undermining the very foundation upon which it presumed to stand? And how, on the other hand, could monarchy maintain any sense of security at all if, for example, a disloyal subject were permitted to amass more resources than the crown itself could command?[2]

It was this immediate issue which united Richard's powerful subjects against him. With that union he lacked the means to cope. The great dramatist's instinct was a sure one. The treatment of Henry Bolingbroke was the incident which brought the king 'down, down . . . like glist'ring Phaeton'. Yet given the nature of his overall programme such a catastrophic incident must sooner or later have occurred. Deliberate policy, let it be said again, not a whimsical act, caused the dynastic revolution of 1399. The examination of the theoretical sources, the development and the operation of that policy is among the most interesting of medieval constitutional studies. At the same time, a selective narrative analysis may serve to modify certain misconceptions about the mainsprings of political action in the late fourteenth century, and an examination of Richard's programme and the reasons for its failure should help to illuminate the constitutional history of the succeeding one hundred and fifty years.

[2] For a sixteenth century statement of this same dilemma, cf. W. Lambarde, *Archeion* (ed. McIlwain, 1957), pp. 66, 67.

Chapter II

THE FORMATIVE YEARS

THE closing fifteen years of the reign of Edward III were an unfortunate anti-climax to a career which had won the admiring envy of contemporary monarchs. What was most apparent was the loss of the prestige and possessions acquired from the French before the peace of Bretigny in 1360. The resumption of the Hundred Years' War brought only costly misfortunes. More fundamental was the gradual withdrawal of royal leadership in the affairs of the realm. Edward had been known to be almost unduly sensitive to infringements of his rights or indifference to his wishes. In the last ten years of his life it was possible not only for his sons, but even for lesser English commanders, to pursue what amounted to private diplomacy in direct opposition to his express command.[1] To domestic affairs he gave increasingly fitful and sporadic attention until by 1376 it had become evident that he had in effect ceased to rule at all. If there was any royal policy in those years it was the policy of the king's third son, John of Gaunt, Duke of Lancaster and of a group of ministers acting more or less in cooperation with him.

This was the condition which excited the protests of the Good Parliament of 1376, but it should be remembered that hostility was directed against the conduct of government, not against its structure or form. In fact, it is entirely probable that even the most virulent among the critics of the behaviour of the king's ministers would have viewed with dismay a resumption of vigorous control by the monarch himself. The earnest desire of lords and commons alike in the late fourteenth century was for a central administration which could conduct its military operations successfully and manage its affairs economically without interfering extensively in local concerns. If influence in determining the policy of the realm and in the distribution of the manifold

[1] Cf. P. E. Russell, *The English Intervention in Spain and Portugal in the Time of Edward III and Richard II* (1955), pp. 42, 46, 120–2, 125.

B

privileges which were the property of royalty were widely shared, so much the better. What the parliament of 1376 sought to remedy was neither impotence nor tyranny, but merely maladministration. There is no evidence that any of the reformers suspected that a central authority which was too weak to curb special privilege in one quarter would also be powerless to check abuse in another. A crown surrounded by disparate councils, subject to pressure, friendly to privilege, honest, parsimonious and competent; such was the ideal of the aristocrats, the knights, the clerical hierarchy and the great corporations.

It is apparent that from the very outset of the reign of Richard II an entirely alternative notion of kingship was congenial to the throne. What is not so clear is its source. It has frequently been attributed to Lancaster, on the basis of his status, his pre-eminence in the final years of the late reign and the interpretation of the hostile comments of a contemporary chronicler. These reasons are inadequate. Against them must be set his behaviour in the early years of Richard's reign, his character and interests, and his relationship with the members of the intimate court circle including the king himself.

John of Gaunt's role in the affairs of the realm from the death of his father until his departure to make good his claim to the throne of Castille in 1386 was much smaller than his birth and position would have warranted. Indeed, it might have been natural for him to have assumed the place if not the title of regent during the minority. He was not even a member of the initial council which was to act in the king's name. From what is known of his character it is much more likely that his relative public withdrawal represented acquiescence in the wishes of others rather than a statesmanlike sacrifice on his own initiative. When he had a free hand he seldom exhibited moderation where his rights, privileges or position were concerned. He insisted on the exercise to the last letter of the prerogatives of the seneschal at the coronation, though there is no evidence that he either directed the organization of the ceremony or instructed his nephew and his associates in the proper estate of kingship. If he had wished prudently to prevent his own unpopularity from casting a shadow over the new reign he would surely not have been so punctilious about his ostentatious precedence at that most impressive of public rituals. Only a few months earlier he had behaved outrageously at the trial of Wyclyf before the Bishop of London, and until the Princess of Wales intervened urging the interests of the king, he had been intransigent toward the indignant Londoners. That intervention and its effect provide a clue to Lancaster's actual relationship to the throne from Richard's accession until his death in 1399. Whatever his own interests or whatever his hostility to the inner court circle, he was always willing to accede to a plea involving the safety and welfare of the king. He was guilty on more than one occasion of the violation of explicit royal instructions, or of setting his own interests above those of the crown.[2] But because actual opposition to the throne was alien alike to his nature and his sense of propriety he made submissions which must have been galling to his great pride when Richard in person requested him to do so.

Prior to 1386, then, Lancaster frequently served his nephew's government, more often than not in diplomatic or military missions where his prestige was a valuable asset. Some of his assignments were in conflict with his personal interests and preferences. But he always fulfilled them, often it may be suspected perfunctorily rather than enthusiastically. As the years passed he watched the steady growth of the influence at court of men who were either his personal enemies or the opponents of his ambitions and his clients. From time to time he quarrelled with them and even with the king. But the most odious and unfounded of allegations could not destroy his loyalty. In the meantime he persevered in the face of seemingly inevitable frustration in the pursuit of the dynastic hopes in Spain to which he continually attempted after 1382 to divert the resources of the English crown. Nothing betrays more clearly his lack of ascendancy at his nephew's court than his failure to control, and in crucial matters even substantially to affect, its foreign policy in these years. It might be concluded that Lancaster has been designated as the author of the official expressions of ultra-royalism which were a feature of the early years of Richard's reign, rather because of the sense that he ought to have been than because of any evidence that he was.[3]

[2] Cf. Russell, *op. cit.*, Ch. XIX, for a most conspicuous case of default on commitments.
[3] See Appendix A.

A more probable source is not difficult to find in the household of the late Prince of Wales. Richard's mother lacked the experience and the disposition to have been named as regent even if political conditions in that time would have permitted a regency. Of the adherents and associates of her husband who who stood loyally by her, none was qualified to hold the chief position in a minority government. Though some of them were to be placed on councils and commissions most were too obscure to be eligible even to such offices. But they could fill inferior posts in the bureaucracy as well as in the household.

Like Lancaster, the Prince had entertained grandiose visions of his role in the affairs of western Europe and of the Iberian peninsula in particular. Unlike Lancaster, he was a great military hero who had been the leader of the outstanding English captains of the generation. Much of his life had been spent overseas where he was in constant contact with the aristocracy and the royal families of France, Castille and Aragon. There pomp and display were the order of the day. His views on the nature of kingship may only be surmised, but in any event his followers were in a position to be acquainted with the most extravagant claims which were made on the continent. Their influence with the princess was paramount, and it was to them that the tutelage of the young king was entrusted.

The major share of this responsibility was delegated to Guichard d'Angle and Sir Simon Burley. Guichard d'Angle was a Gascon nobleman and experienced soldier, who had long been a close associate of the Prince of Wales, and for whose services to father and son the earldom of Huntingdon was not considered to be too distinguished a reward. He was perhaps too old to be particularly active but his sentiments were in all probability those of his colleague. Of Simon Burley much more is known. Like d'Angle he was a seasoned warrior who enjoyed the respect of most of his contemporaries. He was also a man of taste and refinement to whom the theory and practice of kingship were serious affairs. Richard, throughout his life, reserved for him an affection which in its warmth far surpassed his feelings even for the close members of his own family. The organization and direction of the courtier following in these formative years was in all probability largely his undertaking. He was to figure prominently in the arrangements which brought Anne of Bohemia to England as Richard's queen, and from that time forward he enjoyed her unstinted respect and confidence. As sub-chamberlain he held an office of great administrative importance. His was likely to have been the influence which filled the other household posts with men who, like himself, were either former servants of the Prince of Wales, or were known to be devoted to the crown. His kinsman and follower, Baldwin Raddington, was controller of the king's wardrobe. Until 1388 the two great household offices were, therefore, under his close supervision.[4]

In seeking associates among the great nobility it was natural that a man of Burley's position should have turned to younger members of the great houses who could be companions of the boy king.[5] Of these, the most notable were the Mowbrays, John and Thomas, who were successively Earl of Nottingham; the heir to the Earl of Stafford; and above all others, Robert de Vere, Earl of Oxford. Richard's attachment to them, and to de Vere in particular was not a mere matter of politic interest. Oxford was loaded with honors by his adoring master, whose careless generosity only served to arouse widespread resentment of the favourite. As events proved, he was at best not a strong ally, and in the long run the king's inordinate partiality for him alienated others such as Thomas Mowbray upon whom in time of crisis he should have been able to depend. For the time being, however, the hereditary possession of the chamberlainship in the house of de Vere was extremely useful to Burley and his friends.

Either from the outset of the reign or early in the formative years, the royalist clique found other allies among the aristocracy who were men of greater maturity. The most conspicuous were the Earls of Salisbury and Stafford, the king's half-brothers, the Hollands, and Sir Michael de la Pole, who was to become Earl of Suffolk. Neither Salisbury nor Stafford was so active politically as were other courtier partisans. The temperament of the Hollands made their alliance sometimes of dubious value. But de la Pole was to play a constructive part both in the building up of a following and in the formulation of policy,

[4] N. B. Lewis, 'Simon Burley and Baldwin Raddington,' *E.H.R.*, LII (1937), pp. 662–69.
[5] *Polychronicon*, IX, p. 145.

which was secondary to that of Burley alone. Like Burley and Salisbury, he had once been a comrade in arms of the Prince of Wales. Other members of aristocratic families who were close to the court were John de Montagu, Aubrey de Vere, and Sir Richard Stafford. The circle also included such career clerics as John Fordham, William Pakington, Reginald Hilton and Robert Braybrook.[6]

As has been said, the views of the group are evident in certain official pronouncements from the very day of Richard's accession. The most impressive occasions upon which an exaggerated reverence for royalty could be enunciated were, of course, the ceremonies of the coronation and the opening of the king's first parliament.

The coronation was delayed to permit a decent interval for grief over the death of Edward III. A full half-century had elapsed since the community had been privileged to witness such a ritual. Attention has already been called to the evidence of the decline in the predominantly feudal character of the monarchy which was to be found in the untroubled succession. That fact is certainly not without importance, but even more portentous were the substantial revisions of the coronation procedure designed specifically for this occasion.

The bulk of the changes listed in the document which summarized the ceremonies were purely formal; yet their sum denotes an alteration in the relative position of king and subjects. In response to the questions of the Archbishop of Canterbury, Richard swore on the cross to confirm the laws and customs of the people, to protect Holy Church, and to maintain peace and justice throughout the realm. This was essentially the old three-fold coronation oath with certain modifications. Especially noteworthy were the pains taken to remove any doubt that the laws which the king swore to confirm were those which had been established in the reign of Edward the Confessor, not those which had been ordained by the legislation of Edward I. In 1308, too, on the occasion of the coronation of Edward II a fourth promise had been exacted, whereby the king swore to uphold whatever laws the people might elect for the glory of God. For these

[6] T. F. Tout, *Chapters in Medieval Administrative History*, (1928) III, pp. 327–32; IV, pp. 189–205; V, p. 45, and infra Ch. X.

phrases there was substituted in the coronation oath of 1377 an ambiguous reference to the laws of the church. It is plain that Richard II's advisers desired, insofar as it might be possible to do so, to suppress any anti-royalist tendencies of the oaths of 1307 and 1327. The fourth clause, modified in the official record, may even have been omitted entirely at the ceremony, since an otherwise reliable informant mentions only three promises. Then turning to the four corners of the 'theatre', the archbishop 'demanded of all the commons if they would have the prince Richard for their king and obey him as their lay lord. And they in a loud cry responded, "Yea, we will have him".' The most significant changes in the pageant were the absence of the forms of secular election prior to the procession to the cathedral, a probable alteration of the wording of the oath itself, and the emphasis on obedience to the king as lay lord.[7]

It would hardly have been possible for contemporaries to draw from the record of this ceremony the inference that the king owed his right to the throne to the 'election' or approbation of the people following the oath. It was on the contrary easy for the archbishop who administered the oath and for many of the witnesses to assume that the monarch had reached his estate through indefeasible hereditary right alone, the act of acceptance by the populace being taken to be nothing more than proper recognition of the privilege of blood. This portion of the ceremony, therefore, would merely have been a symbolic survival of an ancient right. The opinion of the primate was shared by the advisers and the family of the king.

It was the archbishop also, rather than the chancellor, who delivered the opening speech to Richard's first parliament. This was less a plea than an exposition of a point of view. It was featured by an explicit statement on the source of royal power which might easily be interpreted as establishing a basis for an untrammelled authority. Inheritance, rather than election or any other artificial procedure, was reaffirmed as the sole source of

[7] *Anonimalle Chronicle*, ed. Galbraith (1927), pp. 108–14, 186, 187. I have relied for the above discussion upon the research of Dr. Thayron Sandquist. The standard authority on the subject is P. E. Schramm, *A History of the English Coronation* (1937). The coronation of Edward II has a considerable literature of its own. Dr. Sandquist's researches are to be published shortly.

regality, and the subjects were exhorted humbly to obey the king whom God had graciously set above them.[8]

Simon of Sudbury, the archbishop, is unlikely to have been the sole innovator of so daring a doctrine. Constantly the object of criticism, both in his own lifetime and later, for his lenient treatment of heretics, his virtues were those of unselfishness, scholarship and humane devotion to duty rather than originality or militant leadership. A man of humble origin and refined artistic tastes, he appears in the records always as one who respected authority and abhorred violence. The unswerving allegiance which in the year of the Great Revolt could prompt him cheerfully to sacrifice his life in the cause of the monarchy would have been little strained by the acceptance and promulgation of a theory of absolute right dear to the hearts of those who guided the young king.[9] There was nothing haphazard about either the modifications of the whole ritual of the coronation or the archbishop's choice of a text for his parliamentary welcome. Both were well prepared in advance. The popularity of the princess and the general fear of other influences would have made it an easy matter for a determined group of men, though they were relatively insignificant as individuals, to exploit her prestige for the purpose of publicizing their high royalist notions. No other likely identification of the guiding hand in these affairs can be ascertained.

Apprehension among the commons concerning other influences was reflected in a series of petitions which have often been misinterpreted as an assault on the power of the crown. They were on the contrary, perhaps quite unnecessarily, directed against the prospect of an abuse of the minority by Lancaster and his associates. Their spirit is identical with that of the Good Parliament of 1376. The speaker requested as the express will of all the commons assembled that it might please the king and lords to ordain in parliament a commission of eight who would consult constantly with the king's officials in council on the needs of the

[8] *Rot. Parl.*, III, p. 3.
[9] For contemporary hostility, *Hist. Ang.*, II, pp. 11–12. His conduct in 1381 is interpreted by B. Wilkinson, 'The Peasant Revolt of 1381,' *Speculum*, XV (1940), pp. 12–35. A recent appraisal by W. L. Warren emphasizes his firmness, his tact and his devotion to order, as well as service to the crown. 'A Reappraisal of Simon Sudbury, bishop of London (1361–75) and Archbishop of Canterbury (1375–81)'. *J. E. H.* X (1959), pp. 139–52.

realm; that likewise, the king and lords would appoint in parliament those who were to surround the person of the royal minor until he became of age, a petition which was coupled with the request that the ordinary revenues of the kingdom should be carefully supervised and that extraordinary grants should be expended only for war and not diverted to any other purpose; and, finally, that all old laws, customs as well as statutes, should be confirmed and that whatever was ordained in this parliament should not be repealed except in parliament. The words and the setting suggest that the petitioners were fearful of a return to the state of affairs which had provoked the parliamentary outburst in 1376. When the king became of age there would be no place for such unusual devices. It is manifest that they were expected to be terminated upon his attainment of majority. The fact that this commission and those which succeeded it were shortly to be utilized as precedents for anti-royalist action should not encourage transplanting back to 1377 a set of motives which grew out of the events of 1386 and 1388. Richard had not yet posed a threat to the self-interest of the magnates and the knights. The propaganda campaign against Lancaster on the other hand was fresh in mind.[10]

An examination of the personnel of the commission reveals further evidence that it was not the intention of the petitioners to limit the power of a courtier faction. Some of its members had been closely associated with the late Prince of Wales. None were hostile to the court of his son.[11] It would be unjust to attribute the weakness of the central authority to the commission. Flabbiness was inevitable in a minority without a regent. Things fared badly for England abroad. At home the rumblings of disorder and discontent foreshadowed the Great Revolt of 1381. In the parliament of 1377 a demand for more rigorous legislation to control labourers had been made. It was repeated with more success in 1378 at Gloucester, where parliament was also the scene of the enactment of a law establishing severe penalties for slandering the great men of the realm. Violators were to be imprisoned until it could be discovered by whom they had been

[10] *Rot. Parl.*, III, p. 5. Cf. Tout, *Chapters*, III, p. 339 and A. Steel, *Richard II*, (1942) p. 45.
[11] They were the Bishops of London, Carlisle and Salisbury; the Earls of March and Stafford; Richard Stafford and Henry Scrope, bannerets; and John Devereaux and Hugh Segrave, bachelors. *Rot. Parl.*, III, p. 6.

prompted. The readily apparent uneasiness of the magnates and commons proved to be only too well justified by events.

The Great Revolt was the first, and in some respects the most spectacular, of the major crises of the reign of Richard II. Though from first to last it was principally a socio-economic movement, it was by no means lacking in constitutional significance. The very vindictiveness with which the rebels pursued the ministers of the crown is ample indication of an awareness on their part of a relationship between the conduct of government and the existence of the problems they were seeking to resolve. That their wrath fell upon those who were in no sense particularly culpable is evidence only that they failed to comprehend that the responsibility for their grievances rested with a general social structure rather than a group of individual men. In fact, one of the most remarkable aspects of the whole revolt is the amazing solidarity which it demonstrated among the classes in whose hands the economic and political control of society was vested. Factionalism of the most bitter sort might be rampant among the great men of the realm, but in the face of a threat against the system from which all derived whatever power they possessed, they closed ranks to present a solid front. Both the labours of the justices whose task it was to punish the leaders of the uprising, and the painstaking researches of students of the movement have failed to reveal the slightest hint that any factions or any individual magnates attempted to turn the revolt to their own profit and the discomfiture of their rivals. This is all the more noteworthy in that there was throughout the period of disturbance, and particularly in the environs of London, a constant demonstration of hostility toward John of Gaunt. Yet the men who had been most zealous in their recent political opposition to the duke were at least equally zealous in their demands for the prosecution of the rebels.

There was thus no connection between the rebels and the reformers of the Good Parliament. There was, of course, a relationship of another sort. The rebels showed that they had been influenced by the propaganda which had spread from the parliament of 1376 and held a place in the popular memory.[12]

---

[12] T. F. Tout, 'The English Parliament and Public Opinion, 1376–88,' *Mélanges d'Histoire Offerts a Henri Pirenne* (1926), p. 557, calls attention to the publicity which surrounded the acts of the Good Parliament.

Yet that parliament and its successors had taken the initiative in re-enforcing the statutes of labourers and preparing to suppress civil unrest. Furthermore, while the members of the November parliament of 1381 did not scruple to point to the recent disturbances as evidence of the bad governance of the kingdom, they were unanimous in their condemnation of the rebels, their demand for severe punishment, and their approbation of the withdrawal of the king's enforced promises of immunity. This unity in the face of attack among the important people of the kingdom, whether magnates, clergy, ministers, country knights or guildsmen is another indication of the absence of basic divisions among them on fundamental questions of 'constitutionalism' or reform.

The consistently reverent attitude of the insurgents toward the king, on the other hand, gives rise to interesting constitutional speculations, the significance of which was surely not entirely lost to contemporary observers. No young king or king to be was ever presented with a more remarkable opportunity to observe the nature of the relationship between the ruler and the masses of his subjects. The government's strategy for coping with the uprising was in all likelihood directed by the chancellor, Archbishop Sudbury, and the treasurer, John Hales, whose lives were to be forfeited to it. The vigorous action of the Bishop of Norwich in his own and the neighbouring diocese demonstrated the relative helplessness of rebel hordes when faced by efficiently directed soldiery. But, given the size of the movement against London, the decision to use force would have been extremely costly in human life. Procedure by conciliation and negotiation relying upon loyalty to the king may have involved some risk to his person, but the councillors must have been certain that only an accident could endanger him. It would have been inconceivable to the rebels that he should be deliberately injured. Whether or not Richard shared this assurance at the outset, he quickly acquired the confidence and courage to assume direction of the movement after Mayor Walworth's murder of its leader, Wat Tyler.[13] At fourteen he had learned that miracles might be worked by one who wore a crown. In the meantime he parleyed in person with the spokesmen of the mob and promised redress

[13] This generally follows the reconstruction of events by Wilkinson, 'The Peasants' Revolt of 1381'.

for their grievances. His assurances of amnesty sufficed to disperse the malcontents without a blow having been struck except that by Walworth.

The demands of the rebels, most particularly those made at their final meeting with Richard, posed an important political question. Might not a centralized and authoritative royal power be made the instrument at once for the elimination of privilege and abuse, and for the reformation of the legal system necessary to the easy accommodation of society to the altered social and economic conditions of the late fourteenth century? It was vested local interest which on every hand through its influence in government at all levels stood in the way of such reform. This is not to say that any fourteenth century English king made the alleviation of the suffering of the common people his particular concern. It is only to say that those elements in society who preferred a relatively weak regal power were likewise attempting to maintain a *status quo* in the national economic and social structure, and that the leaders of the Great Rebellion clearly so identified them. There is, in fact, strong evidence that many of the rebels believed themselves to be acting in cooperation with the king. In their minds this may have assumed the proportions of nothing more than assistance in relieving him from the unwelcome tutelage of Lancaster and corrupt ministers; or it may have appeared to be a blow in a common cause against common enemies. In any case, the suggestion of the supremacy of royal power over all other jurisdictions, whether lay or ecclesiastical, had been made. The king and his personal advisers were susceptible.

As Richard's own philosophy of government matured, it remained conventional in the sense that it involved no hint of a reordering of society which would have eliminated either social classes or the clerical hierarchy. The most radical of the rebel proposals found no echo in royal policy; but Richard as king expressed views on the subject of regal sovereignty which were not dissimilar from those attributed to the leaders of the uprising.

The revolt together with some of the questions of policy and of the distribution of power which it raised may have been responsible for the expression for the first time of a concerned interest on the part of the magnates of the great council in the education of the king and in the attitude toward his position which he might be developing. The council may deliberately have directed his attendance at the trials in which his grants of amnesty were most flagrantly repudiated. To the same leadership may be attributed another move which must surely have been galling to the king who could have recalled that at his age his father had been considered mature enough to be entrusted with an important military command in a decisive battle. This was the appointment in parliament of two guardians over his household. The humiliating effects of the arrangement could hardly have been lessened by the fact that he had just been married.[14]

The new guardians were Richard, Earl of Arundel, and Michael de la Pole. Arundel was the head of one of the great feudal houses. He was just beginning in these years to assume prominence in the affairs of council and government in which he was to be active as an opponent of the king for the rest of his life. De la Pole, as has been noted, was either at the time, or soon to become, a leader in the royal circle. The grandson of a London merchant, he had earned honour both as a soldier and an administrator, yet the stigma of his bourgeois heritage was never forgotten by the many enemies which his loyal service to the royal house created for him. There is little to show what these two guardians actually did in the way of policing the king's household. It is only clear that they were incompatible both in personality and in interests.

The king's marriage represented a triumph for his advisers in an important area of diplomacy. It was their decision to bring England and the Empire into a close accord. Even before it became evident that the move had failed to produce the benefits for which they hoped, it was subjected to bitter criticism.[15] Lancaster would have preferred a union which might have forwarded his Iberian interests. Others hoped that Richard might wed the richly endowed daughter of the lord of Milan. The decision of the courtiers, however, was in accord with the wishes of the pope. The marriage, profitless in other ways, was extremely felicitous. Anne of Bohemia was universally acknowledged as a

[14] The lords had been cautious about interference with the household at the beginning of the minority. *Rot. Parl.*, III, p. 6. Richard himself was to continue to be unusually touchy about it.

[15] *Hist. Ang.*, II, p. 46.

gracious and virtuous queen who retained in person and in memory her husband's devoted loyalty until his death. Furthermore, she joined the king in his affection for his friends and personal advisers, an esteem which they uniformly reciprocated in kind.

Whatever may have been the design of those who humiliated the king after the collapse of the Great Revolt and burdened the royal household with appointed guardians, Richard, having once experienced the full power and prestige of regality, was determined never again to be a cipher in his own government. It is difficult to know how much active interest he took in matters of policy as early as 1382. Certainly, he was concerned in surrounding himself with a group of men who would be bound to him not only by ties of personal allegiance, but also by gratitude. It was here that he crossed the chancellor, Sir Richard Scrope. Scrope had long been associated with the Duke of Lancaster, but he wore no man's livery. His brief tenure of office was characterized by an energy and independence of action which won for him the plaudits of many who would have been most distrustful of any man with previous Lancastrian connections.[16]

He devoted himself sedulously to the task of administrative reform and economy. His programme, indeed, was so far the reverse of that which had been characteristic of the years of Lancastrian supremacy in the last reign as to have removed any trace of suspicion about his association with John of Gaunt. In the process of cutting expenditures he gave attention to the royal household. This, in itself, was irksome, but when Scrope refused to execute Richard's orders in the matter of affixing the great seal to grants of land and income to his friends, the king asserted himself and the chancellor was summarily dismissed.[17] His successor after an interval was his brother-in-law, Sir Michael de la Pole, the ruler's former guardian. While Pole's policy, like that of Scrope, was vigorous and constructive, he displayed from the first, as his predecessor had not, a marked interest in strengthening the personal position of the king.

The dismissal of Scrope and its cause indicate the progress of Richard and his advisers in establishing the royal position. The

<hr>

[16] E.g. ibid., pp. 68–70.
[17] Ibid.

task was far from complete. New adherents had to be attached to the royal following before it could face with assurance the prospect of an opposition united by the common peril of concentration of power in the king's hands. A beginning, nevertheless, had been made and the capture of the chancery was a significant victory.

Support from other quarters was required before the court could feel free to act as it wished. No great clergyman was numbered among the inner circle of royal adherents; the only bishops to be counted on were those who had risen from humble clerical estate by grace of royal favour. Furthermore, the steady support of some powerful element among the municipal corporations would be useful. The clerical magnate remained lacking until 1386, when Archbishop Neville of York associated himself with the king's partisans, but the municipal ally was more readily discovered.

Among the corporations of London the grocers and fishmongers were probably sympathetic to a strong monarchy even prior to 1382. They had benefitted, as had Lancaster, from the reversal of the acts of the Good Parliament.[18] Certainly from this time forward until late in 1387 the connection between town and crown was very close. The court had probably been instrumental in the election of the grocer, Nicholas Brembre, as mayor in 1383. He had replaced Lancaster's protégé, John of Northampton, whose radical policies had terrified the conservative, strongly entrenched corporations. By 1385 Brembre, having in the meantime twice secured re-election, was even reconciled to Lancaster, who then had more pressing immediate interests than the protection of John of Northampton. These concerned the organization of a grand expedition against Spain which after 1384 began to appear feasible.

Lancaster did not in any way control or direct government in the years immediately after the accession of his nephew, but many great nobles and commoners alike, recognizing the magnitude of his wealth and influence and recalling the events of the last decade, feared that he might do so unless he were carefully checked. Jealous suspicions directed towards him diminished, of

[18] J. H. Round, *D.N.B.*, II, p. 1163; E. Lipson, *Economic History of England*, (1931), I, p. 454. R. Bird, *The Turbulent London of Richard II*, (1949), Ch. II.

course, in precise proportion to the growth of those directed towards the court. By 1384 some aristocrats who had been most unfriendly were even prepared to defend him from the accusations of the king's friends. The long list of incidents which go to make up the record of mutual suspicion between the court and the duke from 1381 to 1386 is in all probability a reflection of the initiative of neither. There is no evidence that the charges publicly aired either by Lancaster or by Richard's associates had any basis in fact. Lancaster was quite simply too powerful a subject; the fear which his very position inspired in those who surrounded the king had its counterpart in his own fear that pre-eminent position alone might make him the object of their attacks.

The last reign had clearly indicated what this one and its successors were to prove: that the crown must either fail to serve its traditional function or become sufficiently strong to control even a united opposition among the magnates. Lancaster's fundamental personal loyalty was always ultimately with the hereditary king. Given his relationship with the court his situation was unusually difficult. The Spanish démarche was thus doubly attractive as a relief from embarrassment and the fulfillment of old ambitions. Official support for his expedition, at last in 1385, came because the magnates were no longer so concerned about him, while the government looked upon it as the least costly means of satisfying the popular clamour for a show of arms.[19]

The withdrawal of John of Gaunt for a few years from the English scene marked a real turning point in national affairs. The magnates were normally divided in their pursuit of self-interest. A common apprehension concerning the power of the king's friends had begun even before 1385 to enforce unity among many of them. The central figures in this opposition were Richard, Earl of Arundel, an inveterate enemy to court influence; his brother, Thomas, Bishop of Ely; Thomas, Earl of Warwick; and the king's youngest uncle, the Duke of Gloucester. In the Easter parliament of 1384 Arundel bitterly denounced the government. In a parliament of 1385 his brother Thomas attacked the chancellor.[20] In that same year Archbishop Courtenay was

[19] Russell, *English Intervention*, pp. 402, 403; E. Perroy, *L'Angleterre et Le Grand Schisme D'Occident* (1933), pp. 233, 234.
[20] *Polychronicon*, IX, pp. 32, 33, 69; *Hist. Ang.* II, p. 141.

persuaded to act as spokeman for an unidentified group of magnates in complaining to the king about his choice of advisers and
friends. It was a rash move. Only the mediation of de la Pole,
himself a principal subject of the complaint, prevented Richard
from seizing Courtenay's temporalities and banishing him from
the realm.[21] It was the archbishop's last intervention in politics.
He remained aloof from the serious controversies of the next
three years.

On the whole, despite certain setbacks and losses in the years
prior to 1386, the architects of the royal programme laboured to
good purpose. De la Pole's administration did not escape
criticism, but modern verdicts have generally commended both
his policies and his integrity. The court party entrenched itself
in the household and in the great offices of state. Lancaster's
position was so weakened as to cause his withdrawal from
domestic politics. The court gained the alliance of the most
powerful elements in the city of London. The pope was entirely
favourable. The Archbishop of Canterbury was neutralized
either through fear or through gratitude at his restoration to
favour. The power and influence of the king's closest associates
had been enhanced by rewards of titles and lands.[22]

Richard himself had responded very favourably to the
teaching of his mentors. His attachment to de Vere and his
impulsive fits of temper were his most conspicuous weaknesses.[23]
Neither was in itself serious. He developed the high sense of the
dignity of his own position which was necessary to an exalted
conception of the royal prerogative. Consistently, even courage-
ously, he defended his ministers and his partisans from criticism
and abuse. At the same time he demonstrated on more than one
occasion a degree of independence which proved him to be no
mere instrument in the hands of others.

The government, too, had dared to act more and more
independently. It answered complaints about local injustices
with a series of statutes which seriously curtailed the abuses of the

---

[21] Ibid., pp. 127, 128; *Polychronicon*, IX, pp. 59, 69, 70.
[22] This, of course, aroused criticism, some of it very harsh. *Hist. Ang.*, II,
pp. 140, 156.
[23] The impulsive temper may have been exaggerated by modern historians.
Cf. L. C. Hector, 'An Alleged Hysterical Outburst of Richard II,' *E.H.R.*, LVIII
(1953), pp. 62–66.

C

barons and justices of the peace.[24] In 1383 the commons had
secured a renewal of royal assent to an oft-repeated demand that
sheriffs be eligible only for a term of one year, after which they
must wait three years before re-election. The king's acceptance
of the statute reserved the rights of his prerogative. A year later
the commons' complaints concerning violations were boldly
answered by de la Pole, who stated bluntly that it was prejudicial
to the king's interest to remove at the end of one year an official of
proven efficiency. The king would do what seemed best for him
and for the people of the realm.[25]

These steps in the direction of breaking down local privilege
and establishing a more effective central government were quite
naturally resented by both the magnates and the main body of the
knights of the shire. Their resentment, however, did not prevent
Richard in 1385 from replying to a request in parliament for an
investigation of his household and revisions of administrative
personnel that he would look into his household when it pleased
him to do so, and that his present ministers, who would be changed
only at his pleasure, were quite satisfactory.[26] In the past he had
never felt strong enough to treat similar petitions in so cavalier a
manner.

The knights may to some extent have been inspired in these
actions by the more restless of the lords. On the other hand it is
not unlikely that many among them shared the discontent of their
superiors. What they desired from the crown was the security
assured by royal leadership, not a close control over local affairs.
In short, like many other people at many other times they wanted
protection, but they did not welcome supervision. It would
require all of the turmoil and the disorders of the fifteenth century
to teach them that in that age to enjoy the necessary minimum of
the one they must endure a substantial measure of the other.

Another two or three years of similar progress might well
have provided the court party with the semblance of invulner-
ability. If the opposition were to hope for success, it could not
long delay action. The Duke of Gloucester and his associates

---

[24] *Rot. Parl.*, III, pp. 200, 201; *Statutes of the Realm*, II, pp. 36, 37. Only stringent
measures concerning King's Justices and Barons of the Exchequer were declared
invalid at the next session of parliament. Ibid., p. 38.
[25] *Rot. Parl.*, III, pp. 149, 201.
[26] Ibid., p. 213.

might have hesitated to declare war on the court while Lancaster remained in England, but ostensible necessity must, in any event, soon have overruled hesitation. It is possible that the king and his partisans may themselves have been over-confident. Yet the contest when it came was not of their making. There was no way for them to forestall it, short of the voluntary sacrifice of everything for which they had toiled. Their success would greatly have undermined the independent personal power of the magnates who amply appreciated the threat. They joined together to crush the monster before they should themselves be destroyed by it. When that aim had been achieved and a normal equilibrium restored, they could resume their own individual squabbling over place and prestige.

This may seem to be an unduly harsh judgment upon the aristocracy and gentry. In reality it is not. In three generations their sense of responsibility to the community had become blunted. It would be convenient if the change could be explained by some inclusive reference to decline of function or the dissolution of the manorial economy. Its causes were more complex. The war and the plague, among other factors, had operated along with more subtle and profound phenomena to modify the ideals and the aspirations of the upper classes. It is their conduct, however, not its causes, which is immediately relevant to an understanding of the events of 1386. As in the year of the Great Revolt they were on the defensive. It was easy for them, as it has been for others at other times, to confuse right with rights, allegiance to law with the maintenance of privilege, and the interest of the realm with self-interest. There was probably as much sense of honour, as much uprightness, as much generosity and as much self-righteousness among them as among any similarly placed group of their ancestors or descendants. But they possessed no positive programme. They were unconcerned with the perfection of the instrumentalities of justice. They responded to no call to remedy widespread abuse. Hence leadership fell naturally to ambitious men who could play upon a sense of insecurity. The watchwords were issued by Gloucester, the Arundels, and their associates. The opposition to the court was general to all who had social position to defend or to improve.

Chapter III

THE CHALLENGE OF 1386

THE destruction of the royalist faction was rather a development than an event. The opposition, which had crystallized among the magnates, planned no strategy at the outset of the struggle in 1386, nor did its leadership possess clearly defined aims. Nothing beyond an attack in parliament upon the chancellor as the official representative of the courtier following was initially projected. No one was likely to have suspected that further measures might be necessary. The court would be publicly humiliated; the official power of the clique would be broken; and the king would be taught to feel the weight of the combined action of his most powerful subjects. Such optimistic predictions, however, reckoned without both the stubborn devotion of Richard to his own principles of regality and the steadfast loyalty of those who had associated themselves with him. An outright revolution culminating in the wholesale proscription of the royalist adherents was required to assure the maintenance of the results of the easy parliamentary victory.

Lancaster with his household retinue and such troops as he could muster had barely departed for Spain, when the French began to organize their forces for a large scale invasion of England to be led by Charles VI himself. The English ministry took prompt action to prepare the coast against the threat of an attack which was never to occur. Richard's advisers could not know that the French mobilization would be managed with such incredible inefficiency as to produce no result other than an enormous but useless expenditure for the Valois king. They were consequently forced to assemble a parliament in October for the uncongenial purpose of raising a war fund.

The chancellor's opening speech fell on unresponsive ears. The knights and their superiors had other interests than the provision of revenues for the defense of the kingdom. They had manifestly arranged in advance an attack on the administration, in which they persevered with 'a serene indifference to the danger of the realm.'[1] To the chancellor's sober discussion of the necessities of war they returned only complaints about misgovernment coupled with a demand that both he and the treasurer be removed from office. The king withdrew to Eltham obviously annoyed at the criticism of his government. It was there that the petition for the dismissal of his officers reached him. It could hardly have taken him by surprise, though there can be little doubt that he and his advisers failed properly to gauge the seriousness of the parliamentary revolt. His well known reply that he would not at the request of the lords and commons remove the meanest scullion from his kitchen must, therefore, be accepted as a deliberate statement of the royal position rather than an impulsive surrender to temper. Richard merely seized the occasion of an assault upon his ministers to define further the point of view represented by his more polite refusal to accept parliamentary inquiry into the personnel of his household in the preceding year. Already, before his departure for Eltham, he had given evidence of his reaction to complaints against his advisers by the elevation anew of Robert de Vere, who had recently been granted a marquisate. On the thirteenth of October, parliament confirmed the royal favourite in the title of Duke of Ireland.

The king perhaps believed that in absenting himself from parliament and thereby manifesting his displeasure he could reduce the critics to a more conciliatory frame of mind. He may, too, have conceived in advance the plan to treat separately with the knights, who, drawn apart from the magnates, might lack the courage to resist their sovereign to his face. In either event he was doomed to disappointment. He had definitely underestimated the strength of the forces with which he had to deal. The lords and commons paused in their attacks on the chancellor long enough to invite the king to return to join them. His proposal that a deputation of forty of the most prudent and worthy of the knights be sent to Eltham to discuss the entire matter with him in person was scorned as a ruse to get the leaders of the commons in his hands in order that they might be assassinated.[2] The magnates did not intend that the loyalty of the knights to the common cause should be tested by the risk of royal intimid-

---

[1] Oman, *Political History*, IV, p. 101.
[2] *Hist. Ang.*, II, p. 150; cf. *Leyces. Chron.*, II, p. 216.

ation. There came to Eltham, instead of the requested delegation, the Duke of Gloucester and Thomas Fitz-Alan of Arundel, Bishop of Ely. These two feared no assassination.

As unsolicited emissaries from the rebellious parliament they are said to have made some astounding declarations to the already offended monarch. They quoted to him a series of alleged 'ancient statutes', no one of which was really in existence. The king was informed that he was required to hold a parliament every year; that, if he deliberately remained absent from his parliament for more than forty days, the members might legally return to their homes; and, finally, that if he persisted in a wilful course despite the protests of the lords and commons he might be deposed and some other member of the royal family be elevated to the throne in his place, the very thing which had taken place not so many years before. This last extraordinary declaration was said to have been prompted by the king's announcement of a determination to seek, if necessary, the aid of the king of France against his own subjects.[3]

The reminder of the fate of Edward II, whether issued in parliament or at Eltham, was nothing more nor less than a threat of rebellion. No one concerned could have been so naive as to have supposed that the resolution of grievances drawn up against Edward of Carnarvon had the force of a general statute. It was a specific set of charges to justify a specific act of rebellion. The citation of the precedent, nevertheless, served to bring Richard to terms. He returned to Westminster and agreed to the dismissal of his chancellor who was promptly replaced by Bishop Arundel. Gloucester and his colleagues, however, now required more than the removal of the chancellor from office. They determined to crush the court party by a thorough demonstration of its impotence to protect its adherents, and at the same time to establish a form of administration more suitable to their own interests than that which de la Pole had headed. These aims were realized in the impeachment of de la Pole and the creation of a commission to control the affairs of the realm. Strictly speaking, both were unprecedented actions, though neither was more than a further step in a direction which had already been foreshadowed.

The action against the fallen chancellor was initiated by the

[3] *Leyces. Chron.*, II, pp. 216–20; *Cont. Eul. Hist.*, III, pp. 395, 360.

commons, who 'all together and of one accord' came before the king and the lords to accuse him of a variety of crimes. The complaint employed the word 'impeach', as had the actions against Lord Latimer and Richard Lyons in the Good Parliament of 1376.[4] Neither in that earlier instance nor in this is it probable that the term possessed its later technical meaning. It was applied frequently in the fourteenth century to legal accusations. In the record of this parliament it no doubt stood for nothing more. The lords and commons may not consciously have devised a new procedure equipped with a distinctive label. They could not, however, have been unaware of certain extremely significant novelties in the nature of what they were undertaking. Petitions of accusation had been levelled by the commons against unpopular public officials in the past. The king's ministers themselves had brought demands for punitive action before parliament. In no prior case, however, had the whole body of the commons come initially into the presence of the lords to request that the peers render judgment. Petitions had previously always been addressed to the king in council. Now for the first time royal authority had been entirely sidestepped in the prosecution of an officer of the state. The great crisis of 1388 was to evoke an even more extreme example of this transfer of authority. While no system had been devised, the leaders of the magnates seized upon whatever precedents were available in the formulation of a technique for carrying out what even they recognized to be a revolution. In such a situation it was only natural that every precedent was strained to the utmost, that alteration in procedure occurred with great rapidity, and that every step which was taken marked a more decisive break with the law and custom of tradition.[5]

The complaint against Suffolk was divided into seven separate articles, of which three were charges of official misconduct and four of abuse of position for his own financial benefit. He was alleged to have failed to carry out in accordance with his responsibility the investigation of the state of the realm which had been ordered in the last parliament; to have spent funds granted by that parliament for other than the specified purposes; and, by

---

[4] *Rot. Parl.*, III, p. 216.
[5] Cf. T. F. T. Plucknett, 'State Trials under Richard II,' *T.R.H.S.*, Fifth Series, II, (1951) pp. 159–66.

failure to relieve the city of Ghent, to have wasted the three thousand marks interest on the money which had been borrowed for that purpose. In addition he was charged with the sale of pardons, the diversion to his own pockets of funds properly belonging to the crown, and the exercise of the influence of his office to procure advantages to himself in private business negotiations.[6]

The personal charges were petty in nature. The specific offences, had they been proved, would have been more shocking to the political morality of the twentieth century than to that of the fourteenth. Even so, the most that could be established was that the chancellor had been guilty of sharp but not dishonest business practices in one instance. The accusations of official misconduct were even less substantial. Indeed, the facts and the official records demonstrate conclusively that de la Pole was a diligent and efficient executive officer who was not only obedient in the main to decisions made in parliament, but also prompt in putting them into effect. If this was made plain at the trial no record of it appears in the parliamentary rolls, where de la Pole's defence, ably conducted by himself and by his brother-in-law, the former chancellor Sir Richard Scrope, consisted chiefly of rebuttals to the charges of personal dishonesty and the showing that the entire council must share the responsibility for the actions upon which the other accusations were based. Scrope, who apparently was prepared to answer in de la Pole's behalf to all of the charges, was restricted by parliamentary rule largely to the role of a character witness. His assistance was, nevertheless, valuable since he could be suspected of no connection with the court party. No defence would have been sufficient to secure an acquittal. Suffolk was fined, deprived of all grants, save that which accompanied his title, and sentenced to an indefinite term of imprisonment.[7]

The line taken by Suffolk in answering his accusers is interesting. He and the king, who was naturally deeply concerned in this case, were in a position to avail themselves of the best of legal talent. That they chose not to contest the legality of the whole proceeding must be accepted as an exercise of strategy and not a concession of principle. This is made abundantly evident

[6] *Rot. Parl.*, III, p. 216.
[7] Ibid., pp. 217–20.

by the tenor of the list of questions which Richard submitted to
his justices in the following year. Some recognition of the
jurisdiction of the lords would have been implicit in the very
presentation of the argument of improper procedure. Furthermore, from the day of his return to the session, the king was
quite conscious of the momentary strength of his opponents and
his own corresponding weakness. He did not choose to come to
blows with Gloucester and his associates under such circumstances.

From the standpoint of the magnates the assault on the
minister was undoubtedly intended as an object lesson. The king
was almost immediately able to release him from what, at its
worst, had been only a nominal imprisonment in the hands of
Sir Simon Burley. He retained his title and suffered no persecution
in the months which followed his removal. The attack had been
not so much personal as exemplary. Had it been otherwise, the
target would in all likelihood have been the Duke of Ireland.
Suffolk's impeachment had been chosen as the medium through
which the king was to learn the limitations of his own position.
Also, the shift in the heads of the two great offices of state was a
blow to the royal party which might promptly have been nullified
by Richard as soon as parliament adjourned. The impeachment
tended to secure the victory of the opposition. For regardless of
the extent to which precedents had been stretched, the judgment
had the ceremonious sanction of action in parliament with all
attendant publicity.

The real permanence of that victory, however, was to be
guaranteed by a more stringent measure. The leaders of the
parliament virtually wrested all power over the government from
the king by the establishment for the term of one year of a
commission to which was entrusted final authority to supervise
the offices of state, the household, and the courts of law, as well
as to hear and amend all grievances which might be presented.[8]
This commission was in essence a reversion to the system of
continual councils employed in 1376 and early in Richard's
reign, but it was directed against the power of the king as none
of them had been. It represented to many of the peers the ideal
form of government for such a time. It was a scheme which

---

[8] *Statutes of the Realm*, II, pp. 39–44.

involved so careful a balance of important personages as to render a near paralysis of the central authority likely. The members of the Commission of 1386 included, in addition to Gloucester and the two Arundels, such moderate participants or neutrals in the recent anti-royalist moves as the Duke of York, the Archbishops of Canterbury and York, the Bishop of Winchester, and Sir Richard Scrope. The others who sat with them included the Bishop of London, the Abbot of Waltham, Lord John Cobham and Sir John Devereux, none of whom could be described as an adherent either of Gloucester and Arundel or of the courtiers.

The momentous parliamentary session closed with the granting of a subsidy which was preceded by requests that the king swear to abide by the ordinances of the commission and that he replace the steward of his household by someone acceptable to the proctors of the estates. To the first, Richard had perforce responded affirmatively; to the second, he returned the reply that he would take favourable action as soon as possible. In the process of adjourning the assembly, he made a final face-saving gesture with the declaration that nothing to which he had assented was to be taken as an abridgement of the liberties and prerogative of the crown. This conventional sop to the royal pride was small compensation for the humiliation, the loss of his ministers, and the new tutelage which he suffered. But Richard meant it seriously. It was indicative of the spirit with which he accepted what had been done, as was his violation of his enforced pledge to select a steward with the advice of his new councillors. Without their consultation, he named to the office Sir John Beauchamp of Holt, one of the most active of the courtier knights.[9]

In all of the activities of this parliament, the records provide only the usual appearance of unanimity among the members. No word of debate, no hint of dissension is anywhere preserved. Certainly the king had supporters among both the peers and the knights; but the reports record the actions, which must have been decisions of a majority not a totality, as the will of all the lords and commons in a body. The role of the commons throughout the session must be defined. It would be fatuous to accept at face value the implication of the contemporary accounts that the

---

[9] *Polychronicon*, IX, p. 90. Beauchamp 'bene se habuit in officio antedicto.'

assault on Suffolk originated with them. Their conduct in 1386 was in keeping with their conduct in any other great political crisis of the period. The vision of the knights humbly and soberly petitioning the peers to hear their indictment and pass judgment on the official whom the magnates themselves had designated for punishment is not without its element of irony. Yet the use to which parliament was put was of great consequence. The great men of the realm had upon occasion in the past combined to crush unpopular favourites of the monarch. Never before had they made the commons in parliament their instrumentality for doing so. That such a device could be employed is a testimony to the growth in importance, if not always in independence, of the commons in the six decades which had elapsed since the outbreak of the final rebellion against Edward II and his ministers.

CHAPTER IV

THE FAILURE OF THE ROYALIST STRATEGY

THE revolution of 1386 was accomplished entirely without resort to violence. Its only victim endured no more than loss of his office, temporary restriction of his freedom, and a financial penalty. The victory of the enemies of the court was, nevertheless, genuine. If they had not visited Suffolk with the fate of Gaveston and the Despensers it cannot have been because they lacked power to do so. So much must have been obvious to the king himself. Richard was left, then, with only two alternative courses of action. The immediate reassertion of his own independence was impossible. Either he might submit to be bound by the fetters which had been forged for him, or he might prepare his forces for a more timely battle against an opposition whose power for the instant was paramount. The goads of his friends could hardly have been required to induce his decision not to resign himself to defeat.

The king, nevertheless, had need to proceed very gradually, testing his ground at each step. His appointment of Beauchamp as his steward was the first move. That was followed by the remission of Suffolk's fine, and by a journey to York to assist Archbishop Alexander Neville in a quarrel with the monks of Beverley. The archbishop had perhaps already given evidence of tractability. From this time forward he was among the most trusted associates of the king. Richard celebrated Christmas at Windsor, where he terminated the nominal captivity of the Earl of Suffolk by taking the former chancellor into his own household and treating him in public with the utmost respect.[1]

Although no official cognizance of these actions was taken by the commission, as early as November, Chancellor Arundel had exercised the authority of his office to deny the validity of writs issued over the king's signet.[2] The chancery and the great seal were not to be bypassed. The king was left to carry on his

---

[1] *Polychronicon*, IX, p. 90.
[2] Tout, *Chapters*, III, p. 417n.

programme of party reconstruction without any official means of securing funds.

Stripped of his power and resources, Richard found the atmosphere of London, where he was faced with constant reminders that he was a monarch who could not rule, intolerable. He therefore broke up his established residence and withdrew from the vicinity of the commission. For the next several months he wandered about the kingdom organizing his forces for the overthrow of those who had usurped his power. From time to time he held councils of his own, attended by the members of his household and whomsoever among the peers he could assemble. He devoted attention, too, to the development of a standing army. The nucleus of this force was drawn from Chester and Wales, but recruiting was carried on over a large portion of the realm.[3] In this last enterprise a leading role was taken by the Duke of Ireland who had been making ostensible preparations to subordinate the unruly inhabitants of his new duchy. His troops, however, were probably being made ready for action in England itself in case of need.

Even more important to Richard's plans than the development of an army was the effort to provide security for himself. In 1386 he had been taught a bitter lesson. A determined opposition composed of a combination of lords who were able to control parliament had easily rendered him politically impotent. He did not propose to have that experience duplicated. It might be difficult, even impossible, to break up the coalition of the magnates. He strove, therefore, to do whatever he could to prevent the repetition of their mastery of parliament. Whether he went so far as to request that the sheriffs permit the return only of members favourably disposed toward him is doubtful. But he did at least try to get some indication of public sentiment from local officers of government. A contemporary story credited him with encouraging them to prepare the counties for a rising in his behalf.[4] The precise subject matter of his conversations with such folk is difficult to determine, since he would have taken every precaution to keep them secret and would have made

[3] *Polychronicon*, IX, p. 94.
[4] These reports proceed largely from the St. Albans scriptorium. *Hist. Ang.*, II, pp. 160, 161.

no records. Rumours of all sorts were abundant. The wildest of them may well have seemed credible to the lords of the opposition when they received a first-hand account of other conversations which could be verified by sealed records. These were the king's late summer discussions at Shrewsbury and at Nottingham with the justices of the great courts of the realm. They, too, were intended to be guarded with the strictest confidence, but the Duke of Gloucester was promptly informed of their substance by the Archbishop of Dublin who had been present at the Nottingham conference.[5] The anxiety of Gloucester and his associates when they had heard the archbishop's tale is easy to imagine, for Richard's questions and the replies of the justices amounted to more than a preparation for war against the commission. They raised ghosts which had been dormant for more than half a century. The awesome word '*treason*, with all that it implied of forfeiture, hanging, quartering, disembowelling, and attainted blood' had been introduced into the controversy.[6] Taken as a whole, furthermore, the questions constituted a more explicit and elaborate statement of certain aspects of the royal theory of prerogative right than any which had yet appeared.

The inquiry was thorough. Though some of the questions appear repetitious, each attacked the conduct of the parliament of 1386 from a distinct point of departure. After a general statement that the statute establishing the commission was illegal in that it was made against the king's will, the justices pronounced as worthy of the punishment of death all those who had procured the making of the statute or who urged the king to give his assent to it. Those who constrained the king to consent to the statute and 'prevented him from exercising the powers pertaining to his royal prerogative', together with those who encouraged parliament to ignore the business which the crown had prescribed or who in any way prevented royal dissolution of the session, were declared to merit the full punishment accorded to traitors. The distinction is a nice one, but the phraseology of the record

---

[5] *Polychronicon*, IX, p. 103. Cf. infra p. 39, n. 9.
[6] The phrase is Steel's, *Richard II*, p. 133. The historian need not be over subtle. Treason had been introduced whether or not an actual judgment had been declared. But cf. Chrimes, 'Richard II's Questions to the Judges, 1387,' *Law Quarterly Review*, LXXII (1956), and B. Wilkinson, *Constitutional History of Medieval England*, II, (1952), pp. 237 ff.

indicates an unmistakable hierarchy of values. The establishment of the commission, though derogatory to the king's rights was not in itself treasonable; no more was the act of persuading the unwilling monarch to accept the derogation. Both were grave offences, but in both instances the justices chose to add to their response that the offenders merited the death penalty the phrase 'unless the King of his own free will wishes to extend his grace to them'. No such clause, in these cases tantamount to a recommendation of leniency, was appended to any of the judgments on offenders for whom the punishment meted out to traitors was designated as appropriate. These included the participants in the impeachment of royal officers against the king's will, and 'he who moved that the statute whereby Edward, great grandfather of the present King was adjudged in Parliament, should be sent for, by the inspection whereof the aforesaid statute and commission were contrived'. The responses to the questions terminated with a sweeping denial of the legality of the judgment against the Earl of Suffolk, which was 'erroneous in all its parts'.[7]

The answers of the justices were recorded as being unanimous to every one of the ten inquiries which were made, and this uniform response was given on two separate occasions by a judicial panel which consisted of Robert Tresilian, chief justice of the king's bench, Robert Bealknap, chief justice, and John Holt, Roger Fulthorp and William Burgh, justices of the common bench, and John Lockton, justice *coram rege*.[8] A week intervened between the two sessions, yet only one of the justices who had attended the first failed to appear at the second. That fact, taken together with the complete lack of evidence of the use of force in assembling the panel at Nottingham, and the failure of any of the group to violate the royal confidence by a complaint to the commission is a sufficient refutation of the subsequent claim of all except Tresilian that they had acted under constraint.[9] The

[7] *Rot. Parl.*, III, p. 223.

[8] *Polychronicon*, IX, p. 99. Fulthorpe was present only at Nottingham. He was substituted for Sir John Carey, chief baron of the exchequer who had joined in the judgment at Shrewsbury. Tout, *Chapters*, III, p. 423.

[9] Two chroniclers refer rather circumstantially to constraint, though it is probable that neither account was composed until after the meeting of the Parliament of 1388. *Leyces. Chron.*, II, p. 237; *Cont. Eul. Hist.*, III, p. 363. There is a question concerning Fulthorp. He and his heirs alleged that he had informed the Earl of Kent about the Nottingham deliberations. Kent's own position throughout the whole period is ambiguous. He probably had more to gain than to lose through a triumph of the court. Cf. Chrimes, op. cit., p. 285.

justices in fact had made to the king's questions the only replies which they could make in accordance with the law and custom of the realm. All had sworn a solemn oath to respond as faith to the dignity of the law demanded, and so they did. They knew they were providing grounds for the condemnation of the most powerful men in England. Yet they had no other alternative if they were not to violate their oath. The king had broken no statutes. Parliament had no independent legal rights as against the monarch. It would be several centuries before any doctrine of ministerial responsibility to parliament would become enshrined into the constitution. The royal power had been usurped. The novelty of all of the proceedings of October, 1386, was apparent. There were no well established legal precedents for any of those actions.[10] The king's questions were carefully drawn so as to indicate that only one answer was anticipated in each case.[11]

Although the medieval monarch was not an absolute sovereign in the modern sense of that term, his rights and prerogatives as a ruler were absolute and unfettered. His subjects may theoretically have retained the power either to force him to exercise his regality or to depose him. There had been no question of Richard's failure to rule. Custom and precedent established the authorization for subjects to band together to resist the invasion of their own rights by the crown. No such invasion had been attempted. In his function as ruler, the king was universally acknowledged to possess exclusive jurisdiction. So long as he adhered to his obligations and violated no customary right of his subjects, there was none who could question his conduct or restrict his authority. Any active fourteenth century king would have looked upon the performance of the parliament of 1386 as revolutionary. To Richard, schooled as he was in exaggerated doctrines of regal dominion, it assumed the ultimate proportions of treason. Confident of the validity of his own position, his questioning of the justices was for him both the provision of

---

[10] Cf. Plucknett, 'State Trials', p. 167. The procedures of impeachment may well have been forged in the preceeding decade; but, as has been pointed out above, they had not been employed for purposes of direct assault on the monarch or indirect assault through his own chosen ministers.

[11] The author was one John Blake, 'juris apprenticius'. *Hist. Ang.*, II, p. 162; *Rot. Parl.*, III, p. 233. He probably had the assistance of Tresilian.

legal confirmation of opinion upon which actions might be based and an expression of his views on the estate of royalty. For the time being it must be withheld but it could be given wide publicity when circumstances were favourable.

The most important issue with which the questions dealt was, of course, that of treason. A definition had been authorized by the statute of 1352. The terms were specific. Treasonable offences were, for the most part, acts against the person of the king, such as conspiracy against his life, or the life of his queen or his eldest son; the violation of his queen or his eldest unmarried daughter or the wife of his eldest son; the levying of war against the king; or giving aid and comfort to his enemies. Added to this list, however, were a group of actions which might properly be considered offences against the welfare of the realm. These were the counterfeiting of royal monies or of the great and privy seals, and the slaying of royal officials in the act of pursuing their prescribed duties. Other things not designated as treason by terms of the statute could officially be declared to be so only by the king in parliament. Private warfare was established as felony, not treason, and the statute was notable for its omission of any ambiguous phraseology such as 'accroaching the royal power'.[12] This had been the rubric under which numerous prosecutions in the early decades of the century had been carried out.

Certainly the declarations of the justices in 1387 went far beyond the letter of the law of 1352. It must be remembered, however, that they were delivering merely a considered legal opinion and not a formal condemnation. They were advising, not legislating. Since the statute provided no guides to the questions with which they were confronted, they could answer them only by the test of custom and precedent. By those standards there could be but one verdict if the usurpation, threatening or accroaching of the power of the king could be established to have taken place and if the king were to be protected from force, intimidation and deposition. The real question, therefore, on which the advice of the justices was demanded was that of determining whether the royal power had been accroached or threatened. In 1327 Edward II had been deposed and murdered. No one could pretend sixty years later that royalty could be secure

[12] *Statutes of the Realm*, I, pp. 319, 320.

D

in the face of threats of deposition simply because they were unaccompanied by evidence of intent to do bodily harm. The framers of the statute of 1352 were aware of the difficulty of phrasing legislation which would safeguard both kingship and kings while protecting subjects from arbitrarily vindictive royal action. They had preferred to sidestep the issue, as their successors were to do in 1388. To Richard, and indeed to later kings, definition was of such paramount immediate consequence that it could not be reserved in accordance with the letter of the statute for individual parliamentary declarations as need might arise. In 1386 he learned that law must prevent attacks on the estate of royalty. In 1387 the judges were wary of employing language which might controvert the terms of the statute. They named no traitors, and they established no new forms of treason. Their findings, however, were, as has been said, precisely what the king expected them to be. They left no ambiguity on the score of the peril of tampering with the prerogative. Taken altogether they also represented a more explicit statement than any which had yet been articulated in England of the right of the monarch to select his own ministers and advisers without interference, to summon and dissolve parliament when he chose, to prescribe the business with which parliament should be concerned, and to be the final unquestioned executor of national policy. Even the terms of the discussion of policy with the estates were his to set.[13]

The news of the interviews with the justices stirred the lords of the opposition to action. They dared not risk condemnation as traitors. It was imperative for them to take the offensive while yet there was time. When Richard returned to London in November, he made the strategic error of coming without troops into the centre of a region where his enemies were armed and prepared.[14] He counted, perhaps, too heavily on the loyalty of the Londoners which he had been at some pains to secure. Not satisfied with the influence of Brembre alone, he had utilized, to his own advantage, the local fear of John of Northampton. By subtle intimation that a royal pardon might be extended to restore

[13] With some variations in emphasis these views on the judicial declarations are those of Chrimes, op. cit., pp. 365 ff. On the issue of late medieval theories on the relationship of king to councillors which would have reinforced the judicial declarations cf. Ernst Kantorowicz, *The King's Two Bodies* (1957), pp. 154 ff.

[14] *Leyces. Chron.*, II, p. 242.

to John his privileges in the city, the king combined threats with blandishments to bind the mercantile oligarchy to him in his struggle against the magnates. It was an alliance, however, which despite sealed oaths, was quickly transferred when the military superiority of the opposition became apparent.[15]

The powers of the commission were to have expired on the nineteenth of November. None of its members had manifested any disposition to cease to exercise the authority which had been delegated to them for the term of one year. It is apparent, nonetheless, that the king did not expect armed rebellion to prolong their power. His invitation to Gloucester and Arundel to meet him at Westminster betrays more than a little naiveté, as does his dispatching of the Earl of Northumberland to arrest Arundel at Reigate, where he was amassing his troops. Richard evidently supposed that with his acceptance by the city and the expiry of the legal term of the commission, the opposition would simply collapse. If so, he was completely mistaken. Arundel's family had recently known the stigma and the disabilities of treason. The earl's pride and his devotion to self-interest left little likelihood that he would stop short of revolt to escape a like penalty, while Gloucester's soaring ambition already extended to the throne itself.[16]

It was only after their levies had been assembled, despite a royal proclamation prohibiting the giving of aid to Arundel or those who might join him, and the loyalty of the London citizenry to the king had been completely undermined, that Gloucester, Arundel and Warwick, through the mediation of Northumberland, appeared at last before their sovereign. They came to tell him to his face what already they had publicly announced: that their actions were directed against the traitors who surrounded him, and neither against him nor the welfare of the realm. Order could be restored to the kingdom only by the arrest and punishment of the friends and councillors of the king. The magnates had chosen to fight fire with fire. In their own turn they revived the definition of treason which had terrified their forebears prior

[15] H. J. Mills, 'John of Northampton's Pardons', *E.H.R.*, LII (1937), pp. 477–79. A contemporary report that de Vere had interceded with the king on behalf of Northampton is rejected as improbable by Miss Bird, *Turbulent London of Richard II*, p. 88. Cf. *Polychronicon*, IX, p. 93.

[16] Cf. the report of the Monk of Westminster, *Polychronicon*, IX, pp. 109, 110.

to the enactment of the statute of 1352. The king's ministers, like Gaveston and the Despensers before them, were to be treated as traitors who had accroached the royal power. The entire aristocracy, however, was uneasy. The judicial opinions and the reaction to them had reopened the question of treasons not only in the definition of offences but also in terms of penalties. Later while the proceedings against the king's friends were in progress the parliament of 1388 would enact legislation to protect entailed estates and the property rights of widows of proscribed traitors.[17]

Richard was quite helpless. He could do nothing but entertain the appeal of treason which was levelled against Suffolk, de Vere, Archbishop Neville, Tresilian, and Brembre. The accused were advised to flee, while the king, after having discovered that the Londoners would not stand behind him, was obliged to issue orders for his friends' arrest. He proposed that the appeal should be formally aired in parliament.[18] Meantime, he had issued a proclamation that no evil should be spoken of the accused, instructed the sheriffs to permit the return to parliament only of persons who had no concern in the controversy, and resigned himself to await developments.[19]

Of the five accused only Brembre could be found to answer the warrant for his arrest. He had remained to the end in the city working to arouse whatever loyalty to the king might be latent there.[20] Suffolk and Archbishop Neville had fled to the continent, never to return; Tresilian had concealed himself in the city; and the Duke of Ireland had gone to Chester to collect his army. The cause of the court party rested solely on the martial skill of this untried commander, as he marched with some four thousand men at his back down the Severn to do battle with the vastly superior forces of the appellant magnates who had been joined

[17] Cf. C. D. Ross, 'Forfeitures for Treason in the Reign of Richard II', *E.H.R.*, LXXI (1956), pp. 560 ff.

[18] The contemporary testimony is that this was Richard's preference. *Leyces. Chron.*, II, p. 248; *Hist. Ang.*, II, p. 155. The Lords Appellants may also have desired it. Cf. Plucknett, 'State Trials Under Richard II', p. 167; and Wilkinson, *Constitutional History*, II, pp. 254–7. Also, Alan Rogers, 'Parliamentary Appeals of Treason in the Reign of Richard II', *American Journal of Legal History*, VIII, (1964), pp. 95–124.

[19] *Calendar Letter Book H.*, p. 321; *Foedera*, VII, p. 566; *Polychronicon*, IX, p. 108.

[20] The Londoners had reacted in despite of their sealed oaths through fear. R. Bird, *The Turbulent London of Richard II*. Cf. *Calendar Letter Book H.*, pp. 315, 317, 320, 321.

by the earls of Derby and Nottingham. Outmanoeuvred and outmanned, although he gained a slight initial success against the forces led by Arundel, his army was destroyed by the troops of Derby and Gloucester at Radcot Bridge in Oxfordshire. The defeat left the king's friends entirely at the mercy of the Appellants.

Popular sentiment, both at London and in the country, was probably congealing on behalf of the lords. A careful campaign of publicity accompanied all of their movements. In addition to publicizing their charges against the royal favourites, they spread rumours of collusion between the court and the king of France. Their efforts to secure the city included an open letter to the citizens which was a model of well conceived propaganda.[21] Many of the moderates among the nobility were won over to a position of sympathy for their cause. Sir Richard Scrope read their charge to the king. There is even a hint that de Vere's troops were disaffected before the battle at Radcot Bridge. The duke himself escaped through the fog on the night of the disaster, but his baggage and papers fell into the hands of the victors. Letters to the king of France promising the delivery of Calais in return for aid against the rebellious lords were alleged to be among the loot, although the documents were never exhibited. The chroniclers combine to present an impression of the growth of widespread suspicion of the court.

The lords celebrated their triumphant return to London from Radcot Bridge by a considerable extension of the list of the proscribed. To the five names contained in the original appeal were now added those of Thomas Tryvet, Simon Burley, John Beauchamp, Nicholas Dagworth, James Berners, William Elmham and John Salisbury, all knights of the court, together with the king's clerks, Richard Medford, Richard Clifford and John Lincoln. Richard made a last stand by shutting himself in the tower and refusing to give the necessary assent to the arrests and trials. His resistance on this occasion must have been particularly stubborn for it culminated in what most certainly appears to have been his temporary deposition. His throne was in all probability saved for him only by the inability of the Appellants to agree on an heir. The Earl of Derby could never have consented to the

[21] *Leyces. Chron.*, II, pp. 246, 247.

passing over of the claims of his house in favour of his uncle, Gloucester. Yet the threat of 1386 had become a reality, and there was nothing for Richard to do but yield with the best grace possible.[22] The arrests were made. New summons to the parliament were issued, this time omitting the clause prohibiting the election of persons who had shown partisan interest in the struggle. A number of bishops, knights and ladies were banished from the court. And finally the justices whose advice the king had consulted at Nottingham and Shrewsbury were dismissed from their offices and held for trial. When, on February 3, 1388, the long anticipated parliament assembled, the king was completely helpless. Even so, he probably did not suspect the extent to which his humiliation was to be pushed.

[22] M. Clarke, *Fourteenth Century Studies*, (1937) pp. 91–95; cf. *Polychronicon*, IX, pp. 109, 110, 115; and *Hist. Ang.*, II, p. 172. Derby and Gloucester had private reasons for friction. They continued to quarrel about the Bohun inheritance of their wives until 1393. R. Somerville, *History of the Duchy of Lancaster* (1953), I, pp. 67, 68.

CHAPTER V

THE APPELLANT TRIUMPH

THE February parliament of 1388 was one of the most memorable sessions of the entire medieval period. Even by those who approved its actions it was christened 'the Merciless Parliament'. On no other occasion did a parliament mete out so many sentences of death. In effect these were little more than judicial murders. Since the king's return to London in November, events had rapidly proceeded far beyond that moderate kind of revolution which had characterized the parliament of 1386. Under such circumstances, the men who would normally have held the balance of power among both the lords and the commons were unable to resist the pressure of the extremists. The issue between the court and the Appellants had been decided on the field of battle and in the deposition scenes of the Tower. All who in the early stages of the controversy for one reason or another had extended their sympathy to the victors were now so far compromised as to be in no position to oppose them. Many like the Duke of York, the Archbishop of Canterbury, and Sir Richard Scrope, who had been favourably disposed toward a reduction of the power of the court clique, discovered themselves to be unable to check the violence of Gloucester and Arundel even when they were most eager to do so. As to the Apellants themselves, they were quite correct in assuming that after the declaration of the justices, the appeals of treason, the battle of Radcot Bridge and the temporary deposition of the king, there could be no security for them while any remnant of the court party continued to exist. They set themselves, therefore, ruthlessly to the task of utter annihilation.

The parliament opened most extraordinarily with a declaration by Gloucester that neither he nor his associates had ever planned the death of the king. That such a statement should have been considered to be necessary is, in itself, revealing. The king's clerk, Godfrey Martin, then proceeded to read the details of the charges against the royal advisers.

The appeal against de Vere, Suffolk, Archbishop Neville, Tresilian and Brembre took the form of thirty-nine separate articles of accusation.[1] Some were serious and a few were doubtless accurate, though their status as crimes is questionable. All, however, were taken seriously by the lords and commons, to whom they were presented. The usual claims of bribery, corruption, and frustration of justice, all unsubstantiated, were accompanied by an itemized list of accusations of treasonable collusion with France, and of incitement to civil war. But first attention was devoted to the estrangement of the king from those who were truly loyal and devoted to him, to the procuring of the judicial opinions of 1387, and to the separation of the king from the commission which had been established to assist him in the proper exercise of his power. These acts constituted the grossest treason in that they had combined to 'deprive the king of his free condition'. Commentary on the accusations is unnecessary. Their sum is nothing more nor less than a return to the old charge against favourites of the crown that they had literally bewitched the king into voluntarily transferring to them his sovereign authority. Never had the charge been made by men who were more zealous to wrest his authority from him by force.

Richard's response to the lengthy appeal, which he had heard before, was a grave suggestion that so serious a matter should be referred to the justices and the men of law in order that the correct legal forms for action might be determined.[2] A large group of specialists was apparently consulted. Among the number were most certainly the newly appointed chief justices of the King's Bench and Common Pleas. They returned the answer that no such action as an appeal for treason before parliament was justifiable either by the civil law or by the statutory and common law of the realm. It is noteworthy that some, at least, of

---

[1] *Polychronicon*, IX, pp. 122–40; Knighton's continuator lists only 34 articles. *Leyces. Chron.*, II, pp. 273–93.

[2] Plucknett says, 'At this point the lords felt the need of legal advice and consulted the judges, serjeants, etc. . . .'. 'State Trials under Richard II', p. 168. Just why he attributes the initiative in this move to the lords rather than the king, he does not say. The language of the official record seems reasonably unambiguous, though it may be merely formal. 'A quel temps les Justices et Sergeantz, et autres Sages du Ley de Roialme, et auxint les Sages de la Ley Civill feuront chargez de par le Roi nostre dit Seignur de doner loial conseill a Seignurs du Parlement'. *Rot. Parl.*, III, p. 236. Cf. Wilkinson, *Constitutional History*, II, p. 65; and Rogers, 'Appeals for Treason in the Reign of Richard II', p. 105.

these men were the successors of those who had been removed for their participation in the Shrewsbury and Nottingham declarations. Yet they dared to give advice wholly consistent with that which had cost their predecessors their places. Indeed, the entire procedure of the appeal had been, from the outset, questionable. The Appellants had possibly at first considered other courts. It was the king who had proposed the submission of the case to parliament, evidently hoping either that the whole body of the lords and commons would favour the royal cause, or that whether favourable to him or not, they would recognize the irregularity of the appeal and prevent the revolution from coming to a head. Upon the third day of February only the second of these hopes could have remained, and even that was soon to be dashed. Moderates would probably have been inclined to respect the opinion of the men 'learned in the law' but they could not check the course of the Appellants. The reply to the judicial opinion was written into the official record as the judgment of all the lords in parliament.

It was an epoch-making reply. It denied the competence of either civil law or common law for cases of such magnitude as that of the Appellants. In such high crimes, touching directly the person of the monarch, the lords alone might be the judges, bound by no code other than what they chose to define as the law of parliament.[3] If this was not in fact a blatant claim to supremacy over all established law and custom the king could hardly have viewed it as anything else. It is not to be inferred that Richard's own later assertions are to be interpreted in any sense as retaliatory declarations. But the incapacity of established modes of procedure to fit the needs of either the royal clique or its opponents is evident in the events of 1388 which were recognized even by their authors to be dangerously revolutionary. The statement of 1388 represents no principle of constitutional theory devised by the opposition to the crown in reaction to the judicial declarations of 1387. The events of the parliament both in order and in nature admit no such interpretation. A desperate situation required a desperate remedy.

On the 'lower plane of law and procedure', however, the

[3] *Rot. Parl.*, III, p. 236. Rogers, 'Parliamentary Appeals of Treason,' pp. 110, 111.

effort to preserve some sort of continuity with precedent and traditional usage was much more seriously undertaken.[4] It has been argued that 'the lords themselves had vindicated on a previous occasion the perfect regularity of what they described as "the law and course of parliament" ';[5] that the lords were merely asserting a judicial *cum* legislative, not a political supremacy[6]; and that, impeachment without the active assistance of the crown having been declared by the justices to be illegal, the ancient and well known action of appeal for treason provided the Gloucester faction with 'exactly what they were looking for—a criminal procedure over which the crown had no control'.[7]

Yet even on this lower plane the indications of desperate improvisation are still apparent, despite the assistance of the lawyers. The previous vindication of the 'law and course of parliament' had involved a case in 1380 which was in no way a parallel to the appeal of 1388. Most important among the differences was that in the earlier instance there was no necessity for finding a means of evading the authority of the crown. Furthermore, in that instance it was the justices in the presence of the king and the lords in parliament who made the judgment of treason.[8]

As to the argument that the lords meant only to assert that they constituted the highest court in the realm, a court with supreme authority both to declare the law and to apply it in judgment, they could not have administered justice *ad rem* or *ad hominem* as fancy suited them. This they knew and they searched the history of state trials for guidance. On the crucial matter there was no help. No precedent existed for appeals of treason in parliament.[9]

Finally, the history of the session clearly demonstrates the dissatisfaction of Gloucester and his associates with the appeal procedure and their own lack of assurance that it had been a

---

[4] Plucknett, 'State Trials under Richard II', p. 170.
[5] S. Reznek, 'The Early History of Parliamentary Declarations of Treason', *E.H.R.*, XLII, p. 503.
[6] By H. M. Cam. Steel, *Richard II*, pp. 178, 179.
[7] Plucknett, op. cit., p. 167. Cf. Rogers, 'Parliamentary Appeals of Treason', pp. 103–5.
[8] *Rot. Parl.*, III, p. 75.
[9] Plucknett, op. cit., Also 'Impeachment and Attainder', *T.R.H.S.*, (Fifth Series), III, (1953), pp. 145, 146.

wisely conceived means of destroying their victims. They employed it only in these first five cases. For the subsequent prosecutions of the session it was abandoned in favour of a return to action by impeachment as in Suffolk's case in 1386. Perhaps they became worried about the legality of their acts. It is more likely that, having already gone so far in rebellion, they were more concerned with keeping the support of the main body of the lords and their protégés among the commons until they had completed their work. To this end the maintenance of some form of law was essential. The act of attainder still belonged to the future.

On the eleventh of February in full parliament the verdict of the lords was returned against four of the five accused. All were found guilty. The Duke of Ireland, the Earl of Suffolk, and Robert Tresilian were sentenced to be hanged and drawn, the common penalty for traitors. Archbishop Neville, saved from so severe a sentence by virtue of his cloth, was deprived of his temporalities, and handed over to the prelates for further punishment. No one of the four was present to hear the judgment or to present a defence. It was relatively easy to exercise the full rigour of the law against absentees who would probably never be taken into custody, but when a defendant appeared to argue his case the moderate majority among the lords experienced qualms of conscience.[10]

The case of Nicholas Brembre was separated from that of his four absent associates, and he entered a sturdy plea of not guilty to all of the accusations against him. His demands for counsel and for time to prepare answers to the charges having been denied, he asked that he be permitted to defend himself as a peer by combat. No less than three hundred and five gloves, those of all of the lords and many of the knights and squires there present, were cast at his feet in answer to his challenge. After this demonstration, trial by battle was withheld, and the king having protested Brembre's innocence, the case was remanded to a

---

[10]As a matter of fact the main body of the lords did not respond as hastily as the Lords Appellants might have wished. When they did convict the four, they did so on the dubious grounds of 'notoriety', a procedure which had been circumscribed with safeguards early in the reign of Edward III. The general anxieties about loose construction of treason were reflected in the statute of 1352 and the subsequent reversal of the conviction by notoriety of Roger Mortimer. Cf. Rogers 'Parliamentary Appeals of Treason', p. 112.

special committee of twelve lords for investigation. This group returned the verdict that the accused had done nothing to deserve the death penalty. The angry reaction of the Appellants was interrupted by the report that Tresilian had been discovered hiding in the very environs of Westminster.

The unwary chief justice was promptly haled before parliament and, despite his protestations of the illegality of the proceedings against him and his unwavering pleas of innocence of treason, was dragged off to Tyburn to be executed. He was given no trial since he had already been adjudged *in absentia*. The Appellants at last had a taste of blood. They returned with zeal to the prosecution of Brembre, against whom they were finally able to gain a judgment of treason, not initially from the lords, but from a special group of officials of the city. Condemned on the strength of their opinion that he was likely to have been guilty, he followed Tresilian to the scaffold.[11]

The five of the king's advisers who had occupied public prominence had now been disposed of. From Richard's strategy it is evident that he had maintained a strong hope that even they might escape with their lives. The reserving of the appeal to parliament, the raising of the issues of jurisdiction and precedent, and the special efforts on behalf of Brembre all indicate that, though the king recognized himself as beaten, he was still exercising every effort to reduce the cost of defeat. That Brembre and Tresilian could be so summarily dealt with, even after a show of reluctance by a majority of the lords to take extreme measures, was a severe shock. But the Apellants, having set their hands to the extinction of the royal party, could not afford to halt half-way. They turned at once to the destruction of the inner circle of court knights and curial officials, who, being far less well known than those named in the first appeal, might have been considered to be also far less vulnerable. Gloucester and Arundel, at least, among the Appellants were wise enough to know that the real vitality of the royal party lay with these more obscure men.

The first of them to receive attention were John Blake, whose legal skill had designed the questions to the justices in

---

[11] *Polychronicon*, IX, p. 168; cf. *Rot. Parl.*, III, p. 238; Bird, *Turbulent London*, pp. 93–96 and Rogers, 'Parliamentary Appeals for Treason', pp. 113–7.

1387, and Thomas Usk, the undersheriff of Middlesex.[12] Blake and Usk were prosecuted, as were all the subsequently accused, by impeachment in much the same manner as that employed in 1386 against Suffolk. Both had been mentioned in the original appeal as having participated in a plot for the arrests and judicial murders of 'divers Lords and loyal Commons', including the Dukes of Gloucester and Lancaster. Neither sought to mitigate his punishment by any confession of wrongdoing. Usk's solemn affirmations of his innocence were still on his lips at the scaffold, whither he was carried on the day of his trial. On the following day a similar sentence was passed against the Bishop of Chichester, the royal confessor. Like Archbishop Neville, his life was saved by his clerical status but his temporalities were seized.

The prosecution of the six justices who had been associated with Tresilian in the 1387 pronouncements followed. The discrimination shown in their case demonstrated that the Appellants were concerned entirely with a political question, not a constitutional one. If the Nottingham and Shrewsbury declarations constituted treason, then all who had engaged in them were traitors, and, other things being equal, deserving of a like penalty. Such simple logic was quite enough for the commons who proceeded to issue the same sentence against the six as that against Tresilian. The justices, however, were not members of the court faction; they were quite willing to plead guilty, urging that they had been coerced. The Appellants had nothing to fear from them as individuals in the future. They consequently made no effort to exact the death penalty against them, and may even have joined in the appeal to the commons which resulted in their lives being spared.[13] They were exiled to Ireland, where they remained until, in 1397, they were pardoned by the king with the assent of parliament.

The bringing of the action against them, however, had been an essential part of the Appellants' programme. Ruthless as they were, Gloucester and Arundel were too shrewd to have indulged, simply from a predilection for harshness, in persecutions which might leave sore wounds for the future to heal. A direct assault

[12] Blake was a protege of Tresilian's. Favent, *Historia*, p. 19; *Hist. Ang.*, II, p. 170.
[13] Favent, *Historia*, p. 20; *Polychronicon*, IX, pp. 151, 152, 170. Cf. *Kirkstall Chronicle*, p. 8.

on the validity of the judicial declarations of 1387 and a thorough public repudiation of the principles established by them was required to provide the less partisan lords with a minimum sense of security about their hesitant participation in the trials.[14]

The parliament had been sitting for approximately five weeks by the time that these trials were completed. There was a delay of another week before the Appellants were prepared to carry their attack to the very heart of the royalist clique. This was composed of a number of knights and clerks who had been proscribed by the victors on the occasion of their return to the city from the rout of de Vere. For purposes of trial they were divided into two groups. The first included Simon Burley, John Beauchamp, John Salisbury, and James Berners, knights, all of whom were formally charged with sixteen articles of treason. The second was made up of Thomas Tryvet, William Elmham, and Nicholas Dagworth, knights together with the clerks, Richard Medford, Richard Clifford, Nicholas Blake, and John Lincoln.[15]

The accusations against the first four knights in many respects paraphrased those of the principal appeal. Four, however, were directed solely against Sir Simon Burley, and in four others he received separate attention. It was about Burley that the only protracted arguments of the session centred. The length and fierceness of the controversy are an overwhelming testimony both to the importance which Gloucester and his associates attached to him on the one hand and the extreme loyalty of the king and his many friends on the other. Burley's trial was the climax of a session which had been melodramatic from the outset. His plea, which he presented in person, was seconded by members of the household bureaucracy who, though not among the accused, were apparently quite ready to compromise themselves in order to aid him. Even the Appellants were not united against him, Derby actually having joined in the plea that he be

[14] Cf. Plucknett, 'Impeachment and Attainder', p. 146.
[15] *Rot. Parl.*, III, p. 241; Favent, *Historia*, pp. 21, 23; *Polychronicon*, IX, p. 152, which, incidentally, lists the entire group as being arraigned together. Cf. Tout, *Chapters*, III, p. 434 n. The reason for the discrimination is difficult to fathom. Tryvet had been accused of particular malevolence toward the lords. *Hist. Ang.*, II, p. 163; *Polychronicon*, IX, p. 107. Burley, and possibly Beauchamp, might be expected to have been treated as more formidable enemies than the rest, but the grouping of Salisbury and Berners with them is unexplained. Salisbury was alleged to have been the go-between in the supposed dealings with France, and he was, indeed, singled out for a special fate. Favent, *Historia*, p. 22.

spared. The king's pusillanimous uncle, the Duke of York, mustered sufficient angry courage to offer to defend Burley's innocence on the field of combat against his brother, Gloucester. Yet Gloucester was implacable. When the queen humbled herself to kneel before him, he resisted her supplication with the curt comment that she had best save her prayers for her husband, who himself stood in great need of them. He had the commons well in hand. They continued to clamour for the death penalty, even when York and Lord John Cobham, as representatives of the majority among the lords, were sent to reason with them. As for the king, another threat of deposition was required to terminate his three weeks' refusal to give assent to the sentence. In the end Gloucester's way was made smoother by a demonstration in Burley's favour by a large body of the common people in several sections of the realm. The spectre of the Great Revolt was enough to persuade the bulk of the lords who had been sympathetic to him to acquiesce in the verdict of the commons. With the old companion-in-arms of the Black Prince, his three fellows were also condemned, and all were executed on May 5th. The most that the king could do for his former master was to modify the sentence from hanging to beheading.[16]

With these executions the fury of the Appellants exhausted itself. The other courtiers were freed on bond and never seem to have suffered any punishment at all. The attention of the remainder of the session was devoted to a paradoxical series of actions whose purpose was to secure the work of the parliament and at the same time prevent the use of its procedures as precedents.

The lords showed how little importance they attached to their initial pronouncement of parliamentary supremacy to the common law, by attempting to bind all future parliaments against any modification of what this parliament had done. They betrayed their fear of future possibilities of arraignments by enrolling solemn resolutions to deny that they had in any way altered the general law of treasons, and to prohibit the use of their acts as precedents. They attempted, by statute, by oath, and even by threat of excommunication, to forestall permanently the restor-

[16] Most of these details are supplied in *Polychronicon*, IX, pp. 152, 155, 171, 176–78. The story of the uprising and its effect is from Favent, *Historia*, p. 21.

ation of any of the condemned. Finally, before they adjourned, Richard actually renewed his coronation oath and they, in turn, repeated the oath of allegiance and homage 'as at the first at his coronation'.[17]

Before the proctors of the estates returned to their homes, leaving behind them a puppet king, they took pains to reward the victors and buy the complaisance of powerful non-participants in the controversy. The five noblemen who had declaimed against the lavishing of royal monies upon the king's favourites felt no compunction about accepting from public funds a gift of twenty thousand pounds as compensation for their trouble in saving the realm.[18] No more were their consciences troubled by the grant of the earldom of Huntingdon with the extraordinary annual pension of two thousand marks to John Holland, who had returned from Spain in April. Relationships between Holland and his royal brother had not always been cordial, but personally and as the representative of his father-in-law, Lancaster, he may well have looked askance at the humiliation of Richard and the elevation of Gloucester. The unusual bequest has generally been viewed as an attempt by the Appellants to buy his favour. Lancaster himself was created Viceroy of Aquitaine, perhaps with the hope that the attendant responsibilities would keep him abroad after the termination of his Spanish campaign. In fact the eagerness of both the Appellants and the king to conciliate Lancaster made it easy for him to default on pledges made to the government on the occasion of his departure for Spain.

The official gift was but the beginning of a whole series of rewards to the Appellants. The records are sprinkled liberally with evidences of their recompense.[19] The clerics who had been

[17] *Polychronicon*, IX, pp. 158, 163, 164; Favent, *Historia*, p. 24. C. D. Ross, who calls in for a revision of opinion in favour of the Appellants, emphasizes the care which they took to prevent the undoing of their work and the restoration of the forfeitures by the king at a later date. 'Forfeiture for Treason in the Reign of Richard II', *E.H.R.* LXXI (1956), pp. 560–75, especially pp. 570, 571. His argument that the Appellants did not behave with undue vindictiveness toward the heirs of their victims appears to be consistent with available evidence.

[18] *Polychronicon*, IX, p. 154; *Rot. Parl.*, III, p. 248. The gift was finally discharged by payment to the five of £19, 995, 1sh., 8d. on October 20, 1389. The reason for the slight discount is not apparent. *Issues of the Exchequer*, pp. 239, 240.

[19] The recipients of the confiscated property included Nottingham (*Cal. Fine Rolls*, X, pp. 258, 259); (*Issues of the Exchequer*, p. 235), Gloucester (*Cal. Fine Rolls*, X, p. 273), Arundel (*Issues of the Exchequer*, p. 235), Skirlaw, Bishop of Durham (*Cal. Fine Rolls*, X, p. 253), Braybrook, Bishop of London (Ibid., p. 263), the Bishop of Winchester (Ibid., p. 242), Thomas Mortimer (Ibid., p. 248), the Bishop of Hereford (Ibid., p. 255), and Henry Percy *fils* (Ibid., p. 211).

associated with them received their share of blessings. The pope, hastening to abandon Richard in defeat, now became the servant of the conquerors. He could punish with one hand while he bestowed largess with the other. Alexander Neville was translated from York to the schismatic see of St. Andrews in Scotland. It would hardly have behoved him to risk his life in an attempt to assume his new responsibilities. He spent the rest of his days serving an obscure curate in Flanders. He was succeeded at York by Chancellor Arundel, who, though long a champion of governmental economy, celebrated his elevation by an appeal for royal assistance in renovating the lands and buildings of his bishopric. The assistance was, of course, forthcoming, with Arundel himself affixing the great seal to the charters of bequest. Bishop Rushook of Chichester, the king's confessor, was exiled by papal translation to the wilds of Kilmore in Ireland, while Fordham, Bishop of Durham, paid for his royalist convictions by removal to the less wealthy see of Ely which Arundel had just vacated. Three other clerics whose assistance had been useful to the Appellants became bishops.[20]

The commission had been accorded an ultimate vindication. Though its legal term of authority had long since elapsed, its remaining members continued to administer affairs of state. The appearance of unity among the lords and commons, which the momentary supremacy of the Appellants had contributed to the Merciless Parliament, was maintained in the government for the rest of the year. None of the administrations which in the preceding twelve years had been vested in the hands of carefully balanced continual councils had ever displayed either sufficient vigour or sufficient consistency to have been credited with possessing an executive policy. The ascendancy of Gloucester and the Arundels made the administration of 1388–89 an exception in this respect. Their policy has been characterized as being conservative. Perhaps an adequate definition of the use of that adjective may be derived from the activity of the great offices and the legislation of 1388 in the Michaelmas parliament.

In one category may be included the rather futile moves toward peace with France, the disastrous renewal of military activity on the northern border, the reduction of the use of the

[20] Perroy, *Schisme*, pp. 303–5.

E

privy seal and signet, some attempts at household reform, and a
few minor administrative alterations. The peace proposals, so out
of keeping with the Appellants' bitter denunciation of the French
negotiations of Richard's advisers, were probably nothing more
than a reflection of the recognition that the war was very expen-
sive. The champions of economical government could also afford
to be the champions of a bellicose foreign policy when they were
not in power. As heads of the state they were forced to choose
one or the other. The campaign against Scotland may have
seemed to offer an opportunity for a less costly display of martial
spirit, but the penury of the administration was possibly a
contributory cause of the English defeat at Otterburn, which has
been called the greatest loss of face experienced by England in
half a century. The administrative reforms, including the hiatus
in the use of the signet and the privy seal, were obviously all
inspired by the desire to return as much influence as possible to
the chancery, thereby weakening the less readily controlled household offices. With the chancery in the hands of Bishop Arundel
the Appellants had no fear of extending its power too far.

The legislation of the parliament which met in September at
Cambridge is as interesting as any of the entire reign. One point
of difference was manifested in the aims of the magnates and the
knights who had co-operated so effectively in February. The
members of the lower house expressed a quite justifiable fear of
the growth of private armies which was so notable a feature of the
feudalism of the later fourteenth and fifteenth centuries. They
embodied their fear in a proposal, resisted by the peers, to abolish
all liveries which had been introduced since 1327. This would
have had the effect of destroying the bands of armed retainers
who derived privileges from wearing the badges of the great
lords whom they served, and who already constituted a considerable menace to the security of smaller property holders. The
campaign of 1387, fought by just such troops, provided a fore-
taste of what was to become more common by the middle of the
next century. The threat of constant civil turbulence and unrest
was anathema to the knights of the shire who were in no condition
to build up private armies for their own protection. The difference of opinion was settled temporarily by the enactment of a
statute postponing the abolition of the proscribed liveries until
the following year.

On the other matters with which the parliament concerned itself there was greater uananimity. The conservative sentiment of the lords and knights is easily identifiable. It was this Cambridge parliament which enacted the most stringent of the medieval statutes of labourers and coupled it with new authorizations to the justices of the peace, the officials most susceptible to local pressure, for rigid and extensive enforcement. In this attempt to battle against the economic tendencies of the day, the magnates and the knights were united, and both groups were far more zealous than the crown had ever been. In 1388 they had a free hand. Scales of wages were established; labourers were prohibited from moving about without special letters patent; all members of the lower classes were strictly forbidden to bear arms of any sort; pilgrims were to be treated as vagrant labourers; severe restrictions were imposed upon the teaching of trades to children; and, finally, all preceding statutes of labourers were renewed. A further paragraph provided severe punishments at the discretion of the council for derogatory remarks about the great men of the realm. The statute was applauded by at least one conservative who deplored the wealth, the splendour, and the arrogance everywhere exhibited by the base-born.[21]

At Cambridge also was enacted anew a statute prohibiting the export of money, legislation dear to the hearts of all propertied classes. It applied, of course, chiefly to the flow of gold and silver to Rome. The pope had perhaps expected a more generous recognition of his recent co-operation. That act set the tone of the Appellant policy. It was consistently directed toward the interests of the landholders, who desired a central government so controlled as to protect them against the lower classes, while leaving what virtually amounted to sovereignty over the local communities in their hands. These same groups were fearful of foreign influences, including the papacy, and were suspicious of certain elements among the municipal mercantile oligarchy. It is perhaps significant that the Cambridge parliament ordered the return of the staple from Middleburgh to Calais, thereby restoring the time-honoured monopoly which Brembre and his associates had temporarily broken.

---

[21] *Leyces. Chron.*, II, p. 299. Cf. Nora Kenyon, 'Labour Conditions in Essex in the Reign of Richard II', *Econ. Hist. Review*, IV, (1934), pp. 429 ff. for an analysis of the statute and its effects.

The events of 1386 and 1388 illuminate with unusual clarity the major features of the English political situation in the later fourteenth century. They were also extremely influential in the formulation of Richard's policy in the next decade. His memory of every detail of the humiliating tragedy proved to be acutely tenacious.

It has been customary to refer to the Appellants as the leaders of a party. The label is entirely misleading. That no parties in any meaningful sense existed in the latter fourteenth century is demonstrated by the whole course of the revolution of 1386–88. Gloucester, the Arundels, and Warwick were manifestly united in purpose and intent throughout the three year period, yet even their union was no more formal than that of a temporary coincidence of interests. They joined in no common interpretation of the proper estate of royalty or no well defined conception of the constitution. Each had his own separate ambitions which he served as best he might. All happened to be opposed to the overshadowing of local privilege by extensions of the jurisdiction or the efficiency of the crown. One, at least, may have hoped to become king himself. All were upholders of economy in royal administration, and all, until midsummer of 1388, favoured a vigorous prosecution of the war. These were the sole bases of their coalition other than mere congeniality of personality and ambition.

In 1386 they had been able sufficiently to play upon the fear and self-interest of others who, like themselves, had enjoyed the weak government of the minority, to secure the impeachment of Suffolk. Gloucester's higher ambitions, if indeed he entertained them, would have attracted little support. The celebrated reference to the trilogy of 'ancient statutes', if it was really made, was equally bad as history or as law. There is no evidence that Gloucester ever subscribed to any theory of parliamentary independence or supremacy. He was known by his contemporaries as a clever politician, who had mastered the art of courting popular favour. Such statements as he made were undoubtedly intended to be applied to a specific set of circumstances and were conceived primarily in terms of their propaganda value. His own confession in 1397 indicates the same awareness of the unorthodox character of the parliaments of 1386 and 1388 as that made evident by the enactments of 1388 themselves. Any effort to distill the essence of a theory of the constitution from the legislation of the Merciless Parliament yields nothing but a series of irreconcilable paradoxes. Obviously the men who attempted to impose statutory limitations on all ensuing assemblies of the estates did not adhere to any doctrine of parliamentary supremacy to the law. Likewise, the men who took such pains to guarantee the validity of their actions by every conceivable means, and at the same time insisted that they should never serve as precedents in the future, recognized plainly that they had gone far beyond the law and custom of the day. Since Gloucester's was the major hand in directing all of the legislation, he, like the rest, must be considered to have been acting as the occasion demanded with no reference to any philosophy of government.

If it is misleading to refer to the Appellant group as a constitutional party, or indeed as a party at all, it is equally misleading to speak of a moderate or middle party. There was a well integrated court faction which already in 1386 was beginning to enunciate a coherent royalist doctrine. But the controversies of that and the two succeeding years were carried on entirely at the personal rather than the theoretical level. On that level, the Appellants were the most extreme and the most active of the opponents of the court. Other men reacted less violently; some were quite indifferent while others were sympathetic to the king and his friends. All responded to their own individual impulses not to the dictates of party. It was Richard's own reaction to the removal of Suffolk which brought things to a head and forced everyone to take sides. Under the circumstances, particularly after the defeat of the royal armies, most of those who were not yet committed, together with many who had been moderately attached to the court group, approved the assault on the five subjects of the appeal. Before it became quite clear just how far Gloucester, Arundel and Warwick intended to go, almost everyone was too deeply involved to draw back.

The adherence of Nottingham and Derby was essential to the success of the Appellants' programme, both at Radcot Bridge and subsequently in parliament. No less essential was the limited support of men like Sir Richard Scrope, Lord John Cobham and the Bishop of London, and the neutrality of such people as the Duke of York, the Earls of Kent and Northumberland, the Nevilles of Raby, the Bishop of Winchester, and the Archbishop of Canterbury. All of these important men adopted a moderate position in the controversy, but they in no sense in that year or ever constituted the nucleus of a moderate party. Political action in the fourteenth century was conducted on a sophisticated plane. Whoever engaged in it would need to understand its conventions and its subtleties as well as to assess accurately the relative influence of others. Men sought where they could for alliance or support to advance their interests or protect their positions. They remained strangers, however, to the forms and uses of parties.

The coalition of the magnates was the creature of incident; it was, nevertheless, so long as it could be maintained, omnipotent. The church, the city, and the knights fell rapidly into line. While the pope vied with the mayor and aldermen of London in a show of complaisance to the great men, the commons became the advance guard of the hue and cry. Some of the knights, for reasons of their own, shared the fears of their superiors concerning the too great growth of royal power. Others unhesitatingly followed the great men who were their patrons or to whom they looked for favour. Many were doubtless indifferent or even loyal to the king and his friends. But a very substantial number were likely to have been motivated by the desire to be recognized as active vocal supporters of the group who were clearly destined to triumph. If the behaviour of the Londoners may be taken as at all typical, some groups and individuals who might have been subject to the suspicion of direct or indirect association with the courtiers would have been particularly eager to clear themselves by extreme demonstrations of partisanship. Brembre had been sacrificed to precisely this spirit by the people who had been closest to him and who would have profited most by his royalist connections if the magnates had been crushed.

In general, then, these lesser people among the governing classes were already to some degree exhibiting the traits which were to determine their responses to the dynastic controversies which upset the next century. They were prompt to utilize their positions or their bargaining power to advance their own interests whenever possible. They were concerned about the welfare of the realm. In such affairs they could display remarkable initiative and independence. On the other hand, they did not propose to take great risks out of loyalty either to persons or causes if they could avoid doing so. Most of them were probably quite well aware of the vast difference between the events of 1386–88 and those of 1376. They knew that they had been dealing in the later years with matters of life and death; with questions of treason, not simply of abuse of position for self-enrichment; with assaults on the policy and the power of the king himself through attacks on his ministers and advisers rather than the punishment of corrupt or dishonest officials toward whose fate the monarch appeared to be entirely indifferent. As a group their foremost desire was to avoid being crushed in the struggle. Thus in matters of high politics they became rather the agents than the authors of action. It should be added, however, that despite the prohibitions which concluded the Merciless Parliament, the enactments of the commons were destined to serve as precedents which in the long run, like those of earlier years, enhanced their importance.

No impression of Richard's reaction to the brutal destruction of his following emerges from the pages of the chronicles. It may only be surmised that he was completely stunned. Devoted to his friends, and above all passionately sensitive to the dignity and inviolability of his position, he undoubtedly became only the more earnest in his desire to vindicate before all men the sanctity of his prerogative.

CHAPTER VI

THE PREROGATIVE RESTORED

COMPLETE and decisive as was the victory of the magnates over the king's partisans, it only delayed rather than forestalled the attempt at royal absolutism. The triumph of Gloucester and his associates must have appeared to its executors to have stifled forever the ambitions of the king. In actuality, they had only won the first skirmish in a battle in which Richard was himself to enjoy mastery before his final ruin. Out of the wreck of his fortunes in 1388 a new royalist following was slowly and painstakingly developed. On the strength of this support a genuine bid was made for autocratic power. In the long run the second attempt, like the first, was a failure, but not before there had been an experiment with royal supremacy buttressed by an openly proclaimed theory of monarchical right.

The Appellant government was maintained for nearly a year after the dissolution of the Merciless Parliament. On May 3, 1389, Richard startled a meeting of his great council with a declaration that he would, henceforth, assume personal responsibility for the management of his realm. As he had reached his twenty-second year, the lords of the council could do nothing but agree that it was his right to take control of his own affairs, 'even as the meanest man in the realm might do according to law'.[1] Having received this assurance, Richard thanked the councillors for their services and made a significant speech. He had been permitted to do nothing, he said, without the advice and tutelage of others in whose hands he had been placed. In the meantime, his realm had been in many ways ill-governed and his people oppressed by grievous taxation. As he proposed to remedy these evils by the appointment of advisers of his own choosing, he demanded that the chancellor at once surrender the great seal. Further removals followed. Whether or not they were so sweeping as they appeared to contemporaries to be, they sufficed to create the impression of wholesale change. The old civil

[1] *Hist. Ang.*, II, p. 181.

servants Wykeham of Winchester and Brantingham of Oxford, respectively, succeeded Bishop Arundel as chancellor and Bishop Gilbert of Hereford as treasurer. Edmund Stafford became keeper of the privy seal in the place of the Bishop of Salisbury. The judiciary received a thorough overhaul. But the most striking changes came with the removal of Gloucester and Warwick from the council, and the replacement of Arundel as admiral and captain of Brest by John Holland, the new Earl of Huntingdon.[2]

The ease with which Richard reasserted his authority has frequently been a subject of surprise to historians, who have taken pains to explain the episode as evidence of general discontent with the government of the Appellants. There may have been dissatisfaction but the success of the king requires no elaborate explanation. Except for the duration of the Merciless Parliament, the Appellants had never controlled a majority of the lords, and even during the crisis itself their hold on the main body of the magnates had been a tenuous one. With the royal party utterly broken, few of the great men of the realm had any further reason either to fear or to oppose the king. Indeed, many probably welcomed the termination of the ascendancy of Gloucester whose excessive power would, like Lancaster's in 1376, have been a threat to the independence of some of the baronage.[3] The administration of the commission had, after all, no legal standing. Richard was not a minor; nor does his dismissal of the commission in 1389 mark the official termination of a minority. He had exercised the full responsibilities of monarchy in the years from 1384 to 1386, as Gloucester and Bishop Arundel, for example, had recognized when they visited him at Eltham to demand his return to parliament. His request to be permitted to resume the privileges of his majority was so wholly reasonable that none could deny it, and he had been prudent enough to present it, not to the commission, but to the great council which was never subject to Appellant domination. Finally, he had

[2] The most complete contemporary account of this event is to be found in *Polychronicon*, IX, pp. 210, 211. The scene is described more briefly and perhaps less sympathetically by Walsingham, *Hist. Ang.*, II, pp. 181, 182, and Knighton, *Leyces. Chron.*, II, p. 310. All accounts are in substantial agreement as to the substance and reception of the king's remarks. *Cal. Pat. Rolls*, 1388–92, p. 31; *Cal. Close Rolls*, 1385–89, p. 591; *Foedera*, VII, p. 22.

[3] *Leyces. Chron.*, II, p. 311.

shown great moderation in his selection of ministers, Wykeham and Brantingham, for example, being wholly unexceptionable. Yet he had dared to show his personal feeling. If there was no immediate evidence of an attempt to rebuild a royal party, there was at least apparent disapproval of the Appellants. Gloucester, Arundel, and Warwick all felt the weight of the king's displeasure. The degree of their sensitivity may be gauged by the fact that in November 1389 that indefatigable politician, the Earl of Northumberland, presented to the council a petition pleading for a better understanding between the king and his three recent enemies.[4] In November also the return of the Duke of Lancaster to England removed the last possibility that Gloucester might regain his ascendancy. For Lancaster, with his Spanish ambitions sated and his enemies about the king destroyed, remained a loyal and useful servant to his nephew until the day of his death. His influence coupled with that of the crown was decisive. There was no recurrence of civil strife while he lived.

The restoration of the king to his rightful place may have stirred some hope among those of his subjects who favoured him. Richard, however, was careful to do nothing to create another united opposition. On the contrary, he appears to have been determined to secure to himself the active allegiance of everyone in the kingdom except the three noblemen who had led the attack upon his friends. He showered favours on Lancaster and Nottingham.[5] He admitted the Earl of Derby to his council. He made a bid for public favour by remitting one-half of the subsidy which had been voted for 1389. At Lancaster's request he made his peace with John of Northampton and restored to the one-time mayor his possessions and freedom in the city. Until 1392 he showed no sign of interest in the victims of the parliament of 1388.[6] The culmination of the policy of conciliation was reached with the return to office, upon the resignations of Brantingham and Wykeham, of the treasurer and chancellor whom the Appellants had nominated. The reinstatement of Archbishop Arundel to the chancery, where he remained for more than five years, marks the extreme limit of the king's attempt to placate his former foes.

---

[4] *Proceedings and Ordinances of the Privy Council of England* (ed. Nicholas), I, p. 12.
[5] The liberality to Nottingham actually caused difficulties with the council. Ibid.
[6] On November 5, 1389, Sir Robert Bealknap's hardships were mitigated by a royal grant, with assent of council, of 40 pounds annually; *Issues of the Exchequer*, p. 240. Bealknap was not, however, a member of the royal faction.

Richard felt sufficiently sure of his position in 1390 to provide an interesting demonstration of self-confidence. The ministers resigned in a body and begged the parliament that any or all of them might be proceeded against if there were complaints about their conduct of office. There were none. The parliament itself requested their restoration to office with a vote of thanks for their performance in the preceding year.[7] The king, of course, insisted that this bit of carefully staged byplay in no sense constituted a precedent. It served the dual purpose of reminding the nation in the only possible manner that Richard did not believe his ministers to be answerable in any way to parliament for their official behaviour, and of parading the acceptability of his government before any who might have hoped that he would soon be in difficulty again. The docility of both parliament and council was to continue until 1399. The pacific temper of the commons, so violent in 1388, adds further proof that in these matters they but followed the lead of their superiors. Tranquility was the order of the day.

In the next few years death more than once affected the shifting relationships between the court and the magnates. On July 7, 1394, Queen Anne died quite suddenly at Shene. Richard was inconsolable. The passionate and extravagant manifestations of his grief were viewed with awe by his contemporaries. His remarriage two years later to the daughter of the king of France was a diplomatic move important to his policy of peace. In 1392 Robert de Vere died in 'miserable poverty' at Louvain. He had already fallen heir to the few possessions of his fellow exile, Suffolk, who had preceded him to the grave by three years, and he had barely outlived the former Archbishop of York, Alexander Neville. Thus there could be no longer any fear of an attempt at the restoration of the old courtiers. The position of the king was thereby strengthened with the majority of the great noblemen, though he made a public display of his sorrow for the former favourite.[8] The death of the Duchess of Lancaster in 1394 made it possible for the duke at last to formalize the long standing union with his mistress, Katherine Swynford. The royal approval

---

[7] *Rot. Parl.*, III, p. 258.

[8] Richard had proposed to recall de Vere, and the archbishop, only a few months before their deaths, but had been blocked by his council. *Polychronicon*, IX, p. 264.

of the marriage completed the attachment between uncle and nephew. Richard also gained from shifts in the ecclesiastical hierarchy following upon the death of Archbishop Courtenay, in 1396. Courtenay had caused the crown no trouble in his later years, but neither had he been an ally in times of crisis. Richard utilized the vacancy for a three-fold purpose. He awarded the see of Canterbury to Archbishop Arundel, thereby hoping perhaps to detach him from allegiance to his brother. At the same time, the appointment afforded the opportunity for a graceful removal of Arundel from the chancellorship, since there was a feeling that the king's chief minister should not also be head of the church. The new chancellor was Bishop Stafford of Exeter, a civil servant thoroughly loyal to the king. Richard was also able to reward another faithful cleric with the appointment of Roger Waldby to the see of York vacated by Arundel.[9]

Richard's marriage to the seven-year-old daughter of Charles VI involved an important sacrifice to his peace programme. From his own point of view a settled succession was essential, yet so thoroughly was he convinced of the wisdom of the alliance that he was willing to postpone the prospect of an heir for a number of years in order to achieve the friendship of France.

With the establishment of peace abroad and order at home, Richard appeared to be on the threshold of a long successful reign. The country had enjoyed a period of unprecedented prosperity which was to linger in the minds of men for generations to come.[10] Peace and prosperity contributed markedly to the success of the royal policy of the restoration of prerogative authority. The king worked quietly but steadily toward reversing the verdict of 1388. The council, enlarged by the addition of noblemen who owed their titles to the king's good will and

[9] *Ann. Ric.*, pp. 194, 195. The Waldby appointment is described as being 'contra vota totius cleri Eboracensis'.

[10] The chronicles are sprinkled with commentaries on the national prosperity. E.g. *Leyces. Chron.*, II, pp. 320, 321; *Hist. Ang.*. II, p. 211; *Polychronicon*, IX, p. 275; *Ann. Ric.*, p. 201. The impression which carried over into the next century is witnessed by an anonymous metrical roll call of the kings of England, composed late in the reign of Henry VI. 'Sonne of
      Prince Edwarde,
      Richard kinge ye secounde,
      In whos tyme was peas and grete plente;'
Polychronicon, VIII, p. 520. The relatively high value of English coinage is indicated by entries in the *Issues of the Exchequer*, pp. 249, 250.

knights and civil servants who by 1396 had enjoyed years of service under the king, was completely favourable to him. Many of its members had already shown signs of championing extreme royalist doctrines. In February 1392 the lords of the council took, of their own free will, a solemn oath to commit no act against the king or against the peace in defiance of the law of the land. Late that same year the parliament expressly declared that the king should enjoy his prerogative as largely as any of his predecessors ever did notwithstanding any statute to the contrary. Special reference was made to the so-called statute of Gloucester of Edward II, which had authorized the deposition of that unhappy monarch. The voluntary testimonials of both council and parliament may have reflected a lingering uneasiness about the settlement of 1388, but they likewise clearly evinced a widespread feeling that there should be no tampering with the legitimate authority of the king.[11]

The appearances of universal peace and good will in 1396 were, however, illusory. There had been occasional rumblings. The most notable was a quarrel in 1392 between Richard and the city of London. His excessive impatience with the citizens may have reflected resentment over their failure to stand by him in 1387 after he had taken such pains to court their favour. In any case, with the full support of the magnates Richard forced the Londoners to an abject submission.[12] They in their turn proved to have tenacious memories.

There had also been sporadic outbreaks of violence in Yorkshire and Cheshire with which Gloucester and Arundel were suspiciously connected. These disturbances in the portion of the kingdom where warfare was most popular may have been manifestations of hostility to the proposals for peace with France. Though none of these were extremely serious matters, civil unrest was about to be renewed. Richard sought no personal reconciliation with Arundel who had been severely punished for rudeness at the funeral of Queen Anne. Meantime his growing

[11] See J. F. Baldwin, *The King's Council in England During the Middle Ages* (1913) pp. 132, 135, 138, 489 ff. *Rot. Parl.*, III, p. 299.
[12] R. Bird, *The Turbulent London of Richard II*, pp. 101–9; cf. *Hist. Ang.*, II, p. 208; *Polychronicon*, IX, p. 270; *Cont. Eul. Hist.*, III, p. 367; and *Leyces. Chron.*, II, p. 319.

strength was enough to ensure a return to open hostility on the part of others.[13]

The culminating crisis of the reign is generally considered to have originated with a royal *coup d'état*. The king's sudden display of high-handed autocracy has been viewed variously as the climax to years of vengeful planning, as an unpremeditated outburst against those who had humiliated him a decade earlier, and as the action of a madman. The last merits no serious consideration. There is no contemporary evidence to support it; insanity was not one of the charges levied against Richard by his successor, who clutched at every possible straw to justify his usurpation; and the loyalty of the king's own partisans is ample testimony to his sanity. Nervous, temperamental, sensitive he was, perhaps, but not by any standard mad.

The second position rests upon the assumption that Richard might frequently have felt the impulse to punish his enemies of 1388, but that he lacked the power to do so, and was, furthermore, restrained by the moderation of his queen. By 1397 the restraining influence was gone and the power was ample. Any reminder of his grievances might furnish the occasion. On the surface this explanation of his behaviour has much to commend it. Yet while he had apparently never entrusted Gloucester with his entire confidence, and while his relationships with the Earl of Arundel had always been anything but cordial, his repetition of official pardons even to these two most grievous offenders would seem to deny any deeply concealed urge to destroy them.[14] Furthermore, Derby, Nottingham and Archbishop Arundel had been frequent beneficiaries of the royal good will. No record or rumour originating earlier than 1397 affords the slightest hint that the king intended to do other than let bygones be bygones.

The establishment of the related hypothesis, that the grudge had been borne for years behind a mask of docility, only to be made manifest when the prospect of punishment presented itself, is even less plausible. Nothing that is known of Richard's character credits him with the capacity for such long and carefully hidden dissimulation. By all accounts he was, on the

---

[13] Gloucester also was probably never reconciled. Cf. Froissart, *Chroniques*, XV, pp. 157 ff.; J. G. Bellamy, 'The Northern Rebellions in the Later Years of Richard II', *Bulletin of the John Rylands Library*, XLVII (1965) pp. 254 ff.

[14] *Chronicon Adae de Usk*, p. 153 n.; *Rot. Parl.*, III, pp. 376, 421.

contrary, possessed of an impulsive and ungovernable temper, so much so, indeed, that his mercurial disposition became the most familiar aspect of the Ricardian legend. Furthermore, it is difficult to believe that a systematic programme of vengeance to be executed years in the future germinated and matured in the mind of the young king without his ever having suggested his purpose to any of his associates. No one later either in accusation or confession attributed such a design to him.

The rejection of these familiar hypotheses leaves one further alternative. His intention was the seizure of the plenitude of power in his kingdom and the removal of all who stood in his way. This purpose he acknowledged while he still reigned. The simplest and most logical explanation for the *coup d'état* of 1397 is that Richard had again, as in 1386, achieved a position which threatened the independence and privileges of the magnates, and that Gloucester and Arundel perished not because of what they had done in 1388, but because of the fear that in 1397 they might repeat their old offences. It must be remembered that although Richard had been careful since his humiliation not to give particular grounds for anxiety where it might be risky to do so, he had always insisted even in public that his power was undiminished. Perhaps the aristocracy had accepted such declarations too lightly as mere formalities.

The January parliament of 1397 furnished what is probably the key to the entire episode in the much misunderstood case of Thomas Haxey. The case caused enough furore to fill five printed pages of the official record. Its unusual importance had nothing to do with a putative abridgement of the commons' privilege of free speech. It is not even necessary to inquire into the extent to which such a privilege was a reality in the later fourteenth century, for Haxey was not a member of the house at all. The commons' normal petition of grievances was compiled under four headings, which concerned: (1) the employment of sheriffs and escheators beyond the 'customary' term of one year; (2) the failure properly to guard the Scottish border; (3) the disregard of the statute prohibiting the wearing of 'cognizances' except under certain conditions; and (4) the excessive cost of maintaining the royal household, particularly because of the large number of bishops and ladies who habitually resided therein.[15]

To the first three of these grievances, as enumerated, the king took no exception. He presented argument on behalf of the administrative wisdom of retaining the service of useful officers for a longer term than one year, and he promised to attend to the affairs of the Scottish border as well as to any breaches of the statutes. Of the fourth article, however, he deliberately determined to make an issue. Learning that this particular complaint had its origin in a bill presented to the commons by a non-member, he commanded the Duke of Lancaster to discover the name of the author. The commons made no stir about disclosing the name of Thomas Haxey, a king's clerk. To the king's vehement protest that they had therein tampered with matters which were detrimental to his regality and his royal liberty, they returned, with a humble apology, the plea that such had in no wise been their intention. Richard spelled out to the commons, in a fashion at once precise and thorough, his theory of the untouchable nature of his office, before turning to the lords from whom he easily procured a declaration that exciting the parliament to interfere in any way with the king's enjoyment of his royal estate constituted an act of treason. Haxey was thereupon condemned and sentenced to suffer the full severities provided by law. The clerk actually escaped very lightly. Upon petition of Archbishop Arundel and the ecclesiastical hierarchy he had already been remanded to the custody of the church to await a full pardon which was shortly forthcoming.

Such, in brief, is the story. It has been suggested that Richard recognized in Haxey the cat's paw of more sinister forces in the background; that the king's wrath was directed violently against one whom he considered a personal ingrate in order that an example might be provided to the other members of his household; and that the impetuous display of royal temper is the first sign of Richard's alleged mental collapse. No one of these suggestions satisfactorily accounts for so much sound and fury, particularly since there is another way of explaining the episode which would envelope it with significance quite commensurate

[15] *Rot. Parl.*, III, pp. 339–43. Cf. Tout, *Chapters*, IV, pp. 17–19 and J. E. Neale, 'The Commons' Privilege of Free Speech in Parliament', *Tudor Studies* (1924), p. 259. Also Steel, *Richard II*, pp. 223–29, whose analysis is most valuable.

with the attention it receives in the parliamentary record. Given the reconstruction of the strength of the royal following and the assurance of the complaisance of the commons, Richard was only too eager to reaffirm a position on the matter of treason which he had never abandoned and which was fundamental to his whole theory of kingship. Under no circumstances could he have been presented with a better opportunity for doing so. Haxey may indeed have been a cat's paw for Gloucester or for other restless magnates but he was important to the king in a different role. In speculating upon motivation behind the Haxey petition the possibility should not be overlooked that Richard himself may have inspired its presentation to the commons in order that he might be able to reopen the treason issue in precisely the old terms. Haxey's official position and the overly lenient treatment accorded him would lend plausibility to the notion of royal sponsorship.

An assault by the commons on his chosen minister a decade earlier had led the king to submit to the justices those momentous questions which brought the revolution of 1388 in their train. The incitement of the commons to interfere with the royal household and its officials was treason in 1387; it was treason still in 1397.[16] Haxey's offence was the old one of Gloucester and his associates who in 1386 induced the commons to impeach the Earl of Suffolk. He, like them, had encouraged the members of the king's parliament to exceed their responsibilities and to enter into that sphere of activity which was the province of royal majesty alone. There is no indication that the king ever moderated his early conceptions of regality and of treason. On the contrary, he consistently repeated, even in the hour of his greatest humiliation, that nothing had been or would be accepted by him as an abatement of or an infringement upon his prerogative. Now at last he was in a position to make it plain to all the realm that behind those general declarations remained that same specific definition of law which had caused such consternation among the magnates ten years earlier; and thus the relatively absurd parliamentary petition of an insignificant clerk became an event of transcendant importance.

[16] Cf. Plucknett, 'Impeachment and Attainder', p. 149; also Chrimes, 'Richard II's Questions to the Judges', p. 390.

F

From first to last the initiative in the affair was Richard's. Furthermore, the record contains no hint of an objection from any quarter that Haxey's act preceded the lords' definition of treason and that he, therefore, deserved immunity. His guilt was universally accepted and only a pardon requested. The conviction of Haxey was entirely just in terms of the king's interpretation of the law. The clerk had not even discovered a new way of committing an old crime. He had violated what was and had been the fundamental law, for which the lords declared him to be as guilty as any future transgressor would be. They had returned to the all-inclusive definition both of the crime and its penalties which had been enunciated at Shrewsbury and Nottingham in 1387, and in this instance there was no necessity to use guarded language. Treason received its proper name by the lawful judgment of parliament.

If that was the lesson which the king desired to drive home it would have served as fair warning to all who might be disquieted by his increasing display of power, and particularly to those who had reason to believe that they did not enjoy his confidence.[17] Though there was no immediate overt reaction, the first rumours of dissension were forthcoming in a matter of weeks.

During the course of the session the Duke of Lancaster had been brought even closer to his nephew by the enactment of legislation legitimizing his bastard issue by his new wife, Katherine Swynford, and the provision of an earldom for the eldest of them. In the same parliament the justices who had been banished to Ireland in 1388 were recalled. Their recall was, however, coupled with a specific reaffirmation of the validity of the other terms of the statute of that year. Timed as it was, this action may have been meant to serve as a reminder to all concerned that, despite the Haxey incident, the affair of 1388 would not be reopened by the king so long as there was no evidence of a renewal of discord. If such was its purpose it was a failure; for within a very few months of the amicable termination of the session the old animosities flared into the open again. The lords and commons adjourned in February. Before the middle of July, Gloucester, Arundel and Warwick were arrested for treason.

17 Cf. Galbraith, 'A New Life of Richard II', *History*, XXVI, (1942), pp. 231, 232.

In those intervening weeks the behaviour of the king, though inoffensive, had certainly not been such as to please any who might be jealous of the growth of royal power. He had laboured to strengthen his prestige and position both at home and abroad. New honours were loaded upon Nottingham, while for his half-brother, Huntingdon, Richard procured international distinctions surpassing any which for more than a generation had been held by an Englishman. He was named gonfalonier of the church and vicar-general of the patrimony of Saint Peter. The titles were accompanied by privileges 'which virtually placed the English clergy under his domination.'[18] While this rapprochement of papacy and court was in process, the peace with France was strengthened by the surrender to the Duke of Brittany and the King of Navarre of the forts of Brest and Cherbourg. Even more notable were negotiations for the imperial sceptre held by the incompetent Wenceslas of Bohemia. Though Richard's imperial ambitions ultimately came to nothing, there appeared in the early summer of 1397 to be more than a slender chance of their success.[19]

All of these moves were accompanied by evidences of distinct concern with the sacred character of regal power. Most particularly the king manifested an interest in the predecessor whose ill-fated example had been called to his attention in 1386. The tragic conclusion of the reign of Edward II earned for that unkingly king a place in the esteem of his great-grandson far beyond any to which his merits as ruler or as man would have entitled him. In his person the sanctity of monarchy had been assaulted; as Richard viewed it the assault and its consequences rendered him suited not merely to the role of martyr but even to that of saint. Thus the king employed the months of good relationships between England and the papacy in attempting to secure the official canonization of his unfortunate ancestor.[20]

In the meantime, there were complaints about governmental expenditure. The magnificence of the court, the French marriage,

[18] Petroy, *Schisme*, p. 343; *Ann. Ric.*, pp. 200, 201.
[19] Perroy, op. cit., pp. 342, 343; *Foedera*, VII, p. 858; VIII, p. 3; *Ann. Ric.*, p. 199.
[20] *Issues of thē Exchequer*, pp. 259, 264. Efforts in this direction had begun as early as 1385.

the bid for the empire, and the conciliation of the papacy all had occasioned large outlays in the months since the death of Anne of Bohemia. Those artistic tastes which distinguished Richard from so many medieval monarchs were indulged to an unprecedented degree.[21] A portion of these expenses at least was met by governmental borrowing, a practice which had, of course, been employed many times in the past. There is a contemporary charge that not all of the creditors in 1397 assumed their role willingly; but whether or not the pressure applied was greater than customary, the spectacle of the court living beyond its private means was no more pleasant to the bulk of the magnates than it had been in 1386 or in 1376.[22] Hence, though even an unfriendly chronicler calls attention to the unusual prosperity of the times, there were abundant sources for the nourishment of fear, suspicion, and hostility among all whom the monarch did not delight to favour.[23]

To what extent fear and suspicion led to concerted plans for action cannot be determined. Equally problematical is the question of the degree to which the king would have been apprised of plots and conspiracies, if any did exist. Certainly there was grumbling. There were also evidences of misunderstanding. Gloucester and Arundel are said to have annoyed Richard as early as February by a deliberate failure to attend a meeting of the great council. Only a little later there was, if the chronicler is to be credited, a rumour that the king's chances for election as emperor were jeopardized by the report of his inability properly to control his own nobles.[24] In early summer a heated public discussion between Gloucester and Richard on the subject of the restoration of Brest to the Duke of Brittany was terminated with the duke's abrupt withdrawal from the court to his estates in Essex. Although each of these matters is relatively trifling in itself, taken together they point to a growth of tension comparable to that of the mid-1380's. The extant reports of actual conspiracy are all probable enough, but none is confirmed by any official record. As at any other time of tension, however, the

[21] Ibid., pp. 262–64.
[22] *Ann. Ric.*, pp. 199, 200; but cf. the thorough analysis of Steel, 'English Government Finance, 1377–1413', *E.H.R.*, LI (1936), pp. 45–51 and *The Receipt of the Exchequer, 1377–1485* (1954) pp. 103–48.
[23] *Ann. Ric.*, p. 201.
[24] Ibid., p. 199.

fear of plots and counterplots was as likely to produce conflict as their verified reality.[25]

Warwick was arrested at the conclusion of a royal banquet on July 8th, to which Gloucester and Arundel had also been invited, but from which they had with no very convincing excuses absented themselves. Whether, as the enemies of the king alleged, the banquet was only a pretext to make the premediated capture of the lords easy, or whether the very fact of the absences was taken by Richard to be conclusive proof of the truth of his worst fears, is not of great importance. What is important is that feelings had reached the stage that the king's uncle and his associate feared to appear at the royal table, or that Richard so feared the possible implications of their absence that he determined at once to destroy them. He went in person to Gloucester's castle at Pleshy on the following day to seize without resistance the most formidable of his enemies in his own stronghold. Arundel was persuaded by his brother, the archbishop, voluntarily to surrender. News of the sudden move was startling. Richard had not waited, as in 1387, for his opponents to strike the first blow. To quiet unrest a proclamation was issued prohibiting agitation in defense of the victims and announcing that the action had been taken not because of old, but of new treasons.[26] This was followed by the preparation of an appeal modelled precisely after that of 1388, and lodged with the king by eight noblemen.

In August, the appeal, perhaps previously rehearsed, was made the formal subject of a meeting of the council at Nottingham. The new 'Appellants' included one member of the precedent-making group of 1388, Nottingham, who was joined on this occasion by the Earls of Rutland, Kent, Salisbury, Huntingdon, and Somerset, and Lord Thomas Despenser and William Scrope. All were close personal adherents of the court who could easily have been managed by the king. Their action precipitated the issuance of writs for parliament, from which appropriate judgments for the alleged treasons could issue.

By the time that the parliament assembled at Westminster on the seventeenth of September, all the steps necessary to the

[25] *Chronique de la Traison et Mort de Richard Deux*, pp. 3–7; Froissart, *Chroniques*, XV, pp. 157 ff.; *Ann. Ric.*, p. 201.
[26] *Foedera*, VIII, pp. 6, 7.

assurance of the speedy accomplishment of the king's purposes had been taken. The contemporary charges that the royalists packed the commons and that the king coerced the appellants are equally wide of the mark.[27] The appellants required no coercion; and pains were taken to condition the parliament to a frame of mind congenial to the court. Persuasion, pressure, manipulation, and even intimidation were perhaps employed. Only a few magnates whose loyalty could not be doubted were permitted to bring armed retinues into the city. To these private armies were added Richard's own Cheshire archers, who were reputed to have surrounded the open pavilion where the commons debated. The selection as speaker of a tested manager, John Bushy, widely known to be identified with the king's inner council, was secured. The choice of a proctor to act for the whole of the clergy, a move which presaged the ominous expectation of capital sentences, fell upon another of Richard's close advisers, Sir Thomas Percy, the royal steward.[28]

Of all the staging, no act was more carefully arranged than the initial speech of the chancellor. In both tenor and substance it denoted a distinct advance in the enunciation of royalist doctrine over what the estates had become accustomed in years past to hearing. In 1393 and 1394, for example, the commons had been greeted with discussions of the king's obligations to protect his realm in war or peace, and to maintain the liberties of the church and all corporations. These statements were, of course, primarily phrased in such a way as to evoke a favourable response to the demand for a supply which they introduced. In the parliament of 1395 to which Gloucester returned from Ireland to transmit his nephew's request for more funds, the chancellor's opening remarks had elaborated the same themes. Stress was laid upon the mutual responsibilities of government and governed to assure uniform justice to all. In enumerating the reasons why the community should show honour to the sovereign, Chancellor Arundel even saw fit to draw special attention to the fact that his gracious majesty extended his mercy to all and had no damage to do or vengeance to take against any person. Again in the January session of 1397, made momentous

[27] *Ann. Ric.*, pp. 207, 209.
[28] *Rot. Parl.*, III, p. 348; *Chronicon Adae de Usk*, pp. 9, 10; *Ann. Ric.*, p. 208.

by the Haxey episode, Arundel's successor, Bishop Stafford of
Exeter, touched upon four duties of the king and his parliament.
Holy church should be maintained in its rights and liberties;
the people should be governed justly and malefactors punished as
they deserved; the laws should be upheld, or amended if they no
longer served the welfare of the citizenry; and the realm should be
defended from foes abroad.

All of these were familiar platitudes. On the occasion of
Stafford's second appearance in his official role in the September
parliament of 1397, however, the pattern was abruptly altered.
Significantly he chose for his text the words of Ezekiel, 'There
shall be one king over all'. The emphasis was shifted from the
customary cant about monarchical duties to an examination of
monarchical powers. Biblical authorities were cited to testify to
the necessity of the rule of 'one sole king'. To good government
three prerequisities were enumerated: that the king should be
powerful; that he should be strict in the execution of his laws;
and that his subjects should be obedient. Without severe obedience to the prince there could be, the chancellor urged, no
security of life or goods or the fruits of labour to any man. His
statement was concluded with the promise that the king would
preserve the laws and that he would grant pardon to all but a
few of his subjects.[29]

If the official report is not misleading, those concluding
words merit particular attention. The shift in emphasis from the
monarch's obligation to uphold the laws under all circumstances
to his function as the 'pillar of the law' who has every intention to
provide justice for all the realm is not very subtly disguised. The
history of the session demonstrates that the language of the
parliamentary rolls coincided perfectly with the attitude of
Richard and his advisers.

It may be, too, that this carefully chosen language affords an
explanation of the limitation of the appeal of the eight lords
entirely to the events of 1386 to 1388, without ever so much as a
notation of those 'new treasons' which had been served up as the
published pretext for the three arrests. There is, of course, the
probability that no convincing proof of new treason had been
forthcoming, and that the appellants had been forced to resurrect

[29] *Rot. Parl.*, III, pp. 309, 329, 337. For the 1397 speech, ibid., p. 347.

the ten-year-old offences as a secure justification for destroying their victims. Or there may have been compelling reasons to suppress the details of the recent conspiracy. On the other hand, it is tempting to view the selection as a deliberate choice among alternatives and, if such it was, the speech of the chancellor sounded in public the keynote of a long-range programme which began with the prosecution of Haxey and terminated only with the end of the reign.[30]

The sequence of events in parliament may provide some clues. The appeal was not made the first order of business. Instead, the commons, through their speaker, Bushy, brought in a series of petitions. These called for the revocation of the statutes passed by the authority of the commission of 1386-89; a declaration that the instigators of the commission were traitors; the recall of pardons issued to all who had been associated with the commission; and the punishment of these traitors, especially Thomas Arundel, the Archbishop of Canterbury. Gloucester and the Earl of Arundel were also mentioned specifically, the recall of the earl's individual pardon of 1394 being demanded separately. To all of these requests, except that for the punishment of the archbishop, the king readily assented, and they were duly enacted into law. Consideration of the archbishop's case was reserved for another day, when he was formally impeached and convicted.

In the meantime, a new statutory definition of treason had been announced as the law of the land. By its terms any who should incite the people against the king or make war in the realm were to be adjudged traitors, as were, of course, any who should propose the king's death or deposition.[31] This is substantially the definition of the lords in connection with the Haxey case, and of the justices at Nottingham and Shrewsbury in 1387 in dealing with precisely the incidents now, after a lapse of eleven years, linked so closely to the new statute. Richard, it would appear, was returning systematically to the first episode of his humiliation in order that he might be vindicated step by step. To

<hr>

[30] Richard may, in fact, not have dared to publish what he learned. If Gloucester and Arundel had been using the proposals for peace as a principal excuse for an attack on the king, public accusation might have made them popular in the role of champions against France. Cf. Bellamy, 'The Northern Rebellions of Richard II', p. 274; cf. *Traison et Mort*, pp. 3, 4.

[31] *Rot. Parl.*, III, p. 351.

avoid undue panic he hastened to declare that, except for those whose names had been mentioned by the speaker 'All others who were joined in the said commission . . . especially Alexander Neville' were loyal and faithful subjects free from any taint of treason. This declaration brought the aged Bishop Wykeham of Winchester and the Duke of York to their knees before the king, weeping tears of gratitude for the mercy shown them.[32] As yet there had been no mention of the Merciless Parliament or of the events which immediately preceded it. It is impossible to escape the implication that, since the old issues had arisen again, Richard believed that the effects of the revolution which had begun with the assault upon Suffolk could only be extirpated by a universal recognition of the illegality of everything that had accompanied the destruction of the old royal party. Each of those illegal acts was to receive attention in its proper chronological order.

On the fifth day of the session the new appellants at last appeared, clad in robes of crimson silk trimmed with white and gold. In their accusation of treason they now included the name of Sir Thomas Mortimer with those of Gloucester, Arundel and Warwick. The charges against Gloucester and Arundel began with their behaviour in the parliament of 1386; those against Warwick and Mortimer with the armed insurrection of November, 1387. The appeal referred briefly to incitement to violence, constraint of the king and encroachment upon the royal prerogative. It dwelt at greater length on the execution of Sir Simon Burley despite the expressed will of the king and concluded with an allegation that the four accused had concerted to depose their sovereign, an indignity from which he had been saved only by the intervention of the Earls of Nottingham and Derby.[33]

The trial of Arundel before the lords, which followed immediately, was featured by as many manifestations of partiality as that of Brembre a decade earlier. Lancaster, who acted as lord high steward, engaged in an interchange with the accused which had more the character of a brawl than a judicial procedure. In the use of invective he was outdone by his son, Derby, while Arundel's own conduct was as insolent as ever. He appealed quite justly to the pardons which had been granted him for the

[32] *Chronicon Adae de Usk*, p. 13; *Vita Ricardi*, p. 136.
[33] *Rot. Parl.*, III, p. 352.

offences of which he was now arraigned, only to be reminded that those pardons had been annulled in this present parliament. With less ingenuousness, he denied heatedly that he had ever been guilty of acting against the king in any way. He answered Lancaster's accusation of treason with a counter-charge that he was less a traitor than the duke himself. He refused to argue the merits of his case even after the serious consequences of his stubborn behaviour had been fully explained to him by the highest judicial authority. He cried out that the parliament did not represent the 'true Commons' of the realm. At length, to the king's own single accusation that he and his associates had wilfully caused the death of Simon Burley, he could return no response, and the sentence, of which there had never been any doubt, was declared. He died as boldly as he had lived, the only one of the original Appellants who never abased himself before the king in his hour of triumph.[34]

The Earl of Nottingham, to whose custody Gloucester had been entrusted, was then instructed to produce his prisoner. He produced instead only a statement that the duke had died while imprisoned at Calais, and a signed confession which had conveniently been taken by a royal justice in the presence of two witnesses a few days prior to the death. It is presumed that Gloucester had been murdered to avoid the disturbance which might have been occasioned by bringing to trial a prince of the blood royal whose popular following in the countryside was so large. Such a presumption leaves unanswered the questions of why, given the subservience of parliament, a murder was necessary, or what in view of the confession, which must be accepted as authentic, was to be gained by murder rather than execution.[35]

[34] Plucknett, 'Impeachment and Attainder', p. 150; *Ann. Ric.*, pp. 214–16; *Chronicon Adae de Usk*, pp. 13, 14.

[35] The question of Gloucester's murder, which has a lively literature of its own, presents other difficulties. It was one of the charges made by Henry of Lancaster against Richard in 1399. But Henry had likewise charged Norfolk with the murder in 1398 while Richard was still a king whom he was attempting to impress favourably. Surely no member of the royal circle like himself would have been so foolish as to air such a matter if suspicion of the king's complicity were widespread even among the intimate associates of the court. But cf. James Tait, 'Did Richard Murder the Duke of Gloucester?' *Manchester University Historical Essays*, pp. 193–216; A. E. Stamp, 'Richard II and the Death of the Duke of Gloucester', *E.H.R.*, XXXVIII (1923), pp. 249–51; R. L. Atkinson, 'Richard II and the Death of the Duke of Gloucester', *E.H.R.*, XXVIII (Oct. 1923) pp. 563, 564; H. G. Wright, 'Richard II and the Death of the Duke of Gloucester', *E.H.R.*, XLVII (1932), pp. 276–80; and Stamp's reply under the same title, Ibid., p. 453, and Steel, *Richard II*, pp. 238, 239.

In any event, the condemnation of the deceased as a traitor was attended by no difficulty, although since he was unavailable for trial a different set of procedures had to be adopted in order to legalize the seizure of his property. He was charged with treason in levying war against the king in November, 1387. This issue was raised by the commons who alleged that the fact was 'notorious' and thereupon prayed to the lords for his conviction.[36]

The Gloucester confession is an interesting document. The pains taken by Justice Rickhill, who received it, to secure himself against any possibility of retaliatory action regardless of changes that might occur at the seat of power, place its authenticity beyond doubt. Its tone is one of abject submission. The offences, including by intimation the temporary deposition of Richard, are all admitted with only the excuse that they were committed 'for drede of our lyves'. It closes with a reference to the death of Simon Burley, a most humble plea for pardon, and a pledge of absolute loyalty in the future. There is nothing in it either to confirm or deny the allegation of new conspiracies.[37]

Though Gloucester's servility was confined to parchment, that of his confederate, Warwick, was displayed before the entire parliamentary gathering. Weeping and praying for lenience, he confessed to everything of which he was accused. There is no detailed summary of the charges and admissions of guilt in any contemporary record, but in an attempt at self-extenuation, Warwick did lend some support to the otherwise unsubstantiated account of an anti-royalist plot in 1397, narrated in detail by a contemporary chronicler.[38] His protestations that he had been unduly influenced were to good effect, for his life was spared and his punishment reduced to the confiscation of his estates and perpetual banishment to the Isle of Man.

Before Warwick's conviction, the case of Archbishop Thomas Arundel had already been disposed of. Prohibited from entering a plea in his own behalf, his temporalities were seized and he was sentenced to a life of exile. With peculiar propriety, Richard secured from the complaisant pope Arundel's translation to the schismatic see of St. Andrew's which had been awarded to

---

[36] Plucknett, op. cit., p. 151. This procedure is reminiscent of that employed in the conviction of Brembre.

[37] *Rot. Parl.*, III, p. 378.

[38] *Vita Ricardi*, p. 140; cf. *Chronique de la Traison et Mort*, pp. 3–6.

Alexander Neville in 1388. That was the extent of his persecution. He was permitted to withdraw in his own good time to the continent, where he was not to be molested again.[39] Only Sir Thomas Mortimer remained to be brought to trial, but he had fled before the parliament assembled. There was nothing to do but command him to surrender and confiscate his property.

On September 30, after the imposition of a series of oaths to ensure the permanence of all that had been done, the brief session was adjourned. The oaths were reminiscent of those which terminated the Merciless Parliament, and, as on that occasion, they had been preceded by the granting of honours to the faithful. Richard chose, however, to reward his friends with titles and dignities rather than demands on the treasury. Nottingham became Duke of Norfolk; Derby, Duke of Hereford; Huntingdon, Duke of Exeter; Kent, Duke of Surrey; Rutland, Duke of Aumerle; Somerset, Marquis of Dorset; Lord Despenser, Earl of Gloucester; Lord Neville of Raby, Earl of Westmoreland; Sir Thomas Percy, Earl of Worcester; and Sir William Scrope, Earl of Wiltshire. As might have been expected, this unprecedented number of elevations drew unfavourable comment from those hostile to the court, but it was obviously the king's purpose to demonstrate that the hand which was severe in the punishment of offenders was bounteous in its treatment of loyal servants.

On the whole the more thoroughly the Ricardian triumph of September, 1397, is examined, the more it reveals the character rather of an object lesson in royalist theory than of a well executed stroke of vengeance. The punishments were limited to a very few, as contrasted with the number proscribed in 1388. Of them only Gloucester and Arundel paid the extreme penalty. Except for the five against whom charges were brought, no one suffered. Indeed, every effort was made to provide assurances that there would be no further punitive measures unless there was future

---

[39] He is even said by one chronicler to have received a promise that he would be recalled, and to have had an opportunity to admonish the king for the luxury and greed which abounded in his court. *Cont. Eul. Hist.*, III, p. 376. The treatment of the archbishop argues for Richard's acceptance of the truth of the charge of new conspiracies to which he did not believe the archbishop to be a party. So long as he gave no specific grounds for suspicion no action would be taken against him. But his long attachment to his brother and Gloucester and his record in 1386–88 made it imperative for him to behave with more caution than was natural to his imperious disposition. He could not remain submissive for long.

disloyalty. As has been noted, all who had been parties to the impeachment of Suffolk or members of the commission had received specific exemption from prosecution. The new Dukes of Norfolk and Hereford were not only singled out for individual pardons for their share in the affairs of 1387 and 1388 but were actually commended for services rendered to the king in those years in opposing both the removal of Richard and the execution of Burley.[40] Furthermore, these pardons could never be explained away on the ground that they had been wrung from a reluctant monarch against his will. The argument of constraint which had failed to satisfy Arundel though it quieted the royal conscience, could apply to no action taken in 1397.

It is far more reasonable to assume that Richard was naive enough to reckon fear and gratitude as being sufficient to attach to his cause all whom he had spared than that he was so devious a schemer as deliberately to raise his former opponents to exalted stations in order that their fall might be the more notable. The facts, even as they emerge from the pages of hostile chroniclers, make plain the king's intention to deal with issues rather than personalities. The oaths which terminated the September parliament, for example, had been designed to bind living men and their descendants to accept as permanent those acts of the session which might have been subject to change. No one could ever recall Gloucester and Arundel from death. Richard himself might at some future date see fit to pardon Warwick and the archbishop as he had already pardoned others, or to restore to their patrimonies the disfranchised heirs of the two chief offenders. There is nothing to indicate that he was ever vindictive toward either their wives or their heirs, though under his interpretation of the law of treasons they had forfeited all their estates, entailed or not. An example had been made, and those with whom there could be no hope of permanent peace had been destroyed.[41] What was more important, however, and what must be accepted as final, was that the royal doctrine of sovereign right as expounded

[40] Cont. Eul. Hist., III, p. 324; Rot. Parl., III, p. 353.

[41] The significance of this was fully grasped by at least some contemporaries. Cf. the author of the Dieulacres Chronicle in concluding a brief commentary on the revolution of 1388, 'Sed absurdum est servum vel subditum contra suum dominum esse rebellem. Sed quia nullum malum erit impunitum deus cor regis illustravit ut predictos rebelles quammodo puniret . . .' Bulletin of the John Rylands Library, XIV, (1930), p. 168.

by the justices in 1387 had been confirmed and the whole programme of the commission of 1386 had been condemned. More
remained to be accomplished before the king could now be
satisfied to forget the injury with which he had borne so long,
but what remained was not an extension of persecutions. Parliament adjourned to meet in January, 1398, at Shrewsbury to
complete the business at hand.

The removal of the parliament to Shrewsbury may have had
a symbolic significance. It was there that the judicial declaration
had been made. It may be, too, that Richard found it more
convenient to bring the lords and commons into a hotbed of
royalist sentiment than to attempt again to overawe them by
importing Cheshiremen into Westminster. The agendum was so
well organized that the session lasted only four days, despite the
development of a serious problem which could not have been
anticipated when the meeting of the estates had been prorogued
four months earlier.

Chancellor Stafford utilized the occasion of his opening
address to develop further the argument he had presented in
September at Westminster. He told his listeners that they had
assembled together for the honour of God, and the protection of
the rights of all in the realm. In order that this might be assured,
he pointed out, there must be no other governors in the land but
one, and his laws must be duly obeyed and executed. The
chancellor supplied an indication of the nature of one of the tasks
which confronted the session by a reference to the old subject of
the defence of the realm. Thus informed, the lords and commons
resumed the work they had left in September.[42]

The record shows that two things were required of parliament
at this session. The first was an explicit declaration of the
illegality of the Merciless Parliament, which had been mentioned
only incidentally at Westminster, and the second was a grant of
supply. In addition to these major aims the king had probably
planned the revocation of the sentence of 1321 against the long
dead favourites of Edward II, the two Despensers, and the formal
condemnation of Thomas Mortimer, who had, of course, failed
to respond to the summons issued in September. The haste with
which the sitting was conducted indicates that there had been
little original intention of doing much else.

[42] *Rot. Parl.*, III, p. 357.

The matter of the parliament of 1388 was opened by a return to the questions submitted in 1387 to the justices. Their answers were formally vindicated as 'good law' by the lords and commons and the current justices. The 'parliament of the eleventh year' was thereupon declared to be no parliament, and all its acts were annulled and reversed. The last and most grievous stain had now been officially removed from the royal escutcheon. This service to the monarch's pride was made doubly agreeable by the accompaniment of an unusually generous grant of supply. Richard received a tenth and a fifteenth, and a half-tenth and a half-fifteenth for the ensuing year, as well as a subsidy on wool, woolfells, and leather for life.[43]

The cessation of warfare with France, indeed, fell short of his ambitions for permanent settlement, but if the marriage proved to be successful, as Richard was determined it should, truce might yet ripen into peace. The failure prior to 1396 was not the result of irreconcilable differences between the monarchs. The English magnates who would have led the opposition to some statesmanlike moderation of claims in France had been punished as traitors. Concessions would never have been popular, and peace was by no means an aspiration of everyone in the realm. But after 1397 there was little likelihood that any great lord would attempt to foment rebellion out of popular dissatisfaction with the peace programme.[44] Thus Richard's highest hopes within the realm and abroad seemed on the road to fulfilment but already events had occurred which demanded further action.

[43] Ibid., pp. 357, 358, 360, 368.
[44] J. J. N. Palmer, who characterizes Richard's peace efforts as 'the most statesmanlike since the days of Saint Louis' believes that because the failure in 1396 was the responsibility of the Gascons there was no prospect of success in negotiation thereafter. 'The Anglo-French Peace Negotiations, 1390–96', T.R.H.S., Fifth Ser., XVI (1966), pp. 81–94.

CHAPTER VII

RICARDIAN ABSOLUTISM

THE solemn oaths, the distribution of largess, and the pledges of pardon at Westminster were not enough. Fear of what the king might do remained. There was fear, too, of the influence of certain of his advisers, and even the inner circle of the king's friends was not immune to the prevalence of jealousy and mutual suspicion. For all of this Richard was, to a certain extent, responsible. He had placed himself in a position of supreme authority. He had demonstrated that his will was all powerful, that it was his to punish, pardon and reward as he saw fit to do. Though he had been generous, he was notoriously a man of changeable temper who sometimes acted hastily upon ill-considered advice. Anyone who had enemies or rivals was subject to the fear that the wrath of the sovereign might be stirred against him, the more so if anything in his past conduct rendered him vulnerable. The security of every surviving member of the commission of 1386 was somewhat precarious, and the status of the former Appellants, Hereford and Norfolk, was even less enviable, the official expressions of goodwill of September 22, 1397, notwithstanding. Indeed, all who had taken part against the court in the affairs of 1386 and 1388, great and humble alike, had perhaps some lingering cause for trepidation.

The first manifestation of disquietude came from the most unwelcome possible quarter. If Richard's principal purpose was to induce a permanent acceptance of the position defined by the Westminster parliament, it was most essential that Hereford and Norfolk should remain loyal. To that end he had conciliated and honoured them. It is even possible that in the case of Norfolk he had experienced a revival of the personal intimacy which before 1386 had united them. Certainly no one else, with the possible exception of Huntingdon, had so consistently shared his confidence or enjoyed his favour in recent years. Yet, even before the parliament resumed its deliberations at Shrewsbury, Richard was brought face to face with the fact that either Norfolk or Hereford, or both, distrusted and feared him.

Early in January 1398 Hereford came to the king privately with a distressing story. Richard invited his cousin to put his account in writing and present it before the parliament which was shortly to convene. On the last day of the session Hereford appeared with what amounted to a serious accusation of bad faith against his old confederate. As he stated it, a chance encounter had furnished the occasion for Norfolk to discuss his personal problems in detail and to attempt to convince him that they endured a common jeopardy. The king, Norfolk was alleged to have said, was not to be trusted. The pardons which had been extended would prove to be as worthless as those previously granted to Gloucester and Arundel. This was the more likely to be true since men in high favour at court were constantly plotting their destruction. The Duke of Surrey and the Earls of Wiltshire, Salisbury and Gloucester were named as the conspirators.[1]

Norfolk had not been present to participate in the Shrewsbury parliament. He could, therefore, make no public refutation or explanation of the delation. If his absence was in accordance with official command, Richard had obviously not yet determined how to handle the situation, but the mere existence of this first-hand evidence of a renewal of suspicion and unrest, coupled as it was with the revelation of dissension among his closest advisers, must have redoubled his anxiety about the permanence of the legislation so recently enacted and driven him to take extreme measures to secure his position. The oaths sworn at Westminster were repeated in more grave terms.[2] New evidence of the length of the royal memory and the strength of the punitive arm was given by the conviction of Lord Cobham for his share in the affairs of 1386 and 1388. The re-issue of the general pardon, which followed the grant of supply contained two significant clauses of exception. All who had ridden against the king in 1387 and 1388 were required to sue individually for forgiveness, while the general pardon was to be revoked in the event of any effort to interfere with the lifetime subsidy which had been granted.[3] All

[1] *Rot. Parl.*, III, p. 383.
[2] M. V. Clarke, *Fourteenth Century Studies*, pp. 103, 104, describes the oaths in detail.
[3] *Rot. Parl.*, III, p. 360. Fifty unnamed persons had been exempted from the pardon. Cobham had participated in the judgment against Burley. He had also in company with Gloucester dragged Tresilian from sanctuary. *Polychronicon*, IX, p. 178.

G

of this was a repetition of the pattern of intimidation, bribery and affirmation adopted in September, but intimidation had now become paramount. The king's confidence had sustained a severe blow.

The important business which had been marked out for the parliament was concluded by the fourth day. There were 'divers petitions affecting certain persons' and other matters of slight significance which were not passed upon. Richard was, nevertheless, eager to terminate the assembly. The much more momentous questions called up by the Hereford delation had now received an official cognizance which demanded some sort of action. The king, however, could not at once develop any formula for resolving them, and his impatience to adjourn the parliament was not to be denied. By a final enactment the lords and commons delegated to a special commission the authority to settle the affair of Norfolk and Hereford and to dispose of the other unfinished business of the session.

The nature of this commission has often been misunderstood. Taken together with the lifetime grant of subsidy it has appeared to be the culminating step in a carefully devised scheme to alter drastically the whole structure of the English government. Richard, it has been argued, had gained financial independence; he had published his absolutist principles both by word and by act; and finally he had taken advantage of the subservience of a picked parliamentary assembly to do away with the institution entirely through the simple expedient of requiring it to vote itself out of existence by delegating all parliamentary powers to a committee.

The objections to this line of reasoning are manifold. In the first place the powers and purposes of the committee were clearly defined in the enabling statute. They pertained only to a completion of business left undone at Shrewsbury. At a later date, probably sometime in the following year, the king may have caused the phrase, 'the determination of all other matters and things moved in the king's presence in accordance with what seems best to (the committee)', to be appended to the list of delegated powers. If, therefore, Richard ever planned to do for an extended time without parliament, the idea occurred to him after 1398 and not at Shrewsbury. Furthermore, the membership of the body was fixed, and the size of a quorum for each of its specified tasks was set. No provision for the filling of vacancies was made and no replacements ever occurred, though three members died before the work was completed. There had been precedents, moreover, for such committees in the past.

The most formidable objections to the old theory, however, have to do with the uses to which Richard put the committee, and with his obvious recognition both at Shrewsbury and later that parliaments would be summoned in the future. The oaths, the threats of reprisal in the event of parliamentary action to withdraw the subsidy and the fact that trouble was taken to falsify the rolls, all present irrefutable evidence that parliament had not been forced to commit suicide. Until the death of the Duke of Lancaster forced upon the king a new dilemma, he made no attempt to utilize the committee for any other functions than those which had called it into being.[4]

Of these, as has been noted, the most troublesome was the affair of Norfolk and Hereford. Richard's first impulse appears to have been to attempt to reconcile them, but each of the dukes was manifestly too sensitive to the imputation of bad faith to be satisfied with anything short of a complete clearing of his name. Each gave the other the lie direct, and Hereford amplified his earlier accusations with charges of official misconduct of the command of Calais and the murder of the Duke of Gloucester.[5] A decision of some sort was imperative. In the absence of conclusive proof either of Norfolk's guilt or his innocence, it was determined to resort to trial by combat. The duel was set for September 16, at Coventry.

The resort to the field of honour could hardly have been satisfactory to Richard. Whoever triumphed, there would remain in the realm one important nobleman who patently did not trust him and whom he could not trust. Norfolk and Hereford had been too intransigent to permit him to believe at the last that the affair was all smoke and no fire. Yet he remained hesitant as to how to proceed until the very moment of the combat. Then, acting upon the advice of his councillors, of whom Lancaster

[4] Ibid., p. 368; cf. J. G. Edwards, 'The Parliamentary Committee of 1398', E.H.R., XL (1925), pp. 321–33.
[5] *Chronique de la Traison et Mort*, pp. 14–17; *Cont. Eul. Hist.*, III, p. 399. Cf. p. 82 supra, n. 35.

was certainly one, he stopped the duel with the announcement that both combatants were to be banished from the realm, Norfolk for life and Hereford for ten years. It was a difficult decision, bound to provoke dissatisfaction not only from the partisans of both dukes, but also from the crowd who had assembled to witness the tourney. It was, however, at once the most merciful and the most feasible means of freeing the court of a powerful enemy in the immediate future.[6]

The king had sent two potential enemies abroad, but he had also lost confidence in the security of his own system. From this time forward he became increasingly moody and suspicious. Avoiding his capital, he wandered about the country, accompanied by his Cheshire guardsmen.[7] His very fear that what had been done might be undone caused him to weaken his own cause by giving grounds for an increasing apprehension among all classes of persons. To terrorize any possible opposition now seemed to be his paramount purpose. The result was, of course, that he only intensified the hostility and fear which already existed. The extent to which his behaviour frightened neutral elements has probably been over-emphasized, and his fiscal policies were doubtless misunderstood by contemporaries as well as by later historians, but chroniclers who were relatively friendly to him agree with those who were not in reporting the unfavourable reaction. He demanded repetitions of the oaths of loyalty from every group among his subjects including the clergy. He was accused of extending the exemptions from the general pardon so far that seventeen counties actually were forced to sue for individual release from responsibility for the assistance given to the Appellants in 1387 and 1388. According to other accounts the action against the counties was taken because he feared for his safety among the partisans of the recently banished noblemen. In any event, there is evidence of county suits for pardon. That these were readily granted would not suffice to allay unrest. Finally, he caused men of substance to sign blank charters, which he might fill in at his pleasure as a means of extorting money. Whatever the purpose of all these acts and however slight the

---

[6] *Kirkstall Chronicle*, p. 131.
[7] Tout, *Chapters*, IV, p. 33 presents evidence to support the reports of the chroniclers.

sums of money actually squeezed from unwilling subjects, the cumulative effect of the policy would have been anything but soothing.[8]

At this same time Richard's enemies accused him of having abandoned himself to the company of gross flatterers and false prophets, who promised him that he would become the most important sovereign on earth and who praised him inordinately for the recent crushing of his foes. He was said to have indulged in lavish displays of courtly pageantry, sometimes featured by demands of obsequious subservience to the majestic presence enthroned in the midst of his adulators like an oriental potentate. It was in these years, too, that he was supposed most emphatically to have declared that the laws were in his mouth and in his breast, and that he alone could make and change them. These complaints probably had some foundation in fact. For the first time in his reign, Richard felt free to give public expression to the beliefs he had always cherished and to impress his court and countrymen with the dazzling splendour he felt to be appropriate to royalty.[9]

Another contemporary criticism, unhesitatingly repeated by modern historians, has much less justification. This is the charge that he surrounded himself only with young, incompetent and worthless advisers. The very contrary appears to have been true. Many of his intimates among the nobility were relatively young men, though both Lancaster and York were constantly at his service, and Exeter and Salisbury were more than forty years of age. The Earls of Wiltshire and Worcester were older. Norfolk and Hereford who can hardly have been thought of as inexperienced were among the advisers of the king until the time of their disgrace. Most of the younger favourites represented families intimately related to the royal house. It is, however, the personnel of the official bureaucracy and the council that makes the charge of youth and incompetence an impossible one to sustain.

The chief members of this group were the chancellor and the Earls of Wiltshire and Worcester, both of whom belonged to

---

[8] Perroy, *Schisme*, p. 346; Clarke, *Fourteenth Century Studies*, pp. 103 ff; *Ann. Ric.*, pp. 234–6; *Kirkstall Chronicle*, p. 132; *Dieulacres Chronicle*, p. 170; *Rot. Parl.*, III, p. 420. The *Rotuli Parliamentorum* in particular may be suspect as a partisan document. Cf. Steel, *Receipts of the Exchequer*, pp. 138–40 and Ch. III passim.

[9] *Ann. Ric.*, pp. 233, 234; *Cont. Eul. Hist.*, III, p. 378; *Rot. Parl.*, III, p. 424.

prominent families. Both had behind them long and honourable careers as royal servants. Wiltshire's official record dated back to the reign of Edward III, and Worcester's was to continue into the reign of Henry IV. Chancellor Stafford, the Bishop of Exeter, had risen through the king's service to his position. His professional competence was apparently never questioned. Like many another of Richard's aides, he rendered distinguished service to his successor. Other prominent figures were Guy Mone, the Bishop of St. David's, who was treasurer in 1397 and 1398, the king's knights, John Russell, William Bagot, Henry Green, and John Bushy and the clerk, Richard Clifford. These men formed the nerve centre of the royal bureaucracy.[10]

Bushy deserves special notice. His activities as speaker in three parliaments have already been observed. His parliamentary experience was unusual since he had sat in no less than nine consecutive sessions. He had played an important role in the duel at Coventry where he had acted as the king's spokesman. With Bagot and Green, he had been given responsibility for the collection of the notorious fines and loans of 1398 and 1399. For these and other services he had earned the rich rewards of the king and the vituperative odium of the critical chroniclers. All in all the records show him to have been an able, energetic and loyal civil servant whose life was to be forfeited to his zeal. Indeed, in the judgment of the most competent recent authorities, no previous English monarch had possessed so well trained or so expert a council as did Richard in the last three years of his reign.[11]

Such evidence goes far to gainsay the censures of misgovernment recited above. The fact remains, nonetheless, that however competent the administration may have been, and however unjust its defamers, its growing power provoked fear which was supplemented by an active anti-royalist propaganda campaign. The outcries against abuse came from many independent sources. The chief well-springs of complaint were unquestionably the vested interests, both lay and clerical; hence, the furore about professional councillors, new noblemen and career bishops. More was involved, however, than the displacement of hereditary

[10] Tout, *Chapters*, IV, pp. 49–51; Baldwin, *King's Council*, pp. 138–46.
[11] Ibid., p. 142; Tout, *Chapters*, IV, pp. 50–52; for Bushy, ibid., pp. 11–13 and J. S. Roskell, *The Commons and Their Speakers in English Parliaments* (1965), pp. 99, 132–4, 350.

councillors by men of the king's choosing, important as that matter was to persons of great estate. There was the possibility that a well entrenched, powerful monarchy might break up or destroy the great private holdings which had been amassed during the century. The death of the Duke of Lancaster in February, 1399, furnished a test case.

The duke's death confronted Richard with a more serious dilemma than even that of the Norfolk-Hereford feud. He had never felt any personal warmth toward Henry of Hereford, Lancaster's heir. The affair which culminated in the duel had revived all of the old suspicions, latent since 1388. The banishment, though it had been reduced to six years, would, nevertheless, remain a cause for still more complete severance. Hereford was already a great landholder in his own right. To have permitted the vast Lancastrian inheritance to be annexed to the possessions of a powerful magnate of such doubtful loyalty would have been to erect within the kingdom a principality which could maintain its independence against the crown. On the other hand, to confiscate or diminish the inheritance of John of Gaunt would be to challenge the whole structure of feudal society, and to declare to every magnate that no security of family legacy could be depended upon. Richard chose to try to steer a middle course, but his procedure had all of the appearance of a sequestration of Lancaster's estates. By an illegal extension of the authority of the committee of 1398, Henry's sentence of banishment was revised to doom him to life-time exile, while the lands and holdings which had been his father's were seized into the king's hands to remain in royal custody 'until Henry . . . or his heir shall have sued the same out . . .according to the law of the land.'[12]

Just what Richard's ultimate intentions were—if, indeed, he had formed any—it is difficult to fathom. With Lancaster himself he had enjoyed for some years the most favourable of relationships. The duke had recently shown more interest in the welfare of his children by Kathryn Swynford than in his legal heir.[13]

---

[12] *Rot. Parl.*, III, p. 372; *Cal. Pat. Rolls*, 1396–1399, p. 563.

[13] The *Chronique de la Traison et Mort* records Lancaster as advising Richard on three occasions not to pardon Henry, pp. 41, 54. Such advice would have been very difficult, if not impossible, for him. Feudal lords were always concerned about the perpetuation of a great inheritance; few exhibited more consistent concern

This concern was reflected by the king. The honours bestowed upon the eldest of the Beauforts, as the family were known, have already been cited. A few months prior to his father's death a younger son received the bishopric of Lincoln through royal influence.[14] Richard also manifested genuine consideration for the welfare of Hereford's son and heir, who was later to become Henry V. The financial records show numerous grants in his favour, while other contemporary testimony points toward a relationship of mutual affection. It is more than possible that Richard's care for the well-being of his cousin had a basis in reasons of state as well as in personal esteem. He had no children of his own, nor would he have in the near future. Only the Earl of March, also a boy, stood closer to the throne by primogeniture. The security of the dynasty demanded the protection of so immediate a potential heir to the crown.[15] Whether the estates were to be kept in trust to await the majority of the loyal young Henry or not, the reaction of the English feudality to the seizure was, so far as can be known, one of horrified disapproval.[16] It is easy to condemn the royal action either as a tyrannical injustice or a political blunder. It is not so easy to decide what kind of policy would have been equitable or statesmanlike under the circumstances.

How little the king appreciated the possibility of serious repercussions from Henry's disherison is demonstrated by his behaviour in the ensuing months. He had already planned a second expedition to Ireland, this time to avenge the death of his cousin, Roger Mortimer, who had been his lieutenant there. Apparently convinced that his position in England was not in serious jeopardy he pursued his plans. The withdrawal of his

than Gaunt. His will, which he had prepared before Henry's fall, testifies to both his great interest in the patrimony which would be the joint legacy of his own holdings and those of Blanche of Lancaster, and his love for the Beauforts to whom he could not have bequeathed it even if Henry had predeceased him. S. Armitage Smith, *John of Gaunt* (1904), pp. 420–36.

[14] A hostile contemporary view of the young bishop is contained in *Gestae Abbatum Monasterii Santi Albani* (R. S.) III, pp. 438–40.

[15] *Issues of the Exchequer*, pp. lxxi, 269; Creton, *History of the Deposition of Richard II*, pp. 299, 31 n.; *Ann. Ric.*, p. 247.

[16] Cf. Ross, 'Forfeitures for Treason in the Reign of Richard II', who argues that Richard's interpretation of the law of treason was an important factor in alienating the aristocracy. Of course, this implies that they assumed a likelihood that they might be offenders against it. *E.H.R.*, LXXI, pp. 560 ff.

fighting force to Ireland, and the entrusting of the regency of England to the fumbling hands of the Duke of York, virtually assured the success of a revolution which might otherwise have been frustrated, although under the circumstances it is difficult to imagine that the Ricardian system could have endured for many years.

The seven years of careful planning between 1389 and 1396 had brought at least the semblance of success. When the test of strength was demanded it had been the king who, on this occasion, selected his ground, and it was he who emerged victorious. He had reopened the treason question on terms of his own choosing in the case of Haxey. He had caused the commission of 1386 to be branded as illegal and iniquitous. Everything associated with the attack of that year on his official staff had been declared to be treason. The most inveterate and the most personally odious of his enemies had been smoked out to be destroyed by the very precedents they themselves had set. The judicial doctrine of 1387 had received the official sanction of every important authority in the realm. The statutes of the Merciless Parliament had been annulled, the session itself having been written off as an illegal assembly and no parliament at all. Royalty had triumphed while its foes had been humbled in the dust.

The victory bore the traces of well organized preparation. It had proceeded systematically step by step, and each step had been accompanied by explicit or implicit references to the Ricardian conception of regality.[17] The unmistakable doctrine of the chancellor's speeches, the repeated emphasis on the judicial decisions of 1387 and the insistence that treason, whenever or wherever committed, must be cleared by the pardon of the king in person all served to give public expression to the royal theory. So, too, did the pronounced interest in Edward II and the reversal of the judgment against the Despensers who had perished at the hands of rebels for their association with him. The ostentation of the court, with the elaboration of ceremonial ritual, was, likewise, designed to serve the purpose of impressing all witnesses with the grandeur and the sanctity of majesty.

The establishment of his own position and the cleansing of the record were, then, Richard's major aims in 1397 and 1398. Vengeance was only an incidental matter. Indeed, if Gloucester,

[17] Cf. *Dieulacres Chronicle*, p. 168, and *Kirkstall Chronicle*, p. 129.

Warwick and Arundel had walked so warily as to provide no grounds for renewal of suspicion, the king's vindication might have been achieved without any prosecutions whatever. It is true that a personal note frequently crept into the judicial and legislative proceedings. The name of Simon Burley was constantly brought to the attention of the judges and the accused. The importance attached to Burley in fact cannot be exaggerated. Many references to him have been cited. Other examples may be noted. Arundel was sentenced to be executed near the Tower of London where Simon Burley had been killed.[18] Lancaster in passing sentence on Arundel is quoted as alluding to only one specific offence, the execution of Burley, together with the general condemnation for treason.[19] Participation in the judgment against Burley was one of the two crimes imputed to Sir John Cobham, the other being his membership of the commission of 1386.[20] It is hard to imagine that the king regretted the deaths of Gloucester and Arundel, while he could not conceal his pleasure at the abasement of Warwick. Yet even after the disillusionment of the Hereford revelations, there was little persecution and no further bloodshed.

Everything, however, had not proceeded according to plan. Hereford and Norfolk proved that rewards, threats and testaments would bring no lasting assurance of security. The death of the Duke of Lancaster removed a most important aide to the newly established absolutism, and at the same time hastened its collapse. Richard, as has been said, was probably motivated more by political considerations than by financial necessity in sequestering the Lancastrian estates. His government may have been in financial straits in 1399, but except for the gossip of hostile chroniclers there is no real evidence that he was unusually hard pressed, unless it is to be found in the failure of the crown to repay a relatively small amount of petty loans.[21] The inconsistency of the double accusation of the achievement of fiscal independence by the grant of 1398 and of illegal action in order to get funds to support a bankrupt regime in 1399 should cause the statements of the chroniclers who make it to be reviewed with the greatest of caution. The king unquestionably derived some

[18] *Kirkstall Chronicle*, p. 130.
[19] *Cont. Eul. Hist.*, III, p. 375.
[20] *Rot. Parl.*, III, p. 365; *Vita Ricardi*, p. 143.
[21] Steel, 'English Government Finance', pp. 590–94.

profit from his uncle's possessions, though every effort was made not to disturb the existing Lancastrian dependents. The estates of Henry of Hereford's followers or companions in exile were bestowed on Richard's friends. But the assumption was explicit that when it was safe to do so the ducal rights would be restored to the family.[22] Nonetheless the whole aristocracy was profoundly shaken by the seizure, whatever Richard's motives and intentions.

The problem of the Lancastrian inheritance thus not only brought to a head the smouldering conflict between the king and certain of his subjects, but also revealed a fatal flaw in the royal programme. Richard insisted upon the maintenance of the full sum of his ancestral rights. He asserted, too, that his unquestioned supremacy constituted the only real guarantee of the customary lawful rights of his subjects. But monarchy could not with tranquility permit the accumulation through normal feudal procedure of an extensive independent private patrimony, a virtual state within a state. For this paradox, unfortunately, Richard possessed no adequate solution. His widely vaunted claims to absolutism incorporated no conception of the ultimate validity of reasons of state.[23] His treatment of the Lancastrian estates, far from being a bold stroke, was an evasion of the central issue. Henry, proscribed, would be blocked from mobilizing the vast family wealth to injure him. But one day it might be concentrated again in the hands of a single descendant. This was neither preservation of the pristine purity of the law at any cost, nor a statesmanlike abrogation of the law for the greater safety of the realm. When Richard departed for Ireland the contradictions endemic to his own system had already written for him a doom which might have been delayed but could not be averted.

[22] Special care was devoted to safe-guarding the rights and franchises of Duchess Kathryn, *C.C.R.* 1397–1399, p. 476 (May 23, 1399). Cf. Somerville, *History of Duchy of Lancaster*, p. 135. Nearly 40 entries in the calendar testify to the obligation that Lancastrian holders should not be disturbed 'while [the lands] are in the king's hands'. These begin on March 26, 1399 and continue until June 28. *C.C.R.* 1397–1399, pp. 448, 449, 450, 462, 463, 464, 465, 468, 469, 470, 471, 473, 474, 477, 484, 485, 506. Entries dated June 1 and June 12 involve confirmations which do not contain the clause 'so long as the same are in the king's hands'. Ibid., p. 471. On March 20 Thomas Chaucer was granted recompense for certain offices held of John of Lancaster 'which have now been granted to the Earl of Wiltshire'. Ibid., p. 467. The Dukes of Exeter, Aumerle, Surrey and York and the Earl of Salisbury were among the recipients of grants from the Lancastrian inheritance, all with the proviso that they were to retain them so long as they were in the king's hands, but they probably derived little benefit from them. Somerville, op. cit., pp. 134–6.

[23] Cf. *infra*, p. 184.

CHAPTER VIII

THE KING UNKINGED

ONLY a few months separate Richard's achievement of
absolutism from his final ruin. The zenith of his power may
be considered to have been reached in September, 1398, with the
sentence imposed upon Norfolk and Hereford at Coventry. It
was scarcely a year later that the banished Hereford ascended the
throne as Henry IV. The reversal of Richard's fortunes was even
more sudden than his seizure of power. To have been dashed in
so short a space of time from such splendid heights would have
been cause enough to have reduced a temperamental prince to 'a
mumbling neurotic, sinking rapidly into a state of acute melan-
cholia'.[1] It is evident, however, that the king responded to his
misfortunes in a more spirited fashion.

Except for the insurrection of the lower orders in 1381, the
deposition of the king, as might be expected, has attracted more
attention among historians than any other event of the later
fourteenth century. The traditional interpretations of the
deposition and the revolution which encompassed it have also
been subject to much revision and controversial discussion. The
bulk of this revision, like the record of the episode itself, belongs
primarily to the constitutional history of the reign of Henry IV
but certain aspects of it form an important and useful epilogue to
Richard's history and are essential to an examination of his
policy. These pertain to the Ricardian conception of regality, the
makeup and aims of the group who elevated Henry of Lancaster
to his cousin's throne, and the character and extent in 1399 of
Richard's own following.

The expedition of 1399 to Ireland was considerably less
successful than that of 1395. The rebellious chieftains, who had
violated their pledges of four years earlier and had slain the Earl of
March, could not even be encountered by the royal armies. In
the midst of his disappointments Richard received news of the
return to England of Hereford, who now styled himself Duke of

[1] Steel, *Richard II*, p. 279.

Lancaster. Almost at once the king began to be victimized by that series of treacheries which turned the probability of successful revolution into certainty.

One after another men upon whose loyalty he had counted went over to his enemy. Henry was welcomed by former Lancastrian retainers. These were joined by the adherents of the house of Arundel, under the leadership of the old archbishop, with whom, in violation of the terms of his exile, Henry had for some time been in close touch. Such groups might have been expected to flock to his standard. That the Earls of Westmoreland and Northumberland with virtually the whole company of the north country baronage should have displayed equal enthusiasm for the invasion could not, however, have been anticipated. Northumberland may, in fact, have been motivated by entirely personal considerations. Though Richard had been generous to him and to his family, he transferred the lucrative wardenship of the west march to one of the '*duketti*' in 1397. It was perhaps to the king's advantage to break up the monopoly of power which the Percies held in the north and to compensate them in other ways, but their greed was insatiable. They required both the new and the old perquisites. Richard undoubtedly offended others in the same fashion. In any case, the family of Northumberland led the magnates, both church and lay, who in transferring their allegiance to Henry turned the military enterprise into a triumphal progress. Henry quite literally occupied almost the whole of England without striking a blow.

This amazing success is partially to be explained in terms of the insecurity of the nobility, the well organized campaign of propaganda which both preceded and accompanied the invasion, and the ill-timed absence of the king with the royal armies. But the clocklike precision of the whole movement depended upon more than coincidence and consciousness of grievances either real or simulated. The invader had already been in correspondence with the leaders of the nobility, and he knew in advance upon precisely whom to depend.[2] The pusillanimous regent, York, in the meantime, did virtually nothing to rally the opposition. He

[2] Even members of Richard's inner circle had communicated with him. Cf. *Traison et Mort*, p. 39, which refers specifically to the Marquis of Dorset. The aged Bishop of Winchester also was an active party to the invasion. G. H. Moberly, *Life of William of Wykeham*, (1887), pp. 286, 287.

may not even have been able to decide with which of his nephews to side. Henry had been extremely careful to have it proclaimed that he intended only to recover his rightful inheritance and no more. York, like many who actually enrolled under the Lancastrian standard, may have been taken in by the claim. In any case, he clearly failed to perform his duties as regent, for they would have left him no discretionary authority in the event of an armed assault on the realm. Deprived of any real assistance from the head of the state, Richard's loyal councillors were helpless. Some including Bushy, Green, and the Earl of Wiltshire, fled to the west hoping to join the king upon his return from Ireland. Others made what terms of peace they could with the unopposed conqueror.

While his kingdom was thus melting away, Richard tarried in Ireland. Against the advice of older and wiser men, he chose to be guided by his cousin, the Duke of Aumerle, who argued that the best course of action would be to assemble all the forces under his command in Ireland before returning to meet the rebels. The Earl of Salisbury was to be sent ahead to organize the Welsh and the Cheshiremen. Aumerle had only recently come from England to join the king. What is known of his character and of his later behaviour supports the accusation that he had already betrayed Richard, who 'loved him above all other men', and that he advised delay only in order to give Henry more time to snuff out whatever resistance he might encounter.[3] The delay and the division of forces were fatal. By the time that Richard landed at Milford, Henry had consolidated his position. Bushy, Green and Wiltshire were taken and executed at Bristol. The Duke of York abandoned all pretense of discharging his functions and joined the insurgent forces, while the Lancastrians were well on the way toward heading off Salisbury in Cheshire and North Wales. The troops whom Richard brought from Ireland followed the lead of their betters in deserting to the rival army. Aumerle consumated his treachery by abandoning the king to join Henry in the company of the Earl of Worcester, the royal steward. Richard hastened north with a small band of followers to effect a juncture with Salisbury at Conway, only to discover that he had arrived too late. Salisbury's troops, after two weeks of idleness, had

[3] Creton, *History*, pp. 312, 23–27; *Dieulacres Chronicle*, p. 172.

concluded that the king was dead and despite everything that their commander could do, had disbanded.[4]

This was a bitter turn of fate, but all was not yet lost. Richard was in a well fortified harbour with friendly ships at his back. He retained his life, his independence and his belief in the sanctity of an anointed king. There was still opportunity for energetic action and for an attempt at restoration of authority under more favourable conditions. The sacrifice of this opportunity resulted only from a final betrayal, not from either weakness or irresolution. Henry, too, had made all speed to get to Cheshire where he expected a stand to be made in Richard's behalf. The prize for which he had gambled was now just out of his reach. The seizure of the king's person was absolutely necessary to the fulfillment of his plans, but it could only be effected by luring him from Conway. While the Dukes of Exeter and Surrey were on their way from Richard's camp to Henry's as official emissaries to learn the purpose of the rebellion, the Earl of Northumberland was despatched to encompass, by whatever means he might, the arrest of the king. Northumberland may or may not have been accompanied on his mission by Archbishop Arundel.[5] He also may have been unaware that in putting Richard into Lancaster's hands he was actually effecting a change of sovereigns, though it is unlikely that so shrewd a man could have been so unrealistic.[6] Swearing that the king's majesty and his power should not be disturbed, he persuaded him to go inland to meet Henry at Flint. The game was now up.[7]

[4] This reconstruction of the sequence of events follows that of Clarke and Galbraith, *Fourteenth Century Studies*, pp. 69–73. But cf. Evan J. Jones, 'An Examination of the Authorship of *The Deposition and Death of Richard II* Attributed to Creton', *Speculum*, XV (1940), pp. 461–65.

[5] *Chronicon Adae de Usk*, p. 28; the *Dieulacres Chronicle*, p. 173; *Cont. Eul. Hist.*, III, p. 382; *Ann. Ric.*, p. 249; and *Vita Ricardi*, p. 151, all mention Arundel. The *Kirkstall Chronicle*, p. 134; Creton, *History*, pp. 352–68 (by far the most circumstantial account); and the *Traison et Mort*, pp. 46–52, mention only Northumberland, although Creton cites Arundel as the author of the scheme. *History*, p. 352.

[6] Exeter and Surrey had been required to replace Richard's badge of the White Hart with Henry's own recognizance. *Traison et Mort*, p. 46. That would seem to be definitive evidence. But cf. Wilkinson, 'The Deposition of Richard II', *E.H.R.*, LIV (1939), p. 217. The wardenship of the west march had already been restored to Northumberland, a regal act, authorized under the seal of the duchy of Lancaster.

[7] On this very important point, the *Dieulacres Chronicle*, Creton's *History*, the *Kirkstall Chronicle*, the *Traison et Mort*, *Chronicon Adae de Usk* (partial to Henry), and the Whalley fragment (Harleian Ms. 3600, cited by Clarke, *Fourteenth Century Studies*, p. 76) all agree. Only the official record and the partisan chroniclers, *Ann.*

The story of Richard's agreement to withdraw from Conway is crucial, for it was at Conway that he was supposed, according to the official account of the parliamentary rolls, to have made with 'smiling countenance' his voluntary renunciation of the throne. The Lancastrian programme demanded a record of abdication by a king who, while still his own master, recognized his incompetence to rule and hence vacated the throne. The use to which this fabrication was put by the conqueror is important to an understanding of the relationship between the Lancastrians and their parliaments, but the recognition of its falsehood is equally important as documentary testimony to the tenacity with which Richard clung to his own notion of the sanctity of monarchy. The vacillating monarch of the official legend, the creature of 'incalculable moods' who resigned himself to inactivity, alternately weeping and jesting while his kingdom slipped from his grasp, is obviously not the historical Richard. It was rather over-confidence than lack of confidence which caused him so easily to become the dupe of his betrayers. The only eye-witness who has left a record of the Conway meeting pictures the king as being pale with rage. No thought occurred to him after Northumberland's solemn oath but that he would regain the fulness of his power and ultimately punish his enemies as they deserved. 'Some of them, I will flay alive,' he is said to have remarked. On an earlier occasion he had threatened to put Henry to death in 'such a manner that it would be spoken about, even in Turkey'.[8] The ruler who had lost two armies in as many weeks, who had been deserted by all but a handful of his most trusted followers, and who retained only a border harbour in a kingdom occupied by his rival, could not yet bring himself to believe that men were capable of destroying what God had created.

The truth awaited him at Flint.[9] Where he had expected to be met as a king negotiating with the leader of a rebellion, he was treated as a prisoner, subject to the dictates of his captor. It was

---

Ric., and others which paraphrase it, give any other story. The account in the *Vita Ricardi*, pp. 155 ff., is a confused attempt to make the official narrative square with the facts which had come to the author's attention in the west. Cf. Clarke, *Fourteenth Century Studies*, pp. 74, 75.

[8] Creton, *History*, pp. 358, 314.
[9] Northumberland may have placed him in military custody as soon as he left Conway. Cf. ibid., p. 364; *Traison et Mort*, p. 51.

probably at Flint that he was first informed by Archbishop Arundel that he should no longer rule. He was conducted to London under the most humiliating circumstances. An attempt at his rescue *en route* only resulted in an increase of the severities and indignities which he was forced to suffer, but it was on his arrival at the capital city itself that he endured the ultimate shame. Those among the citizens who most bitterly hated him had ample opportunity to retaliate for the harshness shown them in 1392. While Henry received the ovation of a hero, Richard was hooted through the streets to the Tower.[10]

Lancaster had already issued, in his cousin's name, writs of summons to parliament. The session assembled on September 30, to deal with a *fait accompli*. When the proctors of the estates had heard a recitation of how the king 'being in his full liberty' at Conway had renounced his throne, a delegation was sent to the Tower to secure from the captive a verification of the abdication. According to the official account this was readily given, and with it a recognition of Henry of Lancaster as heir to the now vacant throne. As a token of his desires, Richard was alleged to have withdrawn his signet, a most significant instrument of regality, from his own finger and awarded it himself to his cousin. His demeanor was represented as being extremely cheerful throughout these proceedings, his only request being that he not be called upon to appear in person before parliament to read the speech of resignation.[11]

The patent dishonesty of this record has been demonstrated.[12] That Richard's bearing in the Tower was anything but cheerful is attested by witnesses friendly to both Lancaster and the king. That the abdication was accomplished only by the exercise of pressure is apparent from the narratives of Richard's partisans and neutral chroniclers alike. That the royal signet was taken from the deposed king rather than given by him is stated explicitly by a Lancastrian who was actually present in the Tower. Finally, the king's demand to be heard in parliament, a demand seconded by members of the assembly itself, was summarily denied.[13] In

[10] *Dieulacres Chronicle*, p. 173; R. Bird, *The Turbulent London of Richard II*, pp. 110 ff.
[11] *Rot. Parl.*, III, p. 416; *Ann. Ric.*, pp. 252–58.
[12] By Clarke and Galbraith, *Fourteenth Century Studies*, pp. 76–80.
[13] *Chronicon Adae de Usk*, pp. 30–32; *Traison et Mort*, pp. 67–70; Creton, *History*, p. 387; *Davies' Chronicle*, p. 17; Hardyng, *Chronicle*. pp. 352, 353.

H

light of this accumulation of testimony it may be accepted as certain that Richard had never consented to the abdication at all, and that his supplanter did not dare to permit him to appear either before parliament or any unbiased group, lest he give the lie to the whole concocted story.[14] In fact, there is no independent contemporary verification of any portion of the official report. There is, on the other hand, excellent evidence that a consistent programme of maltreatment, bullying and persuasion had failed completely to shake Richard's faith in the inviolability of his regality. From Archbishop Arundel's abuse at Flint to the final threats in the Tower, he retained his convictions, despite the most offensive allegations of dishonesty, misgovernment, and even bastardy. His only recorded reactions, the prepared Lancastrian statement excepted, are anger and extreme melancholy.[15]

It is evident that the conventional notion of the king's character and attitude requires substantial correction. Some modification, also, of the generally accepted version of the nature and disposition of the assembly which sanctioned the deposition is required. Whether this gathering possessed official status as a parliament or not, its records are subject to the normal criticism of medieval parliamentary rolls, in that they present the impression of unanimity where great diversity of opinion must in actuality have existed. This would, of course, have been equally true of the reports of the sessions of 1386, 1388, 1397 and 1398. The meeting of September and October, 1399, had to be managed with particular caution and skill.

Henry possessed certain advantages which he knew how to exploit with the utmost adroitness. In the first place, he had led the revolution from the outset, and had thus been able to dictate its course until the day of the meeting of the estates. Everyone who had joined him was, therefore, committed to a large extent by the leader's action. Furthermore, he was for the moment, at least, the undeniable hero of the city populace and he still retained

[14] Cf. N. B. Lewis, 'The Protestation of Richard II in the Tower in 1399', *Bulletin of the John Rylands Library*, XXIII, (1939), pp. 146–48.

[15] To York and Aumerle he is said to have declared, 'I am yet king, and I will be king'. *Traison et Mort*, p. 66. Adam of Usk comments personally on the possibility of Richard's illegitimacy, *Chronicon*, p. 29; in the *Traison et Mort*, p. 64, the charge appears as an epithet hurled at the king by the Londoners; Froissart makes Henry the author of an abusive and detailed attack on the king's parentage. *Chronicles*, IV, pp. 535, 536. See also *Traison et Mort*, p. 67; *Chronicon Adae de Usk*, p. 30.

a sizeable military following. His position was not, however, without its weaknesses, the most notable of which was the ever present possibility of a crystallization of opposition to his seizure of the throne. Although his own aims had probably been well formulated from the day he left France, the bulk of his associates had allied themselves with him under the assumption that he had come only to claim his inheritance and, in the manner of 1386, to purge the government of the royal favourites. If there were hazards involved in drawing back from the ultimate goal of the revolution, there was also the danger that reluctant followers might be pushed too fast and too far. The Henrician programme was, therefore, tailored to fit conditions of political expediency, rather than any notion of the proper nature of the English constitutional structure. The most pressing of the political considerations was the prevention at all costs of a union between the known partisans of the fallen king, such as his brother, his nephew and the Earl of Salisbury, and those of Henry's own following, perhaps the majority, who had never envisaged in advance a change of dynasty. An understanding of this essential point goes far toward explaining the necessity, from Henry's point of view, of the story of the cheerful, voluntary abdication, and of the isolation of Richard from all except the few who could be trusted implicitly. If his plan were finally to succeed, there must be no rallying point for the opposition.

That such an opposition not only existed, but was openly articulated, has long been a familiar part of the unofficial legend. Exeter, Surrey and Salisbury, it is true, apparently accepted the olive branch which the victor extended to them and bided their time. Others of Richard's supporters made no effort to disguise their feelings. The speech of the Bishop of Carlisle, immortalized by Shakespeare, has generally been held to be nothing more than the propagandist invention of a partisan chronicler. Its authenticity has, however, been verified beyond reasonable doubt.[16] It was perhaps in response to the questions raised by the bishop of the competence of the lords to pass judgment on the king and of the justice of the condemnation of the accused without a hearing, that the thirty-three articles of indictment were read to the assembly. These articles, because of their obvious purpose, are

[16] Cf. Clarke, *Fourteenth Century Studies*, p. 84; Steel, *Richard II*, pp. 281, 282.

a most valuable source of information concerning the opposition to Richard's policies. They were designed to enlist the maximum amount of support for the usurpation by summarizing a whole series of political grievances. Incidentally they expressed implicit, though unintentional, judgments on kingship and law.

Many of the articles were concerned with the personal sufferings of Henry, Archbishop Arundel, and their partisans. Others dealt with the corrupt behaviour of the recent parliaments. With singular disingenuousness some of the very men who had substituted vehemence for judicial decorum in the prosecutions of 1397 now gravely declared those prosecutions to be worthy causes for Richard's deposition. The victims whom Henry himself had gone out of his way to abuse were designated as heroic martyrs whose only offence had been their efforts to steer the king along the path of good governance. The murder of the Duke of Gloucester at Richard's command was specifically alleged. The whole programme of the commission and the Appellants in 1386–88 was upheld and the royal hostility to it cited as evidence of the incapacity of the king to rule wisely.[17] This series of articles constituted a collective repudiation of the Ricardian system and embodied the alternative notion of the right of the king's lawful advisers to impose their council upon him if he was not prudent enough otherwise to avail himself of it. Henry as king now had little love for such a doctrine. Its prominence attests to the necessity for holding fast to his recent allies, although the immediate reason for clearing the names of Gloucester and Arundel was to blacken that of Richard.

[17] *Rot. Parl*, III, pp. 418–23, 424. There was no specific charge that the rights of the crown had been alienated in violation of the coronation oath, although a recitation of the oath preceded the indictment, the first count of which was that Richard had given the goods and possessions of the crown to unworthy persons and otherwise dissipated them. Ibid., p. 418. In 1388, article IV of the indictment against the Appellees accused them of contriving to alienate the heart of the king thereby causing him to give away franchises of the crown contrary to his oath. Ibid., p. 228. Bishop Stafford made a special point of reminding the parliament of 1397 that the king could not alienate his regalities, prerogatives and other rights. Ibid., p. 347. Alienation as a violation of the oath did not, however, figure as an important count against Richard. On the entire issue see Ernst Kantorowicz, 'Inalienability: A note on Canonical Practice and the English Coronation Oath in the Thirteenth Century', *Speculum*, XXIX (1954), pp. 488–502, especially p. 501; and G. Post, *Studies in Medieval Legal Thought*, pp. 431–3. Cf. also M. David, *La souveraineté et les limites juridiques du pouvoir monarchique du IX au XV⁰ siecles*, p. 255 where articles 26, 17, 22, 16 and 29 of the accusation are cited. David emphasizes the coronation oath as an instrument in the hands of parliament, p. 258. Cf. Schramm, *The English Coronation*, p. 212.

Most of the other articles noted recent abuses: the coercion of of parliament, the interference with free elections, the forced loans, the multiplicity of oaths, the infringement of the rights of the clergy, the violation of the laws concerning the tenure of sheriffs and the variety of extortions including the punishment of the seventeen counties.[18] These were already well advertised items in the Lancastrian propaganda. All probably had some basis in fact. Taken together they comprise an appeal to the fears of the well-to-do classes. They were supplemented by two other categories of complaint.

The first of these might be labelled 'bad government'. Under this heading would be grouped all of the conventional grumbling about improper advisers, excessive taxation, lavish expenditures and failure to maintain the laws, as would the more novel charges of subservience to the pope and of such habitual dishonesty that the kingdom of England had fallen into ill repute among all foreigners.

The second category would contain a hostile analysis of the most extreme features of Richard's theory of state. The statements that the laws were in his breast or in his mouth, that he would be as free as any of his progenitors had been before him, and that the life, lands and chattels of all his subjects were held at the pleasure and will of the sovereign, form the substance of this interpretation of the Ricardian position. Each of the statements is attributed to the king by other records than the impeachment proceedings; each of them was probably known to a large group of subjects to be authentic. Yet none was examined in context. As presented among the articles they all lend weight to the general accusation of a wilful attempt to create an irresponsible arbitrary despotism.[19]

All in all the purpose of the articles was two-fold. They were designed to vilify the king sufficiently to prevent any serious demand that he have an opportunity to plead his own case, and at the same time to appeal to the positive support of as large a group as possible. Thus the fears of the magnates, the local dignitaries and the property-holders were played upon, while by implication the promise of economical government, guided by

18 Ibid.; *Rot. Parl*, III, p. 424.
19 Ibid.

the advice of hereditary councillors, was set forth as the programme of the usurper. The condemnation of the king who had failed to 'live on his own even in times of peace' held out the implied pledge that his successor would surely perform that impossible task. Presumably, then, the revolution was a conservative affair. Dangerous innovations were to be abolished along with novel theories of monarchy. An essential control over the government of the realm and of its separate localities was to be, it would appear, restored to the hands of the magnates, the knights, the guildsmen, the ecclesiastics and abbots and the justices of the peace. These, after all, were the people who could assure by their united action either the success or the failure of the revolution.[20]

In the long run any government which could not command either the support or the benevolent neutrality of these groups had little chance to maintain itself in the England of the later fourteenth century. Richard's system could hardly do other than arouse their united opposition since in one way or another it threatened the power and the privileges of each of them. The bases upon which he proposed to erect his absolutism were totally inadequate. The Cheshiremen and the Welshmen who wore his badge of the white hart did attempt to effect his rescue. Some of the career bishops such as Merke of Carlisle did raise their voices in his behalf. And some of the *'duketti'* did sacrifice their lives in a futile counter-rebellion. But these were the sole sources of his strength, and under no circumstances would they have been sufficient to the cause. As for the capable administrative bureaucracy which he had fostered, its personnel knew loyalty to function, but not to a master. With a few conspicuous

[20] This is not to say that Henry IV considered himself to be bound by any such pledges, although he was, as a matter of fact, more dependent on these groups than his predecessor had been. The impression of a promise created by the thirty-three articles is, however, unmistakable. It is entirely possible that the rebellion of the Percies and other of Henry's difficulties may have resulted directly from his failure to make his conduct on the throne coincide with his attitude as a complainant against Richard. The leader of a baronial opposition, having become king, might very naturally be subject to a change of heart concerning the desires of his late allies. Cf. Joliffe, *The Constitutional History of Medieval England*, (1937), pp. 485–88; Tout, *Chapters*, IV, p. 66. Henry was in fact probably forced to depend heavily on the great magnates for maintenance of local order. G. E. Morey, 'East Anglian Society in the Fifteenth Century', Unpublished Ph. D. thesis (1952) cites evidence for Norfolk and Suffolk, pp. 340, 344. This may have been a reversion to the conditions of the reign of Edward III, to some extent changed under Richard II.

exceptions the staffs of the governmental and household offices continued to serve Henry IV as they had served Richard II. The revolution of 1399 actually brought fewer changes in the administrative force than had the hereditary succession in 1377.[21]

The house of Lancaster derived its royalty from conquest and from the clever manipulation of its following in the assembly of 1399. The tranquil character of the alteration of the dynasty was due primarily to the latter. The fiction of the voluntary abdication, transparent as its falsehood must have been, combined with the explicit threats and the implicit promises of the thirty-three articles to carry Henry to his coveted place on the throne at Westminster and Richard to an untimely death in the dungeons of Pontefract Castle.

Richard is said to have lacked the tenacity of purpose and the strength of character required of a would-be absolute monarch. It is certain that he lacked sufficiently influential support among his subjects. In another century a shrewder, less scrupulous and more flexible monarch, who troubled himself very little about oaths of loyalty and theories of monarchical right, would effect a practicable absolutism because he could learn to build it primarily on other foundations than a loyal aristocracy. It is, of course, unlikely that elements among the population upon whom he relied would have been inclined to support Richard in 1399 even if he had been disposed to turn to them. These were the people of position but often not of great prominence in the towns and chiefly the countryside. Throughout the fourteenth century they were among the most stubborn opponents of royal interference in local affairs. In general, they were taught during the next hundred years that the alternatives for them were a strong central government or dependence on maintenance by magnates with liveried retinues. In the absence of effective monarchy indentured retainers tended to become the only basis for local order.[22] Sometimes they acquitted themselves amazingly well. In general, however, the tenuousness of their own hold on power and the unreliability of *ad hominem* protection by maintenance were persistently reflected in the insecurity of their dependents, in

[21] Tout, *Chapters*, IV, p. 62.
[22] W. H. Dunham, *Lord Hastings' Indentured Retainers* (1955) pp. 7–14. N. B. Lewis, 'The Organization of Indentured Retinues in Fourteenth Century England', *T.R.H.S.*, 4th Series, XXVII (1945) pp. 36–39.

whose eyes a sturdy authority at Westminster came gradually to assume a more favourable guise than any other shift of lordship. The active support of common lawyers and the justices of the peace was vital to a restoration of vigour to the crown. Whether Henry VII's administrative system was novel or conventional there can be little doubt about the prominent part they took in it. Indeed, increasingly after 1487, the litigious country gentlemen were essential to him. Even earlier they had begun to turn to his Yorkist forerunners and relief from the bane of late feudal violence was already in process before Henry gave the realm twenty-five years of stable rule. In preceding generations, however, local privilege, frustration of justice and factional strife had their way, ultimately to be climaxed by an era of dynastic conflict. The repeated revival of the precedent of 1399 and the reduction of the aristocracy to an enforced co-operation with the crown belong, however, to the history of the fifteenth century and the slow emergence of the Tudor state. It remains here only to attempt to trace the genesis of the Ricardian conception of monarchy, and to draw some conclusions concerning the relationship of theory to the policy of the king.

CHAPTER IX

RICHARD II AND THE HISTORIANS

SHAKESPEARE inevitably intrudes on any consideration of Richard II. John, Henry IV and Henry VI are overshadowed by other characters in the dramas which memorialize their names while Richard III is too magnificently melodramatic a villain ever to have been a living king. But the portrait of Richard II, like that of Henry V, remains indelible. Modern research into the records and accredited comments of men who knew him cannot drive the vision of the wilful, capricious, poetic, skipping king from the mind. Thus a conception of Richard, dramatically valid but historically distorted, has held the field for centuries. While it was in no way Shakespeare's intention to justify usurpation, it was essential to his theme that Richard's unsuitability for king-ship be demonstrated without ambiguity. To have endowed him with tenacity of purpose, political sensitivity or capacity for leadership would have defeated the dramatist's objective. Nor could he have been permitted advisers who were statesmanlike or prudent. The supreme tribute to Shakespeare's compelling success is that the king's temperament rather than his policies or his ambitions long continued to occupy the foreground of histories of his life and reign.

To Shakespeare, of course, as to the chroniclers upon whom he drew, king and kingship were one and inseparable. A perverse man enthroned could be nothing other than a tyrannical king. The defects of person would manifest the incapacity for station. Other medieval kings have been removed by historians from the uniquely personal frame of reference of the chroniclers. Richard II, however, whether treated with sympathy or disapproval continues to be construed in terms of instability and frivolity.[1]

Another tradition, almost equally persistent, derives from the seventeenth century. History in the age of the Stuarts was written with frankly didactic, not to say polemic, intent. Twenty

---

[1] Professor Wilkinson would seem to be an exception and V. H. Galbraith a dissenter.

years after Shakespeare's production of *Richard II*, Sir Walter Raleigh set the style for the new mode with *The Prerogative of Parliaments in England*.[2] He made the device of an artificial dialogue between a member of the king's council and a justice of the peace his instrument for commentary on what the ordering of government had been and what it should be. The history of the fourteenth century was particularly instructive. As developed by Raleigh it demonstrated the harmony of interest between king and commons, a harmony broken upon occasion to the great detriment of the realm by self-seeking aristocrats, particularly those who abused royal favour to their own advantage. But the destructive issues were institutional, not personal. Despite their well warranted fears of the injury Richard's favourites intended to do them, the Appellants of 1388, for example, were guilty of treason. The assembly they directed cruelly to condemn to death 'the King's servants who were bound to follow and obey their master and sovereign lord in that he commanded', was no more a peaceful, regal, lawful parliament than that of 1399 which set Richard aside.[3] The incidents of 1386 to 1399 would be repeatedly cited in the Stuart period to exhibit the historic role of the commons and the disastrous effects of royal favouritism. Writers who shared Raleigh's respect for the king's prerogative and his notions of treason were less likely to find in the history of the reign of Richard II material suitable to the elaboration of their themes. The field was left to those who could draw from a recital of Richard's public wrongs and his crimes against the constitution the lessons they desired to teach.

Although the purported subject of the histories of Trussel and Baker, for example, is the last reign of the fourteenth century they are clearly concerned with the failure of Charles I to comprehend his place in the constitution.[4] In 1680 William Petyt could declare in passing that no English ruler except 'that miserable and unfortunate prince Richard the Second' ever claimed a prerogative right to make or change the law.[5] Two of his contem-

---

[2] Sir W. Raleigh, *The Prerogative of Parliaments in England* (1615). Reprinted: *The Harleian Miscellany* (1808–09), IV, pp. 304–46.

[3] Ibid., p. 327.

[4] J. Trussell, *A Continuation of the Collection of the History of England* (1636). Reprinted: Kennett (ed.), *A Complete History of England* (1719), pp. 236–307; Sir W. Baker, *A Chronicle of the Kings of England* (1643).

[5] W. Petyt, *The Antient Right of the Commons of England Asserted* (1680), p. 55.

poraries used more moderate language in narrative accounts, but their bias is made explicit.

'Being very much affected with the Consideration how the Errors of ill Administration produc'd the same Fatal Effects upon those unhappy Princes, Edward and Richard the Second . . . I also consider'd the Proceedings of the Government in the latter part of King Charles' the Second's Reign, and the Short Reign of King James the Second, and perceived how exactly they followed the steps of these two unfortunate Kings, and I then expected to see a Revolution resembling theirs.'[6]

By the time those words were written Raleigh's views of the relative position of commons and prerogative had long been reversed, as had his judgment on the attack of 1388 on the king. In 1641 when the conflict between Charles I and the parliamentary opposition was approaching the climax which broke government asunder, a pamphlet purporting to be a translation of Thomas Favent's account of the Merciless Parliament was distributed. In this version there was no question of the opponents of the court having committed treason by proceeding in arms against king and court. On the contrary they acted out of a public-spirited necessity to thwart royal annihilation of an established constitution. An abbreviated version two years later attributed somewhat more initiative to parliament in saving the land from tyranny, but the message was plain enough in the original to which was appended the assertion that parliament 'the only means to rectify and remedy matters in church and commonwealth much amiss' has established all the wholesome fundamental laws of the land, removed unsavoury favourites, abolished idolatry and papal power and done much else as well.[7] Subsequent writers had merely to add details. Richard II was firmly pressed into the mould designed by critics of the Stuarts, an arbitrary tyrant and enemy to the parliamentary constitution. For such a role, Shakespeare's frivolous prince was inadequate, and although

[6] Sir R. Howard, *The History of the Reigns of Edward and Richard II* (1689), pp. ii, iii; cf. *The Life and Reign of Richard the Second* (1681), By a Person of Quality.
[7] Thomas Fannant, *An Historical Narrative of the Manner and Form of that Memorable Parliament which Wrought Wonders* (1641). Reprinted: *The Harleian Miscellany* (1808–1809), I, pp. 133–52; cf. *The Bloody Parliament in the Reign of an Unhappy Prince* (1643); Reprinted: Ibid., V, pp. 323–7.

much was made of evil council with pointed references to establish the identity of advisers of the Stuarts, the king himself must ultimately be so dangerous as to justify armed revolt when he evaded customary restraints.[8]

Even Tory historians in later generations reflected the influence of prevalent anti-royalist interpretations. Lord Bolingbroke assigned responsibility in the constitutional structure to the people, not to parliament. He was, nonetheless, consistently and harshly critical of Richard as the example *par excellence* of the anti-parliamentary king, governing by favourites and caprice.[9]

Hume was more sympathetic. He repudiated the seventeenth century parallels and attributed Richard's misfortunes primarily to the violence of the age. Gloucester he singled out as a particularly dangerous man, whose murder exhibited not the arbitrary ambition of the king but rather a defect in a constitution depriving the ruler of secure authority to proceed lawfully against so obvious an offender. The events of 1386–8 were manifestations of the power of a selfish and violent aristocracy, whose attack on the chancellor was completely unjustifiable. The commission of 1386 was dangerous both to good government and to the constitution. Hume warmly applauded the speech in 1399 of the Bishop of Carlisle which had been derided by seventeenth century writers. But he did not completely liberate himself from their tradition. He compared Richard favourably with Edward III except for fortune and strength. He had, however, a low opinion of the age and its kings. Richard, he described as indolent, capricious and wanting in judgment. He treated de Vere as a 'conventional minion' through whose hands all power and access to the king passed. Like many who preceded him he might have been writing of the first Duke of Buckingham but not of a court where real power was shared by the Earl of Suffolk and Simon Burley. Finally, the programme of the last years of the reign he explained as a matter of mere revenge, the extreme conduct of one faction of a 'turbulent and barbarous aristocracy' as opposed to another.[10]

---

[8] My attention was directed to some of the above citations by Professor Milton Krieger.

[9] *The Works of Lord Bolingbroke* (ed. 1841), 'Remarks on the History of England', Letter VI, I, pp. 325–8.

[10] D. Hume, *The History of England* (ed. 1850), II, pp. 287–314.

Henry Hallam was a judicious scholar who shared none of Hume's distaste for the Middle Ages. He wrote not to teach but to inform; he, therefore, attempted faithfully to represent the age of which he wrote rather than to persuade the age in which he lived. His respect for the creative significance of medieval society was related to a high Whig view of history and of the emergence of the English constitution. The reign of Richard II he considered to be from a constitutional standpoint the most important in early English history and hitherto the most imperfectly studied. For him it was not an episode in wilful tyranny; it was a decisive turning point. The alternatives were despotism and parliamentarianism. Happily, there was strength available to tip the scales toward the latter. If the saviours of parliament were too turbulent and vindictive to merit comparison with the nation's greatest heroes they, nonetheless, maintained a genuine concern for the public interest and they left government on its right foundation. Given their knowledge of the intentions of the king and his associates the members of the commission of 1386 could not, in consideration of their responsibilities to the realm, have proceeded otherwise than they did. By contrast when Richard attained supreme power in 1397 all regard for liberty was extinct. The revolution of 1399 was a national act.

With all the Whig bias, Hallam's Richard II is for the first time a creature of history. His interpretation resembles in general outline those of the seventeenth century, but the crises with which he is concerned are those of the reign of Richard not those of the Stuarts. Where he employed analogies it was to assist in understanding the nature of the threats to the constitution in 1386 and 1399, not to provide instruction in current affairs. If he attributed too large a role to parliament and too limited a place to prerogative; if a struggle for constitutional rights loomed so large to him as entirely to obscure conflict between the forces of order and disorder; if he discerned clarity of definition in constitutional forms which were in fact ambiguous, confused and often ill-adapted for the problems of the time, he was not the last English historian to devote himself to the theme of the long, invincible march of the commons to final triumph.

Nearly four decades later Lingard, no partisan either of the Appellants or Henry of Lancaster, reverted to the thesis that tyranny and defiance of the constitution were the causes of Richard's fall. He deserved to be abandoned by the people upon whose liberties he trampled. He was driven, it is true, by evil ambitious men, including his uncles. Given the enemies with whom he had to cope, his administration prior to 1388 was creditable and the acts of 1397 though illegal were in all likelihood thought to be necessary, as the concurrence of Lancaster, York, Derby and others indicates. The commission of 1398, for which presumably there could be no such defense, marked the climax of unconstitutional conduct. Motivation was found in the personality and psychology of the king. The personal explanation, pushed into the background by Hallam, is central once more with Lignard. Richard is neither protagonist nor victim in a conflict of forces. He is again, whatever the pretexts provided by the wickedness of Gloucester and however much to be pitied, a capricious tyrant.

Hume, Hallam and Lingard painted Richard into their larger canvasses of the history of the nation. The polemics of the late seventeenth century excepted, no significant work had been devoted especially to him since Shakespeare's play. When in 1864, a full scale history of the life and reign appeared it was not primarily the thorough study of constitutional issues whose lack Hallam had lamented. Its great value, in fact, derived even more from novelty of approach than from the impressive scholarship of the detailed examination of events. Henri Wallon was drawn to the reign of Richard II because of the unique place he attributed to it in the history of the long rivalry of England and France. Macaulay had already pointed to the expulsion of the English from the continent as a main source of British strength in a later age. His sentiments were rarely echoed. Englishmen writing about the Middle Ages continued in the manner of the Elizabethans to dwell on the national glories of Edward III and Henry V and the national disasters of Henry VI. French national pride demanded similar reactions to Charles V and Charles VII on the one hand and John and Charles VI on the other. Wallon's modern attitudes prompted a selection of the reign of Richard II. The king and his circle had, he thought, originated the one serious attempt in the entire era at permanent peace without conquest.

With such a thesis it was difficult for him to present Richard in other than a favourable light. The case for the king and against his opponents throughout the 1380's is substantially argued but Wallon strained the evidence to show him as master of his realm after 1389, able if he had so desired to destroy Gloucester and Arundel as punishment for their actions in the parliament of 1386 and immediately thereafter. During this period of royal ascendancy beginning in 1389 the programme of peace developed. Royal policy engendered an era of domestic prosperity and contentment, characterized by observance of all the forms of constitutionality and respect for the law. But because Wallon's conception of the medieval English constitution was narrowly conventional he could not sustain his defence of Richard after 1397. Believing the worst of Gloucester, Arundel, Warwick, Hereford, Norfolk and Aumerle, he nevertheless condemned the king's acts in his last two years as unjust and illegal. He attributed Richard's tragic change of character to the subservience of parliament, a heady intoxicant to which he succumbed. The Haxey case, accepted without question as a breach of parliamentary privilege, was cited as the turning point. The obsequiousness of both lords and commons encouraged the king to despotism and castastrophe. There is in Wallon's treatment of the last years almost a sentiment of personal betrayal that so promising a programme should have terminated so dismally.

English medieval historiography in the nineteenth century reached its climax in Stubbs' great book. In dealing with Richard II, as in so much else, he displayed an acute sensitivity to major questions despite an inadequate grasp of factual detail. He recognized complexity where others had seen only simplicity. Richard inherited problems which no prince, however wise and good, could have solved without serious trouble. Caught between lords who wanted power and commons who desired good government Richard responded with a policy of his own. He developed a royalist party preparatory to the *coup d'état* of 1397, a carefully planned alteration of the constitution which could be accomplished only through perfection of a counterpoise to the great nobles. His grand stroke was the elimination of parliament, 'a resolute attempt to destroy the limitation of two centuries on the king'. But the assertion of principles of absolutism and the practices of despotism were fatal. His attempt was a failure. Fifteenth century constitutionalism lay ahead.

Stubbs' understanding of the extraordinary difficulties of Richard's situation was often ignored by others who followed his lead on the status of parliament and its attempted destruction by the king. The record of the early 1390's demonstrated, in fact, that a constitutional, that is, a parliamentary, monarch could be quite successful. It was in a sense Raleigh's old formula revived with a shift of balance toward the commons. C. W. C. Oman, as hostile toward self-seeking aristocrats as Raleigh and as critical of Gloucester as Lingard and Wallon, sums up his disappointment:

> 'It seems hard to believe that Richard's constitutional rule during the last nine years had been nothing more than a deliberate preparation for a snatch at autocracy in 1397; but the evidence points this way.'[11]

His motives were revenge and sheer desire for power for its own sake. Since he had no programme, 'he fooled away the crown which Kings intellectually, as well as morally, his inferiors preserved to their death day'. The views of Tait, if more moderately phrased, are substantially similar. At the end of the nineteenth century despite the introduction by Hallam, Wallon and Stubbs of basic issues of institutional conflict and questions of policy, Richard by and large continued to be explained or explained away as capricious tyrant and would-be destroyer of an established constitution.

Prior to 1900 the writing of medieval English political and constitutional history was based largely on literary sources supplemented by a few great collections of documents. Other documentary materials, becoming increasingly available, were occasionally consulted but they had not been systematically studied. Most contemporary chronicles were intensely critical of Richard II. There may have been special reasons for the malice of the St. Albans scriptorium and Knighton as there almost certainly were for the hostility of Adam of Usk and of Hardyng who wrote later about events which had occurred in his childhood. Favent's *Historia* may fairly be classed as an *ex parte* piece to extenuate the Appellant assault on the king. Of the Monk of Evesham, as bitterly anti-Ricardian as any of these, nothing is known to explain personal bias. The Monk of West-

---

[11] Oman, *The Political History of England*, IV, p. 132.

minster, for whose house Richard showed great partiality, was by no means a consistently uncritical defender, while the continuator of the *Eulogium Historiarum* who might, if speculations on his identity are correct,[12] have been expected to be his partisan was often brutally condemnatory. A few minor fragments have come to light which are enthusiastically royalist, although the Kirkstall chronicler, for example, castigated the Appellants in 1388 and Richard in 1397. John Capgrave preserved an Austin tradition of temperate defence for the king into the next century.[13] If French writers, including Froissart, were generally favourable to him, none was so ardent in support as Walsingham was savage in abuse. The *Rolls of Parliament* and the *State Trials* contain the official interpretations of the victors in the great controversies. Since Richard was a loser in 1388 and in 1399 his case as presented in those records appears to be virtually indefensible. For three hundred years the most frequently quoted authorities on the period were the official accounts and the chronicles of Walsingham and Knighton, if for no other reason than that they were the best known and most voluminous. After his narrative was edited by Hearne in 1729 the Monk of Evesham was also widely cited. Ordinarily the French sources were considered to be less reliable and the Monk of Westminster less important. As might be expected, the bias in the conventional treatment of the history of the reign reflected that of the contemporaries upon whom it relied most heavily.

Intensive analysis of all the chroniclers should have modified the general verdict. Creton's narration, for example, may possibly have been as much a case of special pleading as Walsingham's. If so it should not have been so outrageously deficient in verisimilitude as to defeat its propagandist purpose. Especially important is the fact that Creton's portrait of Richard in 1399 is fleshed out with anecdotal detail and intimate personal observation. Walsingham and other anti-Ricardian reporters rely on generalities and invective. This is not to say that the case for tyranny, in effect, may not be closer to the truth than the king's partisans would have allowed. Certainly public opinion had been

---

[12] E. J. Jones suggests Bishop Trevor as the author. *Speculum* (1937) XII; he makes elsewhere a stronger case for Trevor's authorship of Creton's *Histoire du Roy d'Angleterre Richard. Speculum*, XV, (1940), pp. 460 ff.

[13] Capgrave, *Chronicle* ed. F. C. Hingeston (R.S. 1858), p. 102.

I

widely alienated before it ever became necessary to discover justifications for Henry of Lancaster's usurpation. But the testimony of the French chronicles together with scraps of evidence from English sources should at least suffice to raise serious questions about explanations of Richard's fall which concentrate on his defects of personal character and to discredit imputations of insanity altogether.

In the last half century it has been possible to check the official reports and the chronicles against other kinds of evidence. J. F. Baldwin and T. F. Tout made exhaustive studies of the royal council and of the offices of administration. Several scholars have explored the composition of parliament, the business of particular sessions and the operation of local justice. T. F. T. Plucknett and others have re-examined the origins of impeachment, the role of the king's judges and innovations in legal procedure. Most recently Anthony Steel has completed a detailed analysis of late medieval royal finance. As a result of their efforts it can now be established that Richard was served by a well-trained professional administrative staff, that he was advised by councillors who were mature and experienced, that the commons was not organized along party lines, and that Richard's government was neither habitually irresponsible about finance nor on the verge of fiscal disaster in 1399. It is also evident that what men were zealous to protect in parliament and elsewhere was not a liberal constitution but the particular interests and franchises they regarded as theirs by right,[14] and that monarchy in Richard's day possessed virtually no adequate machinery with which to fulfill the expectation that it would effect order in the countryside.

[14] De la Garde, *La naissance de l'esprit laique au declin du moyen age* (1942) IV, pp. 88 ff. By 1399, attendance through their representatives at sessions of parliament would already have become for some of the commons such a right rather than an obligation. Parliament would, therefore, already have progressed far along in the process of transformation from an occasion for treating to an institution with established forms and privileges. It is interesting, however, to speculate on reactions if kings had been in a position simply to let parliaments lapse through failure to issue summons. Of course, kings found the meetings necessary for financial purposes and useful for many other reasons. Attention has been called to Richard II's hopes from a parliament in 1388 and his employment of others in 1397 and 1398; there was little likelihood of their termination through disuse. I obviously do not regard the *Modus Tenendi Parliamentum* as bearing any significant relationship to the actual conduct of parliament in the fourteenth century as it is known from other sources. But cf. M. V. Clarke, *Medieval Representation and Consent* and Wilkinson, *Constitutional History*, III, pp. 64–66, 324–337, for an alternative view.

Most of these things should have long been apparent on the basis of less systematic research, but the allegations of the chroniclers outweighed sober judgment on evident fact. It is more surprising that they often continue to do so despite the conclusive testimony of the data. The frivolous spendthrift king, the youthful irresponsible council, the sycophantic agents of despotism and the constitutional party of opposition in the commons have only slowly and partially been recognized as the literary creations of Richard's contemporary enemies or of later authors whose particular purposes they served. Even Tout, who decried the practice, continued the usage of party nomenclature almost as though he were describing the politics of the Victorian era.

More recent historians have retained and developed the conceptions of party politics and well-defined institutional checks on fourteenth century monarchy. The most persistent notion has been that of an organized Lancastrian party, alternatively presented as a bulwark to a strengthened prerogative or as the mainstay of a traditional parliamentary constitution.[15] Richard has been represented either as falling because he ignored the wisdom of the former or being broken in a self-provoked conflict with the latter.

The notion of an attempt to transform limited monarchy into despotism has been argued with greater sophistication than ever before,[16] while a clinical vocabulary has been pressed into the service of the explanation of failure from personal defects.[17] Knowledge of the long list of prudent, industrious, experienced men who were constantly in attendance at his council board or at work in the royal administration has done too little to modify the established conception of 'Richard the Redeless'. Some of the most respectable of his aides combined deep personal loyalty

[15] The first is the thesis of Clark, *Fourteenth Century Studies*, pp. 36–52, elaborated by Steel, *Richard II*, Ch. IV. It is apparently accepted by M. McKisack, *The Fourteenth Century* (1959), pp. 425 ff. The strongest case for a persistent Lancastrian tradition throughout the century is argued by Wilkinson. He identifies Henry with it both as an opponent of Richard II and as a newly-crowned king in 1399. *Constitutional History*, II, pp. 62, 77. Whether or not John of Gaunt was a Lancastrian in these terms is, for Wilkinson, a complex problem. Certainly he was a 'moderate royalist', Ibid., III, p. 33. Cf. II, pp. 55, 71, 231, 301–4, and III, p. 93.

[16] By Professor Wilkinson.

[17] By Steel. Cf. McKisack, *Fourteenth Century*, pp. 497, 498. Also V. H. Galbraith, 'A New Life of Richard II', *History*, N.S. XXVII (1942), pp. 223–39. Infra, pp. 127–129.

with a highly developed sense of professional responsibility. It is scarcely credible that they could have retained such strong sentiments if Richard had degenerated into the arbitrary despot described by his enemies or the palpable madman invented by modern historians.

There is still no satisfactory history of Richard II. It may, however, be worthwhile to shed the parliamentary preference of seventeenth century constitutionalists, to go beyond the personal drama of Shakespeare and to attempt a brief review of the factors of circumstance, tradition and intellectual environment in the late fourteenth century from which a rational policy of royal absolutism might have emerged.

CHAPTER X

THE ARCHITECTS AND SERVANTS OF
PREROGATIVE ABSOLUTISM

THE attempted absolutism at the end of the reign followed, in the main, lines which had been laid out prior to the debacle of 1386. An efficient, closely integrated bureaucracy, a loyal coterie of chamber knights and career clerics, an experienced inner council and a select aristocratic faction which owed pre-eminence directly to royal largess: these were the elements upon which Richard sought to base his power just as the courtiers had begun to do a decade earlier. He had organized a more extensive private army than that which had been destroyed in 1387 at Radcot Bridge, but the inadequacy of the entire structure must sooner or later have been revealed, even if de Vere had beaten the Appellants or if Henry of Lancaster had encountered a capable regent.

Under the circumstances the strongest factor in Richard's cause was his own unshakable conviction of the sanctity of office. His theory of monarchy had borne him through the misfortunes of 1388 and inspired him to carry out, prior to 1397, the systematic rebuilding of his power. His conception of pre-rogative right was the touchstone from which the programme of his final years took shape. His faith in the inviolability of an anointed king made him dangerous to his enemies even when he was a prisoner in the Tower. Finally, all that endured when he had been crushed was the legend which fixed upon him as the protagonist of sacred majesty. The martyr's role in which he had endeavoured to cast Edward II became with more propriety his own.

The experiences of Richard's early years and the weakened condition of the monarchy bequeathed to him by Edward III might have generated a deep concern with the estate of kingship on the part of a less sensitive and intelligent ruler. His own reactions can hardly be doubted. His introduction to affairs of state came dramatically with the revolt of 1381. As a fourteen-year-old he witnessed in a time of crisis the paralysis of government without authorized leadership. The fighting Bishop of Norwich showed how easily rebellion could be repressed by vigorous action. If the policy ultimately adopted by the king's ministers was more humane, it came too late, and it had to be executed by men who were timid, inexperienced or unsympathetic. The first decisive move from the side of the government was Richard's bold offer to serve as leader of the rebels after the murder of Wat Tyler.

In the meantime he had been given an opportunity to observe that the mass of his subjects, in contrast to the men of family who frequented his court, held monarchy in high esteem. It is not unlikely that he shared initially the panic of the aristocrats whose courage he had been taught to respect.[1] The consistently reverent attitude of the rebels indicated to him, however, that he had little cause to fear them. From the outset they demanded to treat with him in person. They refused to be put off by intermediaries or simply by the king's appearance at a distance. They insisted that they wanted no other ruler. When their professions of devotion were put to the test, they proved their loyalty by accepting his command to disperse to their homes.[2]

His elation in the remarkable personal triumph was destined to be short-lived, but it is unlikely that he would have forgotten it or its sequel. Those few days in June of 1381 had taught him how unique was the greatness which pertained to royalty. In the ensuing months and years he learned how impotent he was under normal circumstances to exercise the authority of his station. The king's word, when it was spoken to the rebel horde, might avert catastrophe; it was of scant importance when addressed to the disparate forces which shared, in a variety of forms, political control of the realm. His complaint of 1389 to the great council that he had been deprived of power while others ruled badly in his name was unjustifiable as applied to the three years immediately prior to the establishment of the Commission of 1386. But it reflected lingering bitterness over tutelage unreasonably prolonged as well as more immediate resentment of the commission itself.

[1] *Historia Vitae et Regni Ricardi II*, ed. Hearne (1729), p. 27.
[2] *Polychronicon*, IX, p. 1; *Hist. Ang.*, I, pp. 455, 458; *Anonimalle Chron.*, p. 139.

In the year after the revolt he had still been too young to direct the government of the kingdom. He was old enough, however, to recognize the parliamentary supervision of his household as an unwarranted intrusion, and to be sensitive to the implications of the enforced repudiation of his oaths to the rebels. The time would come when he would himself plead compulsion as an excuse for the violation of pledges. In 1381 he was permitted neither to make nor to explain a decision which reflected seriously upon his honour. Even when he was gradually assuming more control over government while de la Pole served as chancellor, he had been forced to endure affronts and impertinences which constantly reminded him that many of the magnates entertained too little respect for the king. The most shocking episode occurred in 1384 when the courtiers, prompted by the story of an eccentric friar, accused Lancaster of treason. An unreliable anti-royalist chronicler reports that Thomas of Woodstock rushed into Richard's presence shouting that he would kill any accuser of Lancaster including the king himself. The report cannot be entirely accurate. Even Thomas, audacious as he was, could hardly have made a public threat of physical violence to his sovereign. Yet contempt for his nephew and the courtiers was something he took no pains to conceal, and he may have stopped just short of a horrifyingly unpardonable offence.[3] Complete humiliation at the hands of the Appellants was, therefore, as Richard viewed it in retrospect, the ultimate crime derived from the low estate into which kingship had fallen. This gave substance to the charge of ill governance. A monarchy which could command neither the due respect nor the allegiance of the most important of its subjects could not perform its function.

Before the assault on his chancellor Richard had given evidence of his concern not only by testiness toward the most arrogant of the aristocrats, but also by initiating attempts to secure the canonization of Edward II. Kingship had sustained in Edward's deposition a blow from which, as his own experience demonstrated, it had never recovered. Richard's reading of the

---

[3] *Hist. Ang.*, II, pp. 112–15. The story has been accepted by historians including those whose interpretation of the events of the 1380's is most favourable to the opponents of the court.

century's history may have been faulty in detail. The turning point may have come earlier than 1327; the restoration of authority in the first four decades of the reign of Edward III may have been more complete than he imagined; above all the overthrow of Edward II may have involved much besides the assertion of self-interest by an overly ambitious aristocracy. On the other hand, he did not need to be a profound student of history or an unduly thin-skinned and introspective prince to be aware of the discrepancy between the traditional estate of kingship and his own actual power. His preoccupation with the trappings of royalty might, therefore, have had its origin entirely in the circumstances of his situation.

His complex personality has encouraged even more intricate psychological speculation.[4] His father, it has been pointed out, was a great military hero, as had been his father before him. They had maintained magnificent courts which would have overawed an imaginative child. His half-brothers, the Hollands, were men of action, glorified by the chroniclers of chivalry.[5] The fundamental obligation of the medieval king was that he should lead his arrays on the field of battle. Yet Richard was slight of frame and sensitive of disposition. His tastes were aesthetic rather than athletic. It has been urged, too, that he was profoundly disturbed by rumours that he was not the legitimate son of the Black Prince, but the bastard offspring of an unidentified amour of his mother. He, therefore, developed an acute inferiority complex which found its compensation only in elaborate exhibitions of his power and in extravagant declarations of his majesty. These tendencies were naturally accentuated by the humiliation he was forced to endure prior to his first assertion of independence in 1383, and even more by the annihilation of his hopes in 1388. The ultimate result was neurotic fascination with the symbols of absolutism.

This is a seductive analysis which possesses the merit of providing a comprehensive explanation for everything Richard did or said. It is, nonetheless, unsatisfactory. It would appear, for example, that the English court from 1370 until 1377 was much less splendid than it had been at the time of the childhood of the Dukes of York and Gloucester, yet apparently neither of

---

[4] By A. Steel, *Richard II*, pp. 7, 8, 41, 42, 175.
[5] Froissart, *Chronicles*, IV, pp. 110 ff.

these sons of Edward III developed any abnormal awe of kingship. If others reacted differently no testimony survives. Nor is it by any means certain that Richard was a physical weakling, though he never displayed any notable military skill. His behaviour in 1381 and his conduct of expeditions against Ireland and Scotland cast doubt, perhaps, on his wisdom but neither on his courage nor his physical stamina.[6] The charge of illegitimacy was apparently not widely circulated in his life time. It is improbable that, prior to 1399, he would have heard such gossip. Finally, there is no contemporary corroboration of the alleged 'neurosis'. If Richard could have been disposed of as a madman, the revolution of 1399 would have run an entirely different course. His views were hardly so singular as to indicate mental disease. Their substance and the forms he chose for their expression may reflect upon his judgment but not upon his sanity. Indeed, if the first intimations of a concerted effort at strong monarchy had occurred after 1388, rather than in 1377, they could be explained as a normal reaction to a derogation of authority. The programme of the early years must, however, be accounted for on other grounds than frustration and degradation, though it would be imprudent to discount the importance of experience in shaping and deepening Richard's conception of his role as he grew older.

Attention must be directed to the familiars of his household at the opening of the reign and to the people with whom he was intimate at any time in his life. The former would have launched the programme to rehabilitate royalty in 1377 and supervised Richard's education; all would have contributed to the development of his attitudes and his policy. Because of the nature of the available information, conclusions must be tentative. Little is known, for example, about the training or the background of some of the persons who are likely to have exerted the greatest influence over him. But enough fragments can be pieced together to suggest some patterns.

In the first place, relatively few members of great families were ever particularly close to him either personally or in an

---

[6] Cf. *Hist. Ang.*, II, p. 141. Creton, pp. 24ff. *Traison et Mort*, pp. 66, 67, represents him as challenging his accusers to trial by combat in 1399. Cf. Galbraith, 'A New Life of Richard II', *History*, XXVI (1942).

official capacity. Robert de Vere and Thomas Mowbray were his companions when he was young. Each figured prominently in a courtier faction. Aubrey de Vere and John Montagu, who were later to inherit earldoms, transferred their service to Richard at the death of his father. They were among the very few survivors of the purge of 1388 who were still active royalist partisans in 1399. Archbishop Alexander Neville of York was a leader among the king's advisers in the critical year 1387. His brother, Sir William, was for ten years a chamber knight. Sir Peter Courtenay, brother of the Archbishop of Canterbury, served in the same capacity throughout most of the reign. These seven names complete a limited list. In the later stages of the reign, Richard's uncles of Lancaster and York, his half-brothers and his nephew, the three Hollands, his cousins, Edward of Rutland and John Beaufort, together with Mowbray, Montague, Thomas Despenser, William Scrope, Thomas Percy and Bishop Stafford of Exeter made up a larger group of aristocratic associates. Many were recently elevated. Scrope, for example, was the first of his family to hold an earldom. Even so, they were greatly outnumbered by collaborators of humbler origin. Most of these, who came into royal service prior to 1386, like Aubrey de Vere, had been abroad with the Black Prince. Some were soldiers of fortune or country knights; other were clerks and household officials. As a group they are remarkable for their loyalty and their *esprit de corps*.

The Prince has not fared well at the hands of modern historians who have been critical of his diplomacy, his understanding of the major problems of England and Aquitaine and even of his ability as a military strategist. He has been cited as an exemplar of the superficiality and inhumanity of late medieval chivalry. The record, insofar as it is known, leaves room for doubt only on the scores of military competence and brutality.[7] No constructive effort at the solution of the complicated problems of Gascony redeems his administration there. He organized an efficient official staff but he did nothing to make English rule of the province more secure. His diplomacy was dominated by personal interest which sometimes did not coincide with the interest of the

[7] O. P. Shaw, 'The Black Prince', *History XXIV* (1939), pp. 1–15; A. H. Burne, *The Agincourt War*, (1956) pp. 20–22, 27, 28. Cf. E. Perroy, *The Hundred Years War*, (1951), p. 165.

crown. His handling of affairs in the Iberian peninsula was particularly short-sighted.[8] No figure of his time, however, enjoyed a higher reputation and none inspired more enduring devotion. Intelligent men who knew him well expected from him leadership which gave hope to the future. It is unlikely that his well-wishers would have found in him the king they anticipated if he had outlived his father. His personal following sought advancement and the prospect of better government by attaching themselves to the court of his son. Their numbers were gradually enlarged by the addition of kindred spirits who had fought on the continent with Robert Knollys and John of Gaunt or who had been employed there in diplomacy and administration outside the Prince's service.

The young Richard's circle, therefore, was composed almost entirely of men whose experience and training was more European than insular, who were bound together by close personal ties as well as by common background, and whose loyalty was directed toward him rather than toward either Edward III or the personages who had been most influential in the later years of his reign. The councils of the minority were dominated by people whose connections, patronage and channels of communication were deeply rooted in England itself. The royal household on the other hand, and, to the degree that the household could direct it, the administration were permeated by attitudes and lines of association which had their origins on the continent. If the points of view of council and court were not perhaps substantively different they would at least have been separate.

It would be easy to exaggerate the distinction. Medieval England was, of course, never isolated from the thought and the ideological conceptions common to Western Europe. The Hundred Years War had greatly increased the number of Englishmen who had been brought into direct contact with an alien environment. Intellectual community had been reinforced by the orders of friars and by the development of the universities. The court of Edward III would, like the households of his baronage, or indeed, those of humbler citizens, have accepted in matters which were most fundamental a scale of values, an outlook, shared throughout Christendom. Moreover, it could not escape

---

[8] P. E. Russell, *English Intervention in Spain*, Chs. V–VII.

an awareness of modifications of attitude or of new developments in law or practice which gained currency in France, Italy, Spain and the Empire. Richard's servitors and associates, too, their years away from home notwithstanding, were Englishmen who would have assimilated what they learned or observed elsewhere into a frame of reference deeply surcharged with English particularities. Taken as a group, however, in their receptivity to continental influence, and in the complex fusion among them of the traditional with the novel, they were unlike their predecessors.

For more than one reason their orientation was toward strong central power. The soldiers of fortune readily adopted the codes of conduct appropriate to a sort of military enterprise which was in many ways independent of the niceties of feudal law. Customary right came to be of little consequence to them. They thought rather in terms of possibilities for aggrandizement and actualities of power, however obtained or sanctioned. They were familiar with Sir John Hawkwood, whose Italian successes had been founded upon principles which they understood. The Prince's own ambitions in Spain involved conceptions of politics similar to those currently being exploited in Italy.[9] Where the master showed the way, even though he had feudal rights in England and Gascony to defend, the men whose only property was the sword could be expected to follow. They were neither scholars nor theorists; but they were ready to be the obliging executors of any authority which promised reward.

Among the king's knights such men as Thomas Tryvet, William Elmham, Thomas Blount, and Matthew Gournay were frequently employed on royal business in a strong arm capacity.[10] They were veterans of campaigns in France, Spain and Gascony

[9] Ibid., especially pp. 137, 148 and Ch. VII.
[10] T. Blount, C.P.R., 1381–1385, p. 197; C.P.R., 1385–1389, pp. 33, 37, 39, 550. W. Elmham, C.C.R., 1385–1389, p. 169; C.P.R., 1377–1381, pp. 391, 475, 512. M. Gournay, C.P.R., 1377–1381, p. 22; C.P.R., 1385–1389, pp. 88, 165, 317, 385, 393; C.C.R., 1377–1381, p. 326; C.C.R., 1385–1389, pp. 322, 436; Foedera VII, p. 230. Thomas Tryvet, C.P.R., 1385–1389., pp 88, 165, 317, 385. The behaviour of Gournay and Tryvet, who were kinsmen, brought them frequently into difficulty with the law. C.C.R., 1377–1381, p. 473; C.C.R., 1385–1389, pp. 102, 174, 658; C.P.R., 1381–1385, pp. 4, 143; C.P.R., 1385–1389, p. 550; Foedera VII, p. 425. This last entry relates to charges against Tryvet, Elmham and others in connection with the Bishop of Norwich's Flemish Crusade. The commons were no doubt genuinely angry over what appeared to them to be dishonesty and disloyalty if not treason. To some extent, however, the furore may have been fanned up to make the bishop a scape-goat and to protect others. Lancaster and other lords had behaved in so dilatory and self-interested a fashion as almost to insure the

where they had been schooled in violence. In their matter of fact world, boldness and devious pursuit of the main chance counted for more than traditional rights. Gournay had found opportunities to turn usefulness to the Prince to his own advantage in the Iberian peninsula. Elmham and Sir Hugh Calveley, whose reputation was second only to those of Knollys and Hawkwood, had engaged in a kind of individual diplomacy which, though detrimental to English interest, had made them men of importance in the Spanish kingdoms. As an English commander in Navarre, Tryvet had missed no opportunity to look out for himself.[11] Elmham and Tryvet, along with Calveley, were among the lieutenants of the Bishop of Norwich on his ill-fated crusade into Flanders in 1383. Though a critical parliament censured them for lining their pockets by private arrangements with the enemy, they were doing nothing more than plying the trade in which they were skilled. If they recognized a loyalty other than to the life of adventure and profit, it was to their own fellowship. Their comrades in arms surrounded the court. The king's service gave them a congenial employment. They could use their access to the king's ear for their own advancement and the protection of their friends. Their names figure frequently in the Rolls as petitioners for the pardon of convicted felons.[12] They had little to do with giving shape to royal policy but their importance to its operation was acknowledged by the arrests of Tryvet and Elmham and the banishment of Blount in 1388.[13]

failure of Bishop Despenser's martial venture, a failure which Lancaster turned to good account. Cf. M. Aston, 'The Impeachment of Bishop Despenser', *B.I.H.R.* XXXVIII (1965), p. 148. The king was more sympathetic to the bishop who remained, as did Elmham, a loyal partisan in 1399. Gournay was involved with Calveley in a suit brought by the Marshall of France which contained charges of terrorizing witnesses. *Foedera* VII, p. 590; cf. *C.P.R.* 1389–1391, p. 243.

[11] Russell, *English Intervention in Spain*, pp. 50, 121, 271, 277.

[12] *C.P.R.* 1377–1381, pp. 343, 355, 403, 489; *C.P.R.* 1381–1385, p. 517; *C.P.R.* 1385–1389, pp. 23, 376; *C.P.R.* 1389–1391, pp. 41, 89. Northumberland, Arundel and Derby could also sue for pardons to murderers as could other less likely employers or associates of men of violence, such as the Bishop of Aire. *C.P.R.* 1385–1389, pp. 376, 377; *C.P.R.* 1381–1385, p. 441; *C.P.R.* 1389–1391, pp. 41, 173. Pardons for felonies were commonplace. E. G. Kimball suggests that, during the reign of Henry V, 'few men, even those of position, had failed to purchase at least one pardon'. A standard fee had been established at 16s. 4d. *The Shropshire Peace Roll*, 1400–1414 (1959), pp. 43–5.

[13] *Foedera* VII, pp. 566, 567; *Hist. Ang.*, II, pp. 165, 173; *Polychronicon*, IX, p.116. Elmham engaged in diplomatic missions and naval commands as well as judiciary business. *Foedera* VII, pp. 693, 747; VIII, pp. 17, 32; *C.P.R.* 1377–1381, p. 580. His employment by the court ceased after 1386, as did that of Edward Dalyngrigge. But he was constantly active again after 1390. *C.P.R.* 1391–1396, pp. 87, 234, 238, etc. On October 28, 1399 the horses and harness taken from him without due process

Elmham, who in the meantime had performed more distinguished service, was still a loyal king's man in 1399.

Like them in training and experience, but distinguished from them by a greater sense of responsibility and more conventional ambitions, was another group of knights generally called upon for different sorts of service. Men like Nicholas Dagworth, Richard Abberbury, Richard Stury and Edward Dalyngrigge held inquests, officiated at sessions of the peace, fulfilled diplomatic missions and saw to the administration of justice at the king's command in the company of men learned in the law.[14]

of law at Berkeley and elsewhere were returned to him. *C.P.R.* 1399–1401, p. 39. He was one of the attorneys for the Duke of Norfolk during his exile. *Foedera* VIII, p. 5. Tryvet was also an admiral for a few months in 1386. *Handbook of British Chronology*, Powicke and Fryde, eds. (1961), p. 130.

[14] N. Dagworth, *C.C.R.* 1377–1381, p. 383; *C.P.R.* 1381–1385, pp. 49, 498; *C.P.R.* 1385–1389, p. 195; *C.P.R.* 1391–1396., pp 234, 238; grant of tun of wine for life, *C.P.R.* 1396–1399, p. 492; diplomatic services, *Foedera* VII, pp. 298, 304, 307, 353, 423, 455, 456, 457, 458, 610, 612, 636 ff., 650, 651, 714–22. Dagworth's close associations with John Hawkwood culminated in missions to continental courts in which Hawkwood gave him valuable aid. Cf. Perroy *Schisme*, pp. 278–81, 289, 290, and *Foedera* VII, p. 393 for papal commendation of his activities. R. Abberbury, *C.C.R.* 1377–1381, p. 126; *C.P.R.* 1381–1385, pp. 140, 141, 146, 195, 196, 197, 199, 202, 247, 255, 284, 347, 426, 498; *C.P.R.* 1385–1389, p. 80; *C.P.R.* 1389–1391, pp. 40, 47, 51, 159, 208, 210, 214, 215, 345, 412, 425, 444, 516; *C.P.R.* 1391–1396, pp. 92, 331, 434, 438, 440; diplomatic services, *Foedera* VII, pp. 187, 194, 223, 510–15, 515–24, 595, 667, 785, 805. With Stury, Dalyngrigge and others signed protest at behaviour of the papacy, May 26, 1390. *Foedera* VII, pp. 672–5. Queen's Chamberlain, *C.P.R.* 1381–1385, pp. 263, 291, 335; *C.P.R.* 1385–1389, pp. 116, 154, 156.

R. Stury, cf. W. T. Waugh, *Scottish Historical Review*, XI, pp. 55–92. He was among the abler men recruited to Richard's service from that of Gaunt. He moved via the household of the Princess of Wales, though he had apparently been an enemy of the Prince, pp. 65–67. He was close to A. de Vere, de la Pole and Burley. He was also a friend of Chaucer, p. 69. His diplomatic missions for the king began as early as May 1381, *Foedera* VII, p. 308. He was exempted with others including Chaucer's friend, Philip Vache, from summons to the Scottish wars of 1385 in order to remain with the Princess of Wales as a protector, ibid., p. 474. He was a signer, in distinguished company, of the protest of May 26, 1390 to the papacy. Ibid., pp. 672–5. Activities as justice, *C.P.R.* 1385–1389, p. 307; *C.P.R.* 1391–1396, pp. 7, 41, 68, 76, 166, 167, 290, 292, 340, 378, 388, 435, 441, 531, 570, 576. Died, 1395, *C.P.R.* 1391–1396, p. 655. Edward Dalyngrigge. Possibly also a former Lancastrian protege, cf. E. Lodge and R. Somerville (eds.), *John of Gaunt's Register* II, (1937), p. 368. A king's knight as early as 1385. Tout, *Chapters* III, pp. 411 n., 413 n., 469 n., 470 n. He had been relieved of a judicial suit by the king's favour, *C.C.R.* 1377–1381, p. 474. His judicial and administrative service began in 1380. *C.P.R.* 1377–1381, p. 459. There are 22 entries *C.P.R.* 1381–1385 and three prior to April 1386, *C.P.R.* 1385–1389, pp. 90, 123, 164. They became frequent again after January 1389, e.g., *C.P.R.* 1389–1391, pp. 47, 80, 133, 135, 159, 173, 214, 217, 232, 341, 351, 436, 439, 444, 458, 487, 510, 528; *C.P.R.* 1391–1396, pp. 17, 31, 41, 68, 76, 83, 84, 167, 235, 236, 237, 290, 354, 390. He participated in arrangements for a truce with France and was a signer of the 1390 protest to the papacy. *Foedera* VII, pp. 667, 672. He died early in 1394 before his last commission was fulfilled. *C.P.R.* 1391–1396, p. 388.

They, too, had made their reputations abroad as soldiers, but their talents and their antecedents opened to them the prospects of lordship and the foundation of substantial family fortunes.

Tryvet and Gournay would have been unlikely to have held sovereign majesty in awe. They knew that kings lived and died, not infrequently by violence, like other men. They could also be set aside. But while they ruled they possessed the power to reward or to punish. A king's man would not welcome external interference with the power to reward. If the power to punish were likewise unfettered, he need not be concerned so long as he took his orders. In fact he might find a certain pleasure in being the agent. The preference for absolutism was simple and natural.

The opinions of Dagworth, Stury or Dalyngrigge would have more subtle foundations. Dalyngrigge in particular was a careful and ambitious man. The king's favour had authorized the construction of his beautiful little country castle at Bodiam in Sussex. His standing as an important royalist was later recognized by his appointment as governor of London when the city was taken into the king's hands in 1392. Testimony to Stury's constancy to the king is supplied by Froissart. These two were consistently active in the king's councils after 1389. In fact their experience and their devotion to duty may have placed much of the day-to-day business of government in their hands. As seasoned professionals the degree of their influence over the execution, if not the formulation, of policy was perhaps similar to that of their more notorious successors, Bushy, Bagot, Greene and Russell.[15]

Such landholders could appreciate the conservatism of their peers and superiors whose mistrust of the lower classes they might have reason to share. Their understanding of English law and administration would equip them to comprehend the refinements as well as the surface brutality of the foreign statecraft with which they constantly came into contact. The court of the Visconti was

---

[15] Froissart, *Chroniques* (ed. Kervyn) XV, pp. 157 ff. *Foedera* VII, p. 727. The royal licence 'to strengthen and crenellate' Bodiam was dated October 21, 1385. Its terms 'appear to be unique in designating what was otherwise a privately owned residence and stronghold as forming part of a coastal, or second line, national defence scheme'. W. D. Simpson, *Bodiam Castle* (1961), p. 3. *C.P.R.* 1385–1389, p. 42. For the service of Dalyngrigge and Stury on the council cf. Baldwin, *King's Council*, pp. 133, 300, where they appear as a specially deputed committee, and 489 ff. where the record of Dalyngrigge's consistent attendance is compiled. For the importance of these king's knights cf. Tout, *Chapters* III, pp. 470–2.

as familar to them from personal experience as those of the pope or the kings of France and Spain, and their knowledge was supplemented by intimacy with seasoned observers like Hawkwood and Froissart. At the king's council board they could study the considerations which influenced the shaping of policy while they learned to appraise the characters of the great men of the realm. For them the decision between loyalty and self-interest in a time of crisis could be neither simple nor easy, but for the most part they had been schooled to respect authority. They had seen enough of disorder in the world to have a preference for stability in England, a preference which could only be reinforced by their favour at court. Their allegiance therefore belonged to the king. For this they paid in one way or another when control over government fell into the hands of the Commission of 1386.[16]

Abberbury was also one of the group of knights, including Simon Burley, Baldwin Raddington, Aubrey de Vere, Hugh Segrave and John Montagu, who held posts in the royal administration.[17] In this capacity they were closely associated with

[16] Dagworth was imprisoned at Rochester, January 4, 1388. *Foedera* VII, p. 567. Abberbury was banished from the court, *Polychronicon*, IX, p. 116. The interruption of the constant service and preferment of Dalyngrigge and Stury is evident in the entries in the rolls, n. 13 supra. On March 17, 1388, Dalyngrigge made fine for acquisition from Arundel of lands for which no licence had been issued. *C.C.R.* 1385–1389, p. 415. His son and heir, John, had to receive special pardon for all claims which the king might have had against 'the said Edward having been an adherent of Thomas, Duke of Gloucester in the 10th year'. *C.P.R.* 1396–1399, p. 341. This was on May 3, 1398, when all who had served in the parliament of 1386 were being pardoned. Sir Edward was apparently not so ardent a partisan as Dagworth and Elmham, but the record of his commissions and his place on the council give testimony to his loyalties, cf. also *C.C.R.* 1385–1389, p. 334 and *C.P.R.* 1391–1396, p. 37.

Tout provides a list of Chamber knights, *Chapters* IV, pp. 344–6. Abberbury, Dagworth and Stury served in this capacity. The others mentioned above would simply have been king's knights, of whom, of course, there were a large number during the reign. Those mentioned were both typical in background and unusually successful.

[17] Simon Burley is separately treated at length, infra. Raddington's career and importance are treated by N. B. Lewis, 'Simon Burley and Baldwin Raddington', *EHR*, LII (1937), pp. 662–9 and Tout, *Chapters* IV, pp. 196–9.

De Vere was with the Prince of Wales in Aquitaine in 1366, agreed to abide with him for life in 1367 and bore the king's sword at Mile End in 1381. *Complete Peerage* X, pp. 233, 234. He was driven from the court in January 1388, *Polychronicon* IX, p. 116. His career is summarized by Tout, *Chapters* III, pp. 329, 343–51, 356, 357, 371, 382, 406, 428, 475; IV, p. 340; V, pp. 212, 379. Segrave, an executor of the will of the Prince of Wales, was distinguished enough to serve on the councils of the minority. Tout, *Chapters* III, pp. 328–334. Cf. Ibid. III, pp. 227, 234, 344, 353, 356, 373–8, 380, 399, 401, 402; IV, pp. 146, 149, 156, 157, 160, 203, 408; V, pp. 213, 391. Sir John Montagu was steward of the household from 1381 to 1387. His successors were the unfortunate John Beauchamp, executed in 1388, and John

clerical officials who, like them, had served the Black Prince, the widowed Princess, and the young king. The indifference of the staffs of crown and household offices to the great political crises of the period is remarkable. They stayed at their appointed tasks regardless of conspiracy, autocracy, rebellion or dynastic change. In some instances their superiors appeared to be equally withdrawn from great affairs of politics, but more often than not they were deeply involved. Clerical and lay officials alike were active partisans who either stood by the king in adversity or, less frequently, found it prudent to sue for individual terms of peace with his opponents. During the minority they constituted the inner circle of the royal advisers, assembling a courtier coterie from their associates, their proteges and new recruits who showed zeal for the king's business.

Among the clerical servitors of the Prince, William Pakington, Alan Stokes, John Bacon and others held office in the early years of the new reign.[18] John Harewell, a former chancellor of the Prince, was awarded the episcopal see of Bath after membership on the continual council of 1377–78. He was one of several who moved from the household of the Prince to that of Richard and ultimately to episcopal dignity.[19] John Fordham, a secretary to the father and keeper of the Privy Seal for the son, became Bishop of Durham. His attachment to the court and his loyalty in 1387 were punished by translation to Ely in 1388.[20] Robert Waldby, an Austin friar, who as Bishop of Aire had been attendant upon the Prince in Gascony and tutor to Richard, was successively

---

Devereux, also a one-time follower of the Prince, but not a devoted partisan to his son. For Montague cf. Tout, *Chapters* III, pp. 352, 378, 382, 400–2, 425. His son, the younger John, became Earl of Salisbury, one of the court favourites of the late years of the reign who was executed in 1400. Cf. *Hist. Ang.* II, p. 159; Knighton, *Chronicon* II, p. 181 and Waugh, *Scottish Hist. Rev.*, XI, p. 75.

[18] Pakington's biography is in Tout, *Chapters* IV, pp. 191–5; that of Stokes, Ibid. V, pp. 328, 329; Bacon's briefly, Ibid. V, pp. 380, 381. Tout's view that the Prince's followers dominated the household and private councils of the king until 1386 is distributed throughout the volumes of the *Chapters*. E.g., III, pp. 330 ff; IV, pp. 189 ff., 333 ff.; V, pp. 46 ff.

[19] Ibid. III, pp. 343–5; V, pp. 386–9.

[20] Ibid., III, pp. 330, 331; V, pp. 46, 47. Fordham was obviously a man of training and talent, as well as steadfast loyalty to Richard. After his translation in 1388, he served Ely long and well. *Victoria County History: Cambridge and the Isle of Ely* II, pp. 160, 161. He abstained from court ceremonies during the reign of Henry IV, but was prominent again from the accession of Henry V until his death in 1426. On December 4, 1399 he was granted exemption from parliamentary attendance, *Foedera* VIII, p. 110.

K

Archbishop of Dublin, Bishop of Chichester and Archbishop of York. Two other clerics whose careers were similar proved to be less devoted. Walter Skirlaw, a distinguished canonist, moved through the ranks in the king's service until, apparently annoyed at Richard's preference for a rival candidate as Bishop of Wells in 1387, he joined the Appellants to be rewarded with Fordham's see of Durham. In the meantime, royal influence had made him Bishop of Lichfield and treasurer. His removal from the latter office by parliament, incidental to the fall of Suffolk, was indicative of his relationship to the inner circle of the royalists in 1386.[21] Perhaps Skirlaw, like Fordham, retained fundamental loyalty to his old confederates. He was suspected when an old man of giving encouragement to the discontent against Henry IV which culminated in the battle of Shrewsbury.[22] Robert Braybrook, Bishop of London after 1381, had been an intimate of the royal family and an executor of the Princess' will as well as king's secretary at the beginning of the reign. An old civil servant and civil lawyer with friends in almost every circle, he probably deserted Richard in 1387 for less personal reasons than those of Skirlaw. He did his best to mediate between the hostile forces before the convocation of the Merciless Parliament, and unlike Skirlaw, he did not become an Appellant partisan.[23]

A group of younger clerics less familiar with affairs on the continent gained experience and preferment as staunch royalists during the minority. Representative of them were Thomas Rushook, John Swaffham, John Waltham, Richard Clifford, John

[21] Tout, *Chapters* V, pp. 48, 49 relates the history of his attachment to and breach with the court, cf. III, p. 400. Diplomatic service, *Foedera* VII, pp. 143, 188, 223, 229, 248, 298, 304, 306, 307, 308, 353, 401–3, 412-4, 418, 466, 467, 610, 612, 648, 714–22, 739; VIII, p. 108. The last entry pertains to negotiations with the French in November 1399. These activities together with his regular attendance at meetings of Richard's council in 1392 and 1393 (Baldwin, *King's Council*, pp. 489–504), would seem to modify Tout's judgment that he took little part in politics after 1386. *Chapters* III, p. 436 n. He was granted special permission by reason of past services and age to absent himself from parliament after October 7, 1397. *Foedera*, VIII, p. 19. Unlike Fordham he was probably not a royalist partisan after 1388, but like many another who aided the Appellants he resumed his place as a prominent public servant without apparent loss of the king's confidence.

[22] J. H. Wylie, *History of England Under Henry IV* (1884) I, p. 355.

[23] Braybrook studied civil law at Oxford, *D.N.B.* II, p. 1151. He was a kinsman of the Princess and one of the executors of her will. Tout, *Chapters* III, p. 330. He performed Richard's marriage to Anne of Bohemia and he served in the sixth year as courtier chancellor. Ibid., p. 402. He accompanied the king to Ireland in 1395, Ibid., p. 494. For his role in 1387 cf. *Hist. Ang.* II, p. 162.

Lincoln, and Richard Medford. All but Lincoln achieved the epispocate, although Clifford's elevation occurred only after Richard's deposition. In the early years Clifford was a clerk of the king's chapel. He was to be keeper of the great wardrobe and of the privy seal before he transferred his allegiance to Henry IV. Lincoln served as chamberlain of the exchequer and was king's secretary late in the reign. Both were proscribed in 1388, but neither suffered severe punishment.[24]

Swaffham, Bishop of Bangor since 1376 and an ardent king's man until his death in 1398, was one of the witnesses to the judicial declarations at Nottingham and Shrewsbury. He was a former Carmelite preacher who is said to have won his position by the eloquence of his declamations against vice and luxury.[25] Rushook, a Dominican, was also a preaching friar. As the king's confessor and a special favourite, he advanced rapidly. Archdeacon of St. Asaph's and Bishop of Llandaff in 1382, he moved to the wealthier see of Chichester in 1386. His career was destroyed by the Appellants at whose behest he was translated to Kildare in 1388. The king's affection could not save him from death in exile and poverty.[26] Chichester was likewise for a time the episcopal seat of two other king's friends. Robert Waldby has already been mentioned. Richard Medford, the royal secretary driven from the court in 1388, was one of the first of the Appellant victims to be restored to favour. He became Bishop of Chichester in 1390 and moved on to Salisbury five years later. He succeeded to that rich see upon the death of John Waltham who was also King Richard's treasurer.[27]

The Appellant purge left Waltham unaffected. Family connections assured him a good place in the royal service which he entered prior to 1381. His administrative talents won and held Richard's respect despite equivocal behaviour in connection with the animosities of 1386–88. Whether or not the see of Salisbury was actually a reward for assistance rendered to the king's enemies during the Merciless Parliament, he seems clearly to have enjoyed their confidence without ever forfeiting that of the king.

[24] *Polychronicon* IX, pp. 116, 182, 199. *Foedera* VII, pp. 566, 567.
[25] G. R. Owst, *Preaching in Medieval England* (1926), p. 66.
[26] *Polychronicon* IX, pp. 156, 157; M. E. C. Walcott, 'The Bishops of Chichester from Stigand to Sherborne'. *Sussex Archaeological Collections* XVIII, pp. 52, 53.
[27] Ibid., p. 54.

There were others among those who aggrieved Richard at that time whom he later forgave including two of the leaders. Waltham's case, however, if he actually did desert to the opposition, is unique not only in the constancy of the king's regard for him, but also in the degree to which he was honoured. He was the first ecclesiastic to be buried at Westminster Abbey amidst the members of the royal family.[28]

The attention lavished on these clerics and their fellows by enemies of the court, either to detach them from their allegiance or to destroy their influence, suggests that they were identified with the court's ultra-royalist programme disrupted by the impeachment of Michael de la Pole. In Appellant propaganda and in the declamations of 1388 the names of many of them were linked with those of the proscribed traitors. The later careers of all who were not broken by the Merciless Parliament, or won over by the Appellants, demonstrate their perseverance in their master's cause. Most of these clerics probably developed their respect for authority as a natural by-product of official careers. Only Waldby, Skirlaw, Fordham and Braybrook were conspicuous for their learning. They also had spent much time abroad and it was they who were most intimately connected with the lay associates of the late Prince of Wales. It is not unlikely that they took a leading part both in formulating the policy of the courtiers and in selecting the fellow clerics who were to assist in its execution.

Waldby merits special notice. His tomb in Westminster Abbey memorializes his knowledge and his interest in people. He had studied and lectured at Toulouse. He served for a brief period as Richard's tutor and he was on three occasions an envoy to Spain. As an Austin friar his connections both in England and on the continent were with preachers and men of letters who were vitally concerned about the relationship of temporal society to the divine plan. His elder brother, John, was a friar preacher who rivalled Fitz-Ralph or Brinton in the energy and ingenuity of his moralist declamation.[29] Both brothers had been resident at the Austin priory at Tickhill where they could not have

[28] D.N.B. XX, pp. 721, 722. C. Cb.R. V, pp. 344, 345.

[29] Owst, Preaching in Medieval England, pp. 64, 125, 322. Cf. A. Gwynn, The English Austin Friars in the Time of Wyclif (1940), pp. 115 ff., 272; Walcott, 'Bishops of Chichester', p. 54.

escaped the influence of John Erghum, the Austin Prior of York.[30]

Erghum was both a bibliophile and an author. The most interesting product of his pen was the anonymous pseudo-prophecy of John of Bridlington, an obscure poem attributed by its author to the opening of the fourteenth century with a detailed prose explanation designed to appear as a later addition. It was harshly critical of Edward III, eulogistic of the Black Prince and permeated by the self-righteous moralism characteristic of John Waldby's sermons. For the most part it was an unfriendly review of events which had already taken place by 1370 when it was probably composed. The author's actual prophetic powers were exhausted in the prediction that the English justly would suffer long for their current sins, but would ultimately be rescued by the government of the Prince, who, incidentally, in the meantime would have made good his claim to the French throne. Its ideological teaching, apart from the theme of sin and retribution, is that the monarch alone has the capacity to save the community, or, for that matter, if he be so disposed, to lead it astray.[31]

The admiration of Erghum for the Prince was shared widely among the most influential and most serious minded of English clerics. The president of the Black Monks, Thomas de la Mare, who headed the great monastic house at St. Albans, was the Prince's intimate friend. It was probably he who introduced the Austins to the court. Though he was a preacher of note, his energies were devoted primarily to the administration of his house and his order. He was a vigorous defender of Archbishop Fitz-Ralph and a close associate of friar John Waldby. Whatever their other differences, Fitz-Ralph and the Austins were in close accord in their views on the sources and nature of political authority. In the absence of a record there is no reason to suppose that in these matters Abbot de la Mare was not of their mind. Of his relationship with Richard II, it can only be said that the king was entertained at St. Albans during the aged abbot's lifetime. The scriptorium, of course, reflected de la Mare's feelings for the

---

[30] Gwynn, *English Austin Friars*, pp. 129–138.

[31] The poem and commentary are reproduced by T. Wright, *Political Poems and Songs Relating to English History* (R.S. 1859) I, pp. 123–214. Wright's introduction provides a useful discussion, pp. xxviii–liv.

Prince while preserving the most viciously hostile record of Richard's reign.[32]

In the case of Bishop Brinton of Rochester it is more apparent that respect for the Prince led to service to his son. Brinton may have been the outstanding preacher of an era when sermons were highly esteemed. He spoke with unusual fervour against vice and worldliness. He exhorted all Christians to live in a common allegiance to the precepts of orthodoxy while he censured the excessive concern of the Roman curia with wealth and material power. A scholar of the canon law, his attitude toward monarchy was simple and conventional. Kings and their advisers must be dedicated to high moral purposes; but if he was critical of the shortcomings of rulers, he was a sturdy foe of insurrection or rebellion. He was from time to time a preacher at the court and was probably a confessor to Richard II. He was chosen to present a sermon at the great procession following Richard's coronation, a significant indication of his place among the king's circle. In the early years of the reign he was also employed in diplomatic business in the company of Walter Skirlaw and others. After 1382, failing health forced him into virtual retirement but apparently Richard continued to show him marks of favour. John Sheppey, prior of the cathedral monastery at Rochester who acted often as his deputy in affairs of the bishopric, was also employed on the king's business prior to Brinton's death in 1389.[33]

The regard and esteem of such men was in many ways the most important legacy of the Prince to his son. How Brinton or de la Mare or Erghum might have responded to the programme of Richard and his mentors, had they still been active when the first great crises of the reign occurred, is problematical, but the steadfastness of Robert Waldby and others of the preaching clergy has been noted. A further testimonial to the attitudes of the Austins is provided by the exhortation to his brethren of William Flete, an English hermit at Siena. From a general statement of the disastrous consequences of abuse of royal

---

[32] T. Walsingham, *Gestae Abbatum Monasterie Sancti Albani*, ed. H. T. Riley (R. S., 1869) III, pp. 389 ff.; Gwynn, *English Austin Friars*, p. 122; David Knowles, *Saints and Scholars* (1962), pp. 123–33; L. F. R. Williams, *History of the Abbey of Saint Alban* (1917), pp. 166–189.

[33] *The Sermons of Thomas Brinton, Bishop of Rochester* (1373–1389) (ed.) M. A. Devlin (C. S., 1954) 2 vols. *passim* especially p. 458 and Introduction, pp. xiv–xviii, xxi–xxxi; *Foedera* VII, pp. 412–14.

power, particularly in the matter of clerical appointments, he proceeded to an expression of hope that the new young king might abolish evil customs, and an urgent recommendation that the friars preach concord to the whole kingdom. A kingdom divided against itself, he pointed out, cannot stand. Let all obey and honour the king. The distinguished recluse demonstrated an informed concern with the affairs of his native land. Like Erghum, he looked to vigorous monarchy for remedy to the disorders of a time when the obligation of obedience was too lightly observed.[34] That he should have written at all is remarkable evidence of his intense anxiety. When he left England in 1359 he swore to sever all connections. There was to be no correspondence. The letters urging obedience to royal authority were the only deviations from his vow.[35]

It may be assumed that the Black Prince's friends among the great clerics were bound by personal ties as well as similarity of outlook to the men whom he had placed about his son. Brinton, for example, who had a high regard for Archbishop Sudbury, was a collaborator with Hawkwood and Calveley in founding an English hospice at Rome in 1380.[36]

The central figure in the group was, of course, Sir Simon Burley, the king's *magister*, reputed in his own day to be a man of refined intellectual and aesthetic tastes. As master or tutor he would not necessarily have been responsible for instruction in any arts but those of warfare and chivalry. Even in these matters the tutor's role was often perfunctorily supervisory, but given Burley's interests it is likely that he would have directed close attention to every facet of his charge's education. Whether or not he was a deep student of theories of kingship, he had familiarized himself with doctrines akin to those held by clergymen who were attached to the court.

The evidence, ubiquitous in the records and chronicles of the king's devotion to him and his memory, provides sufficient reason for attention to his outlook. The facts of the crisis of 1388 emphasize the importance of his influence. Burley alone among all the members of the courtier party whose punishment was

---

[34] Gwynn, *English Austin Frairs*, pp. 201–7.
[35] M. B. Hackett, 'William Flete and the *De Remediis Contra Temptationes*.' Watt, Morral and Martin, eds., *Studies Presented to Aubrey Gwynn* (1961), pp. 331, 332.
[36] G. Omerod, *History of the County Palatine and City of Cheshire* (1882) II, p. 768.

demanded in the Merciless Parliament found champions within the ranks of the accusers themselves. Two of the five Appellants, Derby and Nottingham, added their pleas for his pardon to those of moderates like the Duke of York. The king, who had perforce sacrificed Brembre and Tresilian, risked his throne in an effort to save the former tutor, while the queen humbled herself to the extent of imploring Gloucester on her knees that he be spared. Testimonials to his honourable character, his integrity and his chivalry came from many quarters. Gloucester and Arundel remained inexorable. Officially Burley held only the title of sub-chamberlain. He was not a great magnate, and in 1388 his health was already broken. There are only two possible explanations for the intransigence of Gloucester and Arundel. Either they were animated by extreme personal malice, or they knew that Burley was a far more significant personage in the royalist camp than he appeared to be on the surface. Gloucester was too astute a politician and too hard-headed a realist to have jeopardized the Appellants' cause for an act of personal vengeance. Yet he did risk the possibility of a serious division of his own following to insist that the sub-chamberlain be destroyed. It must be concluded, therefore, that Gloucester recognized in Burley the mastermind of the whole court party. The old companion in arms of the Black Prince not only contributed to the development in his pupil of the theories of regality which were to be associated with his name, but he also organized and directed the royal following which supported Richard's first bid for supreme power. Burley was the owner of a fine private library. Since he was neither a wealthy man nor a great aristocrat, his choice in books would have been likely to reflect his personal tastes. Many were romances; the one political treatise was the de Gauchi version of the *De Regimine Principum* of Giles of Rome.[37] He probably studied it well and found in it a fully developed conception of monarchy compatible with less systematically formulated notions prevalent among courtiers and their associates.

Prior to 1388, then, Richard had been surrounded by men whose general attitude toward royal authority was remarkably homogeneous. Though the influence of Burley was paramount, there were others whose adherence to the cause of strong

[37] Clarke, *Fourteenth Century Studies*, p. 120.

monarchy was by no means inconsequential. Simon of Sudbury and Alexander Neville, like Fordham, Skirlaw and Braybrook, were skilled canon lawyers who had spent much time abroad. Together with Thomas Brinton of Rochester, they constituted an able and experienced group of scholarly advisers. Simon, as chancellor and primate, was a consistent spokesman for the courtier group until his death at the hands of the rebels in 1381. Archbishop Neville had developed a preference for strong authority before he became a leader among Richard's partisans in 1387. His associates, Brembre and de la Pole, probably from conviction as well as self-interest, shared his views. He had, in fact, long been close to de la Pole who planned to endow prayers for his own immediate family, Sir Richard Scrope, the king, the late king and the Archbishop and his brothers.[38] Chief Justice Tresilian and John Blake found the basis in English law for the judicial declarations of 1387. Tresilian's colleagues subscribed to his interpretation of the law of the land, but unlike him they manifestly were not ardent royalist partisans. In the reign of Edward I, the eyre had given institutional expression to a power inherent in kingship to provide remedy and see to justice regardless of statute or custom.[39] Justices in the fourteenth century expressed extreme respect for the king's prerogative; it is, nonetheless, likely that in the degree to which he set the crown above ordinary law, Tresilian outstripped all of his predecessors.[40]

The failure to include the name of Chaucer in the list of those from whom something can be learned about the attitudes of the courtiers in the first decade of Richard's reign may require some

[38] *C.C.R.* 1377–1381, p. 228.
[39] W. C. Bolland, ed., *The Eyre of Kent 6 and 7 Edward II*, Selden Society XXVII, (1912), p. xxviii.
[40] In 1341, Edward III assented to a statute of reform which in effect restricted both his freedom of appointment and his officers' freedom of action. It included a requirement of an oath by the chief officials of the realm to which the chancellor, the treasurer, and certain justices protested on the ground of conflict with the oath of office already sworn to the king. *Rot. Parl.* II, p. 131. The chancellor, Bourchier, the treasurer, Sadington, and his successor, Parning, were all experienced common law judges. After parliament adjourned, Edward took the unprecedented step of revoking the statute. *Foedera* V, p. 282. This extreme exercise of prerogative authority followed advice and council with groups which most certainly included Bourchier, Sadington and Parning, as well as other lawyers close to the court. The best account of the episode is that of Lapsley, *Crown, Community and Parliament*, pp. 252–8.

explanation. He was closely connected to the inner circle, having travelled abroad on diplomatic missions with Guichard d'Angle, Richard Abberbury and others. He was an official associate, perhaps a close personal friend, of Simon Burley. With Philip Vache, who suffered for his loyalty to the king in 1388 and survived to retire from royal service after the upheaval of 1399, he was on even more intimate terms. But on high politics the poet is a disappointing witness who left little definite record either of his opinion on the state of monarchy or his reaction to controversies at the centres of power. It may only be assumed that he accepted the outlook of his friends and fellows.[41]

[41] Florence R. Scott makes a strong case for Chaucer's close involvement with Burley and the king's partisans. *Speculum*, XVIII (1943), pp. 80–87. Her evidence is primarily drawn from records rather than the poet's works. Chaucer did withdraw from his appointments in 1386 to return only after the termination of the commission. Cf. H. Braddy, 'Chaucer and Dame Alice Perrers', *Speculum*, XXI (1946), pp. 222–8. There are alternative but, I think, unconvincing views. The most vigorous is that of M. Slauch, 'Chaucer's Doctrine of Kings and Tyrants', *Speculum*, XX (1945), pp. 133–56. More specific but less plausible is M. Wilks, 'Chaucer and Mystical Marriage in Medieval Political Thought', *Bulletin of the John Rylands Library*, XLIV (1962), pp. 489 ff. 'There can be little doubt that when the *Wife of Bath's Tale* was read before the court, Chaucer intended that his king should appreciate the moral of the story', p. 522. Agreement permits doubt that the intended moral was a lesson in political theory. Chaucer's relationship with Vache is examined in detail by E. Rickert, 'Thou Vache', *MP*, XI, pp. 209 ff.

CHAPTER XI

ABSOLUTISM AND THE COMMON GOOD

CHAUCER'S opaqueness on political matters is a misfortune to historians. Two other great poets, his contemporaries, were less diffident and circumspect. Neither Langland nor Gower was a member of the court circle. Their unambiguous statements on kingship and on the king are valuable as expressions of views current at the end of the century rather than as specific insights into the minds of Richard and his friends.

Langland belongs to the tradition of medieval sermonizers. As such his moody complaints are against breaches of the laws of God, of nature and of custom. Kings, if they are to avoid trouble for themselves and their subjects, must be careful both to observe and enforce all laws. They must also avail themselves of prudent council. In a well-known parable the poet points up the folly of aristocratic attempts to nullify royal power. Despite their conservative character and their identification with popular preaching, the doctrines have a secular tone. It is the might of the commons, not the will of God, that makes the king 'to reign'. Langland's great poem, *Piers Plowman*, may in the later recensions have contained specific commentary on contemporary politics. An alliterative poem in a similar style, *Richard the Redeless*, dilates on the themes of tyranny, self-indulgence and evil council in recounting the events of Richard's last years. Whoever was the author, the emphasis, though more crudely phrased, on royal responsibility for order, justice and the common good is much the same as that in *Piers Plowman*.

Two of Gower's poems, *Vox Clamantis* and *Chronica Tripertita*, were inspired by the crises of 1381 and 1399. His greatest work, *Confessio Amantis*, was undertaken at the express request of Richard II, whom he had admonished severely but without rancour in a second version of *Vox Clamantis*. *Confessio Amantis* was written in 1390. It was shortly under revision, and by 1393 when the author became a protégé of Henry of Lancaster, the dedication was addressed to him, all favourable references to Richard being eliminated. These were the years when the king was making every effort to conciliate his former foes, including Henry, who apparently had no reason for criticism of a court where his father's influence was so great. Gower's change of heart, therefore, is puzzling. He retained his devotion to Henry until he died. The *Chronica Tripertita*, composed early in Henry's reign, is an acid recital of Richard's overthrow and its causes.

Perhaps, for reasons which cannot be known, Gower had already determined shortly after 1390 that Richard would never be a suitable ruler. It may even be that he was disillusioned by the king's failure to undertake a programme of reform after his resumption of official charge of the government in 1389. For Gower, 'more than any other poet', was confirmed in the belief that the ruler must assume responsibility for the welfare, morals and integrity of his realm.[1] In its final form the prologue to the *Confessio Amantis* deplores an upside-down world in King Richard's sixteenth year. In the old days law and justice were secure and the privilege of royalty was upheld. People were subservient under good government. Now justice has lost its way, the law is double faced and the advisers of the court inspire little confidence. Discord is everywhere.[2] This pessimistic observation made midway between the none too gentle instruction of the 1380's and the savage condemnation of the *Chronica Tripertita* reflects a final discouragement about prospects that Richard would reform the realm. The complaint against the king, repeated with increasing vehemence, was that he had failed to check corruption and that he was deficient in good council and sound judgment. There was no criticism of failure to observe the rights of parliament. Gower was distressed by royalty's shortcomings, not its excessive power.[3]

It is significant that both Langland and Gower took the positive obligations of the ruler to be a matter of course. There is nothing in either of them to commend the view that temporal

[1] George R. Coffman, 'John Gower, Mentor for Royalty: Richard II', *P.M.L.A.* (1954) LXIX, p. 953. Cf. also Coffman, 'John Gower in his most significant Role', *Univ. of Colorado Studies*, Series B II (1945), pp. 52–61; and Gardiner Stilwell, 'John Gower and the Last Years of Edward III', *Studies in Philosophy*, XLV (1948), pp. 478–91.
[2] For purposes of clarity I have paraphrased Terence Tiller's readable translation into modern English. Penguin Books, 1963, ll. 93–192.
[3] Coffman, 'Mentor for Royalty', p. 964.

power is man's punishment for sin and that wicked rulers may be serving God's mysterious purposes. Their distaste for contemporary society, expressed in such different modes, was in no way a rejection of the world and its affairs. Quite the contrary. Implicit in every complaint is the evil consequence to human society of folly and sin. When they spoke of kings they exhorted and they warned. The justice they prized could be defined entirely in natural terms. The leadership they called for was required to remedy the defects of the community. Their vocabulary, alike in little else, was the vocabulary of men who knew the world and hoped to improve it. When Gower and Langland referred to the uses of power they spoke naturally in terms of polity, not ecclesiology. Secularism in that sense was the commonplace of their day even with deeply religious men who had moral lessons to teach.

In an earlier period it had been otherwise. Throughout most of the Middle Ages in western Europe common assumptions about *respublica Christiana* were so intrinsically ecclesiastical as virtually to exclude the word 'political' from the language.[4] Change accelerated rapidly in the thirteenth century. By 1350 the ascendancy of the lay spirit everywhere was acknowledged in the common idiom. This is not the place for a recapitulation of the developments in the economy and in the structure of society which made the old intellectual framework unrealistic. It should be enough to note that principles of social morality derived from the rejection of the values of terrestrial life were anachronistic in a world where industry, commerce, and banking were highly developed. Ideological bases for a more appropriate outlook were not long in appearing. The change reinstated politics as one of man's major preoccupations and vested royalty with a new importance.

The monarchies of the thirteenth century in responding to external pressures and internal dynamics toward the increase of central authority sought and found theoretical justification for relaxing the inhibitory stringencies of feudal law or communal custom. The role in temporal affairs to which the triumph of the Hildebrandine movement of the eleventh century had committed the papacy inevitably generated increasing demands for universal

[4] Cf. W. Ullmann, *Principles of Government and Politics in the Middle Ages* (1961) who presses the distinction between the East and West in these terms, pp. 110–13.

recognition of ultimate authority in the Holy See. The growth of virtually independent communes, particularly in Italy, created opportunities to establish novel institutions for the promulgation and enforcement of law at the same time providing the means and the excuse for the seizure by despots or oligarchs of what was in effect supreme power over their fellow citizens. Church and commune no less than monarchy required that aspirations and conduct be legitimized by theoretical justification. The extension of interest in Roman law and the rediscovery of Aristotelian philosophy were put to the service of king, municipal autocrat and hierarch alike, while for the latter an extension of Augustinian theology also became a basis for claims to absolute sovereignty.[5]

During the centuries of emergence Western monarchs, striving to reinforce an authority which was often in fact very limited, took comfort in sacramental theory. In traditional terms the right to rule was conferred by God to be exercised in accordance with the precepts of divine law. Civil society was conceived of as a remedy for sin; immutable divine law was reflected in the law and custom of the community to which prince and people alike owed allegiance. Law, whether Christian or customary, stood above the monarch, whose tendency to prefer theocracy to an authority sanctioned through established usage was curbed by ecclesiastical claims to primacy. The intellectual revolution of the later Middle Ages afforded more substantial defences to strong monarchy. Aristotelians and civilians shifted attention from supernatural to natural origins and functions of political authority. In their eyes monarchy was rather a law of nature than a contrivance of God; the measure of the king's success was the degree of his satisfaction of the needs of his people.[6]

[5] Carlyle, *Medieval Political Theory*, VI, pp. 9–14; R. A. Markus, 'Two Conceptions of Political Authority: Augustine, *De Civitate Dei*, XIX 14–15, and Some Thirteenth Century Interpretations'. *Journal of Theological Studies*, XVI (1965), pp. 68–100; M. V. Clarke, *The Medieval City State* (1926), pp. 126–142; W. Ullmann, *Principles of Government and Politics in the Middle Ages* (1961) pp. 158, 159; Carlyle, *Medieval Political Theory*, II, pp. 59–62; cf. F. J. Pegues, *The Lawyers of the Last Capetians* (1962), pp. 226–229; M. Wilks, *The Problem of Sovereignty in the Later Middle Ages* (1963), pp. 354–369.

[6] F. Kern, *Kingship and Law in the Middle Ages* (tr. Chrimes, 1939), pp. 70–79; Ullman, *Government and Politics in the Middle Ages*, Pt. II; W. Berges, *Die Fürstenspiegel des hohen und späten Mittelalters* (1938), pp. 118 ff. Cf. Kantorowicz, *King's Two Bodies*, pp. 231, 232.

There were other facets to the new political discourse. In their quest for wider sovereignty princes and popes created franchises to increase their strength; to defend their gains they sold privileges. Rights, warranted by charter or customary recognition became the jealously guarded possession of corporations. Monarchy itself, even papal monarchy, was an estate buttressed and defined by a set of juridical principles. The feudal king had been held in check by personal arrangements between him and each of his vassals without whose support he would in fact have been powerless. The monarch in the fourteenth century claimed the allegiance of the community of the realm; he was forced, however, to treat with innumerable separate estates. If he could collect them, or the most important of them, together in a responsible parliamentary assembly so much the better for him, and since the realm was an estate which contained them all so much the better for them as well. But treating and parleying must go on, whether in one great forum or many lesser ones.[7] The servants of monarchy laboured to preserve the estate of kingship from infringement by militant and over zealous defence of the competing rights of other estates. Sometimes they failed. The endeavour to elevate the common good as pursued by the head of the polity into a canon transcending all other claims succeeded only in the guise of despotism. Most princes shunned the despotic style. Their apologists urged voluntary abrogation of privilege in deference to the common good.

The canon lawyers may have been the pioneers in launching new secular modes. If absolute power were to be justified by the requirements of the common good, the moral worth of temporal life must be acknowledged. Without bothering about whether the good life was an end in itself or only a means to salvation, canon lawyers in the twelfth century were busily developing arguments from usage and precedent for extension of papal jurisdiction over human conduct. Amplified by the great decretalists of succeeding generations these became the basis for the sweeping claims of Boniface VIII. Their attention was addressed to a frankly political world. What they accomplished was to give

[7] The most illuminating discussion of the growth of the corporate principle is that of G. de la Garde, *La naissance de l'esprit laique au declin du Moyen Age* (1942), IV, Ch. II; cf. O. Gierke, *Political Theories of the Middle Ages* (1900) and the brilliant introduction by F. W. Maitland.

political significance to such concepts as *plenitudo potestatis* which originated in an entirely ecclesiastical context. Though the most extreme statements of papal sovereignty were made by polemicists, the canonists were the architects of papal theory. Its fundamental precept was the right, in fact the obligation, of papal monarchy to intervene in temporal affairs when defects in the law or its administrators made it improbable that people might obtain justice.[8] This respect for authority and its uses could readily be transferred to other temporal princes who proclaimed devotion to similar objectives. Lawyers trained in the teachings of Innocent IV and Hostiensis were likely to be enthusiastic recruits to the cause of royal supremacy for the common good.

In the twelfth century the work of civil lawyers was primarily limited to glosses on the texts of Roman codes. Within a hundred years they began to produce summary textbooks and treatises. In doing so they inevitably, though not exclusively, developed arguments on behalf of strong central government. The teachings of the civilians dominated the legal curricula of the universities of Italy and France.[9] They have been credited with an almost unique contribution to the achievement of lay control of the state and with setting the foundations for royal absolutism.[10] Like the canonists civilians discriminated between law and arbitrary will. They recognized tyranny both in unlawful seizure and improper exercise of power. But they were capable of saying that to the ruler alone belonged the capacity to create law and of attributing to him a jurisdictional authority free from any institutional check. They insisted, of course, on the obligation of the ruler to promote the welfare of his people without agreeing on any means of forcing him to do so or punishing him if he abused his power. The Codes and Institutes furnished no clear guides. It was easier from these sources to determine the

---

[8] Cf. J. A. Watt, *The Theory of Papal Monarchy in the Thirteenth Century: The Contribution of the Canonists* (1965), a subtle and balanced presentation of the canonist position. Cf. G. Post, 'Plena potestas and Consent in Medieval Assemblies'. *Traditio*, I (1943).

[9] W. Ullman, *Principles of Government and Politics in the Middle Ages* (1961), pp. 197–9.

[10] T. Gilby, *Principality and Polity* (1958), pp. 53, 54, 105. 'Roman law had already taught before the revival of Aristotle that political authority originated in human reason and in natural law'. L. Genicot, *Les lignes du faîte du moyen âge* (1951), p. 351.

extensive authority which the king alone could wield for the common good.[11]

Canon and civil lawyers encouraged new attitudes toward polity and royalty. Aristotelian philosophers transformed the entire range of medieval thought. The synthesis of St. Thomas hid rather than healed the breach with the patristic tradition. The hammer blows of Marsilio and the subtle surgery of Ockham exposed the irreparable rupture and elaborated the unique sovereignty of reason in human affairs.[12] Reason was less certain than Roman law to point in the direction of royal absolutism. St. Thomas emphasized the supremacy of law; Marsilio named the people, that is citizens, as the source of authority. The political theory of Ockham is as complex as it is subtle. Temporal dominion and jurisdiction, he believed to have been instituted by God, but their forms, their processes and their legal definition were of human origin. The ruler, receiving his power from the people, had henceforth no superior but God. Yet men retain inviolable rights even when they submit to the will of an autocrat. They may renounce the exercise of franchises and liberties; they are incapable of renouncing the right to them.[13] Ockham dealt with law, authority and rights only in his polemical works directed against the papacy, but in an age when monarchy had long been the normal form of government it was as natural for him as it was for most other Aristotelians to identify the king as the authentic centre of power in the rational polity. Despite the significance of law, natural right and popular origins of authority, St. Thomas, Ockham and Marsilio could all be cited by and large as defenders of wide royal jurisdiction if exercised for the public welfare.[14]

[11] For extreme positions which mingle Roman law and Augustinianism see W. Ullman, *The Medieval Idea of Law as Represented by Lucas de Penna* (1946), pp. 50, 52, 170. Cf. also the civilian precept that 'the prince is under no man, though he is obligated to God'. Kantorowicz, *King's Two Bodies*, p. 399.

[12] De la Garde, *Naissance de l'esprit laique*, V, pp. 33–36. 'Ockham's system with its new conception of the universe and the human being and its new moral and legal philosophy did more to bring about the new lay spirit of the fourteenth century than the more radical position of Marsilio'.

[13] Ibid., VI, pp. 175–83, 214 and *passim*, a comprehensive analysis; P. Boehmer, 'Ockham's Political Ideas', *Review of Politics*, V, (1943), pp. 462–79.

[14] Cf. Jean Dunbabin, 'Aristotle in the Schools', *Trends in Medieval Political Thought*, ed. B. Smalley, who treats St. Thomas' *De regno: Ad Regem Cypri*, and Giles of Rome's *De Regimine Principum* as containing fundamentally similar points of view, pp. 66–82; and Marjorie Reeves, 'Marsilio of Padua and Dante Alighieri,' ibid., who emphasizes the interaction between ruler and people and the tight control over all parts of the community which the ruler must exercise, p. 99.

L

Other authorities were unqualified protagonists of absolutism. The treatise, *De Potestate Regia et Papali*, written at the opening of the fourteenth century by John of Paris, a Dominican familiar with the scholarship of canon law, who admired and quoted St. Thomas, showed the way in defining independence for temporal rulers. The power of princes John accepted as the will of God, valid even when it degenerated into tyranny inasmuch as tyranny 'exists for the punishment of sinners'. So much for theocracy. The proofs that one ruler is better than many, that monarchy is necessary to the common good and that kingship is in accord with the laws of nature and nations are purely Aristotelian.[15]

De Potestate Regia et Papali was written in behalf of Philip the Fair in response to the pro-papal polemic *De Ecclesiastica Potestate* of Giles of Rome. Other partisans of monarchy, notably Remigio de Girolami, made more excessive claims in the same debate, but the most thorough exposition of unqualified power came from the papal side. Giles was an Augustinian, a student of St. Thomas and perhaps the most influential writer of his generation. His works became the standard for Austin scholarship and he was cited with respect by theologians, philosophers and lawyers alike.[16] The fundamental theses of the *De Ecclesiastica Potestate* are Augustinian. His preference for absolutism found in theology a satisfactory authorization which was in no way disturbed by his Aristotelian or legal scholarship. The treatise constitutes a forthright declaration of what can only be defined as papal sovereignty, assigning universal and superior lordship of temporal things to the church and the plenitude of power which is in the church to the pope.[17] There is a peculiar piquancy to the fact that the most widely quoted and studied tract on kingship in the later Middle Ages came from the pen of this champion of papal monarchy. This was the *De Regimine Principum*, a handbook of a type already familiar for the guidance of princes.[18]

[15] Cf. Jean Leclercq, *Jean de Paris et l'ecclésiologie du XIIIe siècle* (1942). 'The contribution of the Aristotelians was that of the state as a collective entity, the source of all rights and good'. Genicot, *Les lignes du faîte du moyen âge*, p. 351.

[16] Cf. A. Gwynn, *The English Austins*, pp. 38, 59–73. Lucas de Penna quoted him admiringly, referring to him as 'frater Aegidius'. Ullman, *The Medieval Idea of Law*, p. 33.

[17] *De Ecclesiastica Potestate*, ed. R. Scholz (1929), Book III, Ch. IX.

[18] Some commentators have stressed the inherent contradictions in the views presented in the *De Ecclesiastica Potestate* and the *De Regimine Principum*, cf. R. Scholz, *Die Publizistik zur Zeit Phillipps des Schönen und Bonifaz VIII* (1903), pp. 95 ff. But J. Riviére argues for their fundamental compatability, *Le problème de L'église et de L'état au temps de Philippe le Bel* (1926), pp. 224–7.

It was written some two decades earlier than the *De Ecclesi-astica Potestate*. Subject matter and form were different, but the predilection for absolutism was already manifest. In fact, the characterization of Giles as a unique medieval advocate of absolute monarchy is based on a textual analysis of the *De Regimine Principum*. He is said to stand 'practically alone in suggesting that the king should rule according to his own will and the laws which he has made, and not according to the laws which the citizens had made.'[19] Such a judgment exaggerates the difference between him and contemporaries who understood and used his text. Giles invoked the authority and adopted the method of Aristotle throughout the work. Much that was fundamental to his view of society, of the nature of man, the function of law and the purpose of political authority was also derived, whether he clearly recognized the debt or not, from Aristotle. The development of crucial themes was his own.

There can be no mistaking the preference for hereditary monarchy as compared with all other forms of government. His arguments from function, purpose and organic analogy had long been commonplace, but he took pains to develop each of them in detail and to underscore the civil order and freedom from strife which one ruler would assure. Like John of Paris and many others he also pointed to the apparent will of God.[20] Positive law, which should embody the principles of God's natural law, he defined as that which has been written by the king with the advice of the wise and honest men of the realm.[21] The king, he held, was the proper interpreter of the natural law to which he would give expression in the form of his statutes. God had implanted his eternal principles of justice in the heart and mind of man. It was, therefore, only incumbent upon the worthy prince, supreme above all positive law, to search his heart and there discover truths which he alone could frame into legislation. 'It is better,' he insisted, 'to be governed by a good prince than by

---

[19] R. and A. J. Carlyle, *A History of Medieval Political Theory in the West* (1936), VI, p. 10.

[20] *Li Livres du Gouvernement des Rois* (ed. S. P. Molenaer, 1899), Book III, Pt. II, Chs. II and III. Since the de Gauchi version was widely known in fourteenth century England and was owned by Simon Burley, I have cited from this text. All citations have been checked against the Venetian edition of 1498 to verify their identity with the original.

[21] Ibid., Bk. III, Pt. II, Ch. XXXIII.

good law.'²² But if the prince were to deserve his place as 'Dei minister' he must strive to maintain justice and promote the common good; he must be equally prompt in generosity of reward and severity of punishment; and he must make it his ultimate purpose to bring the blessings of peace and security to all the realm.²³ The exercise of power for the welfare and happiness of his subjects distinguished the true prince from the tyrant motivated by concern for his own advantage and profit.²⁴

Giles included advice for subjects as well. Strict obedience by all to the will of the sovereign, he designated as the source from which the values of the commonwealth were derived. Honour, safety, both from enemies abroad and evildoers in the realm, and an abundance of prosperity were the rewards to be expected by obedient citizens.²⁵ Even tyranny would engender no misfortunes comparable to the sacrifice of such blessings. It was not for the subject to risk so great a loss by failure to obey the commands of the monarch, though the commands might in actuality be the mandates of a tyrant. The evils of tyranny were to be preferred to those of civil disobedience.²⁶

Civil obedience Giles associated with the necessary punitive power exercised by the magistrate. The prudent monarch, he asserted, was at once generous and stern. Indeed, the obligation to deal severely with all who violated his law was one which the ruler could not escape if he were to fulfill properly the duties of his station. The king who treated malefactors with undue lenience came dangerously close to the sin of tyranny, for in so doing he served only his own tender conscience and not the welfare of the community. He must be rigorous in punishment of all who caused discord or who in any way threatened the peace

²² Ibid., Bk. III, Pt. II, Ch. XXVII.
²³ Ibid., Bk. I, Pt. I, Ch. XII. The obligation to defend justice and promote welfare, though justified primarily by its effect on subjects, extended even to foreigners who might be in the realm. Bk. I, Pt. II, Ch. XI; Bk. III, Pt. II, Chs. XVIII, XIX, XXXIII; Bk. III, Pt. III, Ch. X. This last injunction is the concluding sentence of the work.
²⁴ Ibid., Bk. III, Pt. II, Ch. VI. This was the definition of tyranny, perhaps adopted from Giles, employed by such civilians as Bartolus; Carlyle, *Medieval Political Theory*, VI, pp. 78–81. It was repeated by the Florentine Coluccio Salutati in the year of Richard II's death. *De Tyranno*, ed. E. Emerton in *Humanism and Tyranny* (1925), p. 77.
²⁵ *Gouvernement des Rois*, Bk. III, Pt. II, Ch. XXXII.
²⁶ *De Regimine Principum*, Bk. III, Pt. II, Ch. XXXIV, 'Nammagis est tolerabilis aliqualis tyrannides principantis, quam sit malum quod consurgit ex inobedientia principis, et ex prevaricatione mandatorum ejus'.

of the land.[27] Better the evils of harsh injustice than those of unrepressed malefaction.

This insistence upon unqualified obedience to the king's laws, of course, only magnified the importance of justice in legislation. As the king's armies were the defence of the populace in time of war, so were his laws their defence in time of peace. The one must be strong; the other must be just. Of justice the king was himself the final arbiter; but he required the aid of councillors who could assist him in the discovery of good and true laws. The right to select his advisers, like the final authority to make and enforce the laws, rested with the king, but he was obliged, if he were not a tyrant, to observe the same criteria in performance of the one function as in the other. His councillors should be men whose vision would advance the commonweal. If a monarch shunned the wise men of his realm to follow the dictates of his own selfish desires, he was a tyrant.[28] Yet Giles intimated nothing of inherited or customary rights requiring the prince to accept advice from any other quarters than those which suited him. His pleasure alone conferred lawful power upon his aides.[29]

Moderation was not among Giles' virtues. In his description of the king as 'lexanimata', his explanation of royal powers and obligations, and his enumeration of the blessings of unfettered monarchy, the learned Augustinian produced a more complete delineation of the secular ideal of strong monarchy for the common good than any other in his age. It was a remarkable achievement for the author of the doctrine that all rights to possession are dependent upon Christian moral worth.[30] But the *De Regimine Principum* continued to be read and copied by men who rejected both the moral philosophy and the political theory of the *De Ecclesiastica Potestate*. Among them were Austin friars of the later fourteenth century.[31]

[27] *Gouvernement des Rois*, Bk. III, Pt. II, Ch. XXXIV; Bk. III, Pt. II, Ch. VI.
[28] Ibid., Bk. III, Pt. II, Ch. XVI.   [29] Ibid., Bk. III, Pt. II, Ch. XVII.
[30] For the debt of Giles' theory of dominion to feudal law as well as Augustinian theology see de la Garde, *Naissance de l'esprit laique*, IV, pp. 170 ff. He was by no means singular in visualizing the king as 'lexanimata'. Cf. Kantorowicz, *King's Two Bodies*, pp. 132 ff.
[31] The Austin priory at Tickhill, for example, contained the *De Regimine Principum* in more than one version, a copy of a set of tables made from it by Friar John Kervyle and other works of Giles. M. R. James, *Fasciculus J. W. Clark dictatus* (1909), pp. 46, 47, 49–52. But it did not contain either the *De Ecclesastica Potestate* or James of Viterbo's *De Potestate Christiano*. Gwynn thinks the omissions to have been deliberate. *The English Austin Friars*, p. 132. Cf. also for the reaction against Giles' theories among the Austins.

Theoretical discussion tended to decline in originality by the middle of the fourteenth century. Perhaps after the work of the great canonists and civilians, and especially after Marsilio and Ockham, there was really little that was new to say until the shape of the modern state had begun more fully to be revealed. Theory, after all, must be related to actuality. The papacy, for example, had been acting on the assumption of a reserve of power sufficient to do whatever was necessary for the good of the Christian commonwealth long before the canonists adumbrated the principle into a doctrine.[32] The kings of the later thirteenth century would have behaved much as they did if the Institutes had never been studied and the *Ethics* and *Politics* of Aristotle been remembered only by vague repute. It was comforting, nonetheless, perhaps even inspiring, for them and their successors to enjoy the authorization of absolutist inferences drawn from late medieval adaptations of Roman law and Greek philosophy.

In England as elsewhere the new conceptions met a mixed reception, but whether theories were welcomed or spurned men's ordinary speech implied acceptance of secular values, and few indeed would have cared to contest the view that polity, as natural to humanity, was therefore good.

Roman law, canon and civil, made more impact on English practice prior to 1300 than some common lawyers would have cared to admit.[33] Thereafter, lawyers were usually laymen, trained not principally at the universities but at the Inns. It is the intellectual contribution of the Romanists, however, that is relevant, not their participation in courts and cases. They continued to offer the courses of study at the universities and their students continued to fill places in royal administration. The chief office in the realm was occupied for only eleven years under Edward III and six under Richard II by chancellors who had not been schooled in Roman law. Many studied abroad. English collegiate libraries contained substantial collections in the civil law. Sometimes listings under that heading included such works as Bracton and the *De Regimine Principum* of Giles of Rome

---

[32] Watt, *Theory of Papal Monarchy*, p. 142.
[33] Cf. G. W. Keeton, *The Norman Conquest and the Common Law* (1966), Ch. VI and Post, *Studies in Medieval Legal Thought*, Ch. III. T. F. T. Plucknett, 'The Relations between Roman Law and English Common Law down to the Sixteenth Century: A General Survey', *Toronto Law Journal*, III (1939), pp. 24–50.

along with the Codes and the Institutes. And sometimes the books showed signs of little use although often they were heavily annotated.[34] The experts were asked upon occasion to prepare advice on state matters of the utmost importance. The most famous instance in the late fourteenth century was the consultation by parliament as to the appeals of 1388.[35] Roman law modified by particular English practices was the law of the court of chivalry, the court of the admiral and the church courts. It, nonetheless, affected thought chiefly through the repetition of maxims and principles, rather than through rules and decisions.

The English response to Aristotle was more lively. Much of it was conservative and defensive. Bishop Grosseteste of Lincoln, who spent many years of his life at Oxford, left there a strong tradition of revitalized Augustinianism. Robert Kilwardby, Dominican, and John Peckham, Franciscan, who were successive Archbishops of Canterbury condemned the work of St. Thomas. In the next century Thomas Bradwardine, the central figure of a gifted group of Oxford scholars, reinstated the doctrine of grace and heaped scorn on rationalist attempts to discern ultimate truth. His associate, Walter Burley, persistently attacked Ockham's theory of knowledge. None of these was the unreasoning action of a man attempting to suppress what was unfamiliar and strange. Grosseteste translated several Aristotelian works including the *Ethics* from the Greek. Kilwardby was fully abreast of Aristotelian scholarship. Peckham was quite prepared to engage in disputation with St. Thomas himself. Bradwardine was a broadly learned humanist whose own works consistently employed the Aristotelian mode of argument, while Walter Burley produced more voluminous commentaries on Aristotle than any other scholar of his era. They resisted the conquest of theology by philosophy and the exaltation of free will at the expense of grace. They rejected neither the examination of nature nor the value of human society.

[34] For the loose grouping of titles, see M. R. James, *The Ancient Libraries of Canterbury and Dover* (1903), p. 145. Comment on the collections and their use at the colleges at Worcester and Hereford is made by J. K. Floyer, 'The Medieval Library of the Benedictine Priory of St. Mary in Worcester Cathedral Church', *Archaeologia*, LVIII (1903), p. 564. For another collection before 1376 see M. R. James, *A Descriptive Catalog of the Manuscripts of Corpus Christi College, Cambridge* (1912), pp. ix–xi.

[35] M. H. Keen cites the advice requested on the appeals of the Gascon lords to the *parlement* of Charles V in 1369. 'The Political Thought of the Fourteenth Century Civilians', B. Smalley, ed. *Trends in Medieval Political Thought* (1965), p. 112.

English opinion on behalf of new ideas was as vigorous as the criticism. It included Dominican answers to the assaults on the philosophy of St. Thomas. The Franciscan, William of Ockham, was trained at Oxford where his freedom of mind first attracted attention. Among his earliest works were commentaries on Aristotle. Despite the animosities he aroused, the character of his thought was profoundly shaped by the university, its course of study and the tone of its intellectual life.[36] He left ardent followers behind him, while his influence is plainly evident even in the works of theologians who would have recoiled from his reputation.[37]   Merton in the days of the predominance of Bradwardine, rich as it was in Augustinianism, retained its strong interest in Aristotle.[38]   Among Bradwardine's circle Walter Burley is, of course, a case in point.

Burley's writings have been cited as evidence of English intellectual stagnation in the fourteenth century.[39]   The wide dissemination of his works in western Europe over a period of one hundred fifty years would indicate that contemporaries, nonetheless, attributed considerable importance to him. He was perhaps valued more for careful scholarship and comprehensive range than for originality. His differences with Ockham related to significant issues, but modern scrutiny has revealed that he and Ockham had much in common and that Burley was no mere pedant.[40]   He shared the preference for absolute monarchy common to most medieval commentators on Aristotle.[41]

Sometime in the early 1340's his reputation earned him a call to court to be tutor to the king's eldest son, Edward, perhaps then in his twelfth year. Holinshed reports, on the authority of unnamed contemporary testimony, that it was he who introduced his kinsman Simon Burley to the prince's company. Though Simon would have been only six or seven years of age such

---

[36] De la Garde, *La naissance de l'esprit laique*, IV, pp. 15–17.
[37] Examples are noted by G. Leff, *Medieval Thought* (1958), pp. 291 ff.
[38] Powicke, *Medieval Books of Merton College*, pp. 20–23.
[39] By Roberto Weiss, who argues that no intellectual advancement was made in the entire century. *Humanism in England during the Fifteenth Century* (1941), pp. 9 ff.
[40] Cf. the article on Burley by L. Baudry in 'Archives d'histoire doctrinale et litteraire du moyen-age', IX (1934) and the same author's 'La rapports de Guillaume d'Occam et de Walter Burley', *Journal of Symbolic Logic* (1955); H. Shapiro, 'Walter Burley's *De Deo Natura et Arte*', *Medievalia et Humanistica*, XV (1963), pp. 86 ff.
[41] C. Martin, 'Medieval Commentaries on Aristotle's *Politics*', *History*, XXXVI (1951), p. 38.

differentials were not unusual in royal and aristocratic households. A bright six-year-old in that society might already have been taught to read and would be progressing to the study of foreign language. In any case, the bond which developed between him and the prince was strong and lasting. It is by no means unlikely that Walter Burley contributed to forging it and had some part in instilling both the intellectual interests and attitudes which were crucial to cementing it.[42] Simon served the prince in Gascony, fought at his side at Najera, and was selected by him as tutor for his heir.

Simon's love for books has already been noted, and reference made to his ownership of the *De Regimine Principum*. It was, of course, the kind of manuscript which a bibliophile might collect and prize even if he had little understanding of its tenets or little sympathy for them.[43] Simon Burley may never have brought his pupil into contact with the work or its specific ideas. In view of the character of the programme of the first twenty years of his reign, however, it is tempting to suspect that Richard II, like many another prince in his age, had been set to school to Giles of Rome and had learned his lessons well.[44] In any case the book and others with a not dissimilar point of view were widely consulted by his contemporaries.[45]

[42] Holinshed is, of course, a dubious authority; yet he is uncharacteristically insistent about the documentary evidence for his story of the relationship of the Burleys and the introduction of Simon to court. It is twice repeated. *Chronicles*, II, pp. 709, 795. Both J. H. Round and T. A. Archer accept the story. *D.N.B.*, III, pp. 372, 374. Tout rejects it as unlikely on chronological grounds without giving reasons. *Chapters*, III, p. 331, n. 2.

[43] Both Thomas of Woodstock and Humphrey of Gloucester owned it, although Duke Thomas' copy may have been the one originally possessed by Burley. H. Anstey, ed. *Munimenta Academica, or documents illustrative of academical life and studies at Oxford* (1868).

[44] The treatise was probably written for the guidance of Philip IV of France. It was translated into at least ten different languages before the end of the fourteenth century. Berges, *Fürstenspiegel*, pp. 320 ff. Among rulers acquainted with it was Pedro I of Castille upon whom it may also have had considerable influence.

[45] Copies of the *De Regimine Principum* are known to have been in the libraries of the Prior of St. Martin at Dover, Canterbury College, the Austin Priory at Tickhill, and Westminster Abbey before 1385. At least seven others are identifiable from Oxford collections by that date. A good many more belong to the first half of the fifteenth century. M. R. James, *The Ancient Libraries of Canterbury and Dover* (1903), pp. 145, 169, 463; M. R. James, *Fasciculus, J. W. Clark dictatus* (1909), pp. 46, 52; J. A. Robinson and M. R. James, *Manuscripts of Westminster Abbey. Notes and Documents Relating to Westminster Abbey*, No. 1 (1902), p. 24. *Harley ms*. No. 4385; *Add ms*. No. 17366; M. R. James, *A Descriptive Catalog of Western Manuscripts of Sidney Sussex College* (1895), p. 46. It continued to be copied throughout the century. In the reign of Henry V, Thomas Hoccleve used it as the model (though the

Political and legal disputation at the universities or in the world of affairs continued throughout the century to be carried on largely along the secularist lines initiated with the early enthusiasm for Aristotle and the development of Roman law. The themes had lost their novelty. By the time Richard's advisers and their associates were acquiring their education there were no significant extensions of them which had not been explored. The belief that the world was a Christian community still prevailed, unquestioned in the face of nascent nationalism, papal schism, and Ottoman conquest. But discussion about the ordering of society generally de-emphasized its Christian quality to concentrate on practical matters. Basic principles, as well as derived conclusions, might vary widely. Ockham's theory, for example, though monarchical, was grounded on the notion of indefeasible corporate and invididual rights.[46] Lawyers, English and Roman, sometimes carried respect for law to the point of seeming to assert its absolute inviolability. The conception of a popular source of authority could be pressed to the conclusion that the people might determine who should rule them. And institutional precedents furnished persuasive argument that rulers must not merely take advice but that they must take it from particular groups in particular forms. But discourse had a common quality. Contentions on behalf of either the extension or the limitation of the king's prerogative were likely to be pragmatic even when they invoked morality. A curious treatise addressed to Edward III attacked the royal practice of purveyance by citation of precedent. In elaborating the precept that it is better for the prince to submit to the laws than for the laws to submit to the prince, the author pointed to the suffering endured by Henry III, Edward I, and

absolutist substance eluded him) for his poem, *The Regement of Princes*. John Capgrave writing at mid-century credited Giles' book with helping to introduce the Augustin friars to England. *Chronicle*, (R.S.), p. 152. The history is obviously faulty but illustrative of the continued respect for the work. The *De Rege et Regno ad Regem Cypri* written by St. Thomas and Ptolemy of Lucca was more rare in fourteenth century English collections. There was a copy at Corpus Christi College, Cambridge. M. R. James, *A Descriptive Catalog of the Manuscripts of Corpus Christi College, Cambridge* (1912), p. 71. A fourteenth century manuscript in the University of Cambridge Library contains both the *De Regimine Principum* and the *De Rege et Regno* bound together. Cambridge collections include other copies of the *De Regimine Principum* dating from both the fourteenth and fifteenth centuries. One was the property of Richard de Bury, the close friend of Walter Burley. *Catalogue of the Manuscripts of the University of Cambridge Library*, III, pp. 457, 378, 471, 606.

---

[46] De la Garde, *Naissance de l'esprit laique*, IV, pp. 95, 96.

Ahab and their unfortunate subjects as a consequence of their evil acts.[47] The *De Regimine Principum*, while demanding obedience even to tyranny appealed at every turn to the conscience of the king. If he failed to act for the common good he would suffer in this world and the next. The evidence and the reasoning were strictly of this world.

[47] Simon Islip, *De speculo regis Edward III seu tractatu quem de mala regni administratione conscripsit Simon Islip, etc.*, Thesim Facultate litterarum parisiensi proponebat Josephus Moisant (1891), pp. 113–6. Islip, or the pseudo-Islip, also argued that purveyance was illegal among other reasons because the king was not an emperor able to change the law, since his ancestor had enfoeffed the realm to the pope.

Chapter XII

THE FIGURE OF GOD'S MAJESTY

CONTINENTAL models, the theories of the publicists, canon law, civil law and English law contributed to the courtier notion of exalted monarchy. Most of its adherents were men of affairs. Some were serious scholars. None were mystics. Their opinions on the nature of good governance derived from experience, from precedent and from the scholastic and legal disputation of the past hundred years. It was their design that the king should be in reality the supreme power in the land. For most of them, and for Richard, the validity of their objective was confirmed alike by necessity and by right.

Right was the secular principle of the common good. Necessity was less ambiguously defined. The over mighty subject had proved more than once since the death of Edward III that he could be a dangerous enemy to order. A controversy between Lancaster and Bishop Courtenay in 1377, the threat of conflict between the armed retainers of Northumberland and Lancaster in 1382, the manoeuvres for prestige and power during the minority, the restiveness in the Northern counties in the 1390's,[1] and, above all, the events culminating in the battle at Radcot Bridge demonstrated the fragility of domestic peace dependent upon mutual goodwill among the magnates. Less dramatic but more vital was the disorder endemic in the disrepute of the courts of law and the ineffectiveness of royal justice. For this the aristocracy and the greater clergy were not principally at fault, although royal weakness was an essential precondition to the ascendancy they enjoyed in the affairs of the countryside. The gentry exhibited even more concern for local privilege uninhibited by royal surveillance. The crown suffered grievously from lack of firm lines of communication into the localities. The effort of the knights to defeat their development was unremitting.

At the opening of the century the voice of the king was heard everywhere in the land through the agency of his sheriffs and the

[1]Appendix A, *Infra*, p. 189; *supra*, p. 69.

justices in eyre. Both had succumbed to the ambitious antagonism of the commons. The sheriff was rendered impotent by legislation which robbed him of honour and prestige while leaving his onerous duties undiminished. By the middle of the century the post ceased to be sought by men of standing. The ultimate futility of the office, which had risen to such heights under the Angevins, was defined in the statute requiring annual replacement. No one who served so brief a term would have time either to develop loyalty to the king or to forget his relationship to the class of country gentry to which he belonged. The systematic violation of the statute by Richard prior to 1386 and again a decade later was by no means his least significant move toward the reconstruction of royal authority.

Independent control over local courts was won by the knights less through assault than by assimilation. Before the end of the reign of Edward I the burden of business had become more than the eyre could handle. Its functions were assumed by keepers and commissions of the peace. The statute of 1361 satisfied the desire of the commons by giving official recognition to long standing reality. Within two generations the keepers of the peace had grown from a species of military police into the arbiters of the common law in the communities. As justices of the peace their actual powers were manifold. As members of the king's commissions they sat to investigate the observance of the law and the fulfilment of obligations to the crown in their own localities. They were thus, in effect, the only assessors of their own conduct. The invitation to abusive pursuit of self-interest was manifest. In the thirteenth century the vists of the eyre, not without reason, inspired a fear that sometimes approximated terror. But not everyone dreaded their approach. The Justices in Eyre were in effect 'impersonations of the king' who afforded remedy for 'any complaint that should be brought by any against any other'. Their suitors were often, perhaps largely, very poor people.[2] The disappearance of the eyre was a great misfortune for both king and kingdom. 'In place of one majestic and irresistible tribunal, competent to deal with every injustice, and where every grievance might find a remedy, there was a collection of limited commissions,

[2] W. C. Bolland, ed. *The Eyre of Kent 6 and 7 Edward II*, Selden Society, Vol. XXVII (1912), p. xxviii.

at whose approach fear was too often unmixed with hope of redress'.[3] Strong monarchy was unlikely to attract the allegiance of the Justices of the Peace until experience could teach them that there were worse evils. But a restoration of royal authority wielded in the king's interest by an efficient council might, in curbing self-indulgence among them, have restored some respect for law as well. Whenever his government was free of aristocratic domination Richard and his chosen councillors displayed as avid an interest in local justice as they did in the sheriffs.[4]

During the years after January of 1388, the frequency with which attention was called officially to either the rights or the duties of the king diminished. Richard continued to append disclaimers of the abrogation of his prerogative to acts which in substance infringed upon it. When in connection with the Haxey case the question was at length openly revived, the king's position was stated in substantially the old terms. The attitudes of his councillors in later years were probably much akin to those of the earlier courtiers. Acquaintance with affairs of government, whether derived from domestic experience or from observation of statecraft abroad, prepared men like Bushy and Scrope to serve authority as readily as their predecessors had done. There was, of course, continuity between the two groups. The attachment to the court of a few knights like Vache, Aubrey de Vere, Montagu, Dagworth and Elmham spanned the entire reign. Others who rose to prominence after 1390 were bound by personal or family ties to men of long standing royal service. William Bagot, for example, was a mainpernor for the release of John Lincoln from prison in 1388.[5]

Despite the contemporary attention given Bushy, Bagot, Green and Scrope, perhaps the most important adherent to the royalist cause after 1397 was the chancellor, Edmund Stafford. The son of one of the closest friends of the Black Prince, association with Richard's followers was natural to him. His talents and his family connections had already brought him preferment

---

[3]A. Harding, *A Social History of English Law* (1966), p. 68.
[4] Cf. *supra*, pp. 25, 26; Tout, *Chapters*, IV, pp. 33–35.
[5] *C.C.R.* 1385–1389, p. 414. Among the adherents of Richard arrested at Berkeley Castle in 1399 were William Elmham, Bishop Henry Despenser and W. Burley, who may have been the heir of Simon Burley. *Cal. Inquisitions Miscellaneous*, 1387–1399, pp. 140, 160, 161.

before he became keeper of the privy seal in 1389. His career as a distinguished scholar of civil law included advocacy in the Roman court and appointments at Oxford. Though he possessed and apparently merited Richard's personal confidence, his ultra-royalism was basically official and philosophical. The great seal was returned to his custody for two separate periods in the reign of Henry IV.[6] The extreme declarations with which he greeted the parliaments of 1397 and 1398 perhaps reflected his training in civil law. Consistent in every way with the courtier principles of the preceding decade, they might have served as appropriate extensions of the themes of Simon of Sudbury, and they resembled theories prevalent both in England and on the continent through-out the fourteenth century.[7] But already the king had struck a new note.

The most widely publicized contemporary tradition of Richard is that of the tyrant, a tradition substantially documented by the charges of the parliament roll. Another, which emerged shortly, commemorates him as the protagonist of sacred majesty. If he provoked the first, he deliberately inspired the second, for an overwhelming concern with the ceremony, the symbols and the liturgy of kingship was one of the most notable features of the last years of the reign. He displayed the sun on his banners and standards; he converted ordinary occasions into impressive pageants; and he laid special stress on the properties of anoint-ment.[8] Western kings during the preceding two centuries had permitted the liturgical sanctions of their office not indeed to

[6] Tout, *Chapters*, III, pp. 462, 463; IV, pp. 49–51; V, pp. 51–3. Stafford opened the parliamentary session of September 1402 with a speech on obedience and God's sanction to the ruler. *Rot. Parl.*, III, pp. 485–7.

[7] These views were common in England at the century's close. L. J. Daly draws a remarkably close parallel between Bishop Stafford's summary of the requirements for good government and that of Wyclyf in his *De Officio Regis*, though he attributes the statement of the bishop to Richard. *The Political Theory of John Wyclyf* (1962), p. 131. The sentiments of the (gentleman?)author of *Mum and the Sothseggar* were not dissimilar. Cf. in particular, ll. 1405–62. Ed. Day and Steele (E.E.T.S. 1936) pp. 67–9.

[8] The depth and subtlety of his interest in symbols was a subject explored by Dr. Ernst Kantorowicz in whose opinion Richard's preoccupation with them combined his theoretical speculation and his artistic bent. Hints of the study he might have written are contained in a footnote. *King's Two Bodies*, p. 33, n. 18. Others have seen in the king's fascination with symbols an evidence of his retreat from reality. I am convinced by Kantorowicz. Cf. also J. Evans, 'The Wilton Diptych Reconsidered', *The Archaeological Journal*, XV (1948), pp. 1–5; F. Wormald, 'The Wilton Diptych', *Journal of the Courtauld and Warburg Institutes*, XVII (1954), pp. 191–203.

lapse, but to recede in importance. There were excellent reasons. As monarchies gained in real power and security, the incompatibility of consecration and dynastic aims became manifest. Consecration warranted the authority a worthy man might exercise. Dynasty required the unique association of worth with family and, if painful crises were to be avoided, with primogeniture.[9] While dynastic considerations prompted the exaltation of the office, they also encouraged independence from temporal agents, whether hierarchy or community. There were, moreover, practical and forceful reasons for avoiding questions or delays in the acknowledgement of royal right, which in fact tended increasingly to pass in the instant of life and death from ruler to successor.[10] Thus the coronation gradually assumed rather the character of a ritual of endorsement than an investment with authority.

The Capetians, it is true, had found it convenient to buttress regal authority, which had breached dynastic right, with anointment of a very special sort. They used a holy oil sent from heaven in the beak of a dove on the occasion of the baptism of Clovis. They never neglected to exploit the divine favours claimed as their inheritance from the Merovingians, and they were fortunate enough to number a saint among the members of their line. Even so, the strength of the French crown in the thirteenth and fourteenth centuries rested primarily on other actual and theoretical foundations. The constitutive significance of anointment was little emphasized.[11] It may be, nonetheless, that Richard II, who found much to envy in the French court, visualized in the Merovingian balm an ultimate immunity for kings, an immunity which, in kind if not in particular, could shelter every Christian ruler.

It is equally possible that he need not have looked abroad for inspiration. He had always surrounded himself with clerics. His attachment to his confessors and his fondness for preachers was well-known. Throughout the reign the orders of friars

<hr />

[9] R. E. Giesey, *The Juristic Basis of Dynastic Right to the French Throne* (1961), p. 6. Kantorowicz discusses the transition at length, *King's Two Bodies*, pp. 318–36.
[10] Ibid., pp. 328–30.
[11] Giesey, *Juristic Basis of Dynastic Right*, pp. 4–6. For the contrast between French and English coronation ceremonies in the thirteenth and fourteenth centuries, cf. W. Ullman, *Principles of Government and Politics*, pp. 201–203.

enjoyed his patronage. Robert Waldby, the learned Austin, and Thomas Rushook, the eloquent Dominican, were only the most noted of the friars who frequented his court. Special favour was shown to the Dominicans. Richard often visited the tomb of his older brother in the Dominican church at Langley, where he was himself buried until Henry V removed his body to Westminster. The popularity at court of the Dominican preachers was a tribute primarily to their zeal and their piety. For the most part in England in the later fourteenth century they were not scholars; when they were, they tended to be concerned with philosophy and theology, avoiding disputations on canon law and speculation about political questions.[12] Reverence for royal authority was an obligation to the devout. The fidelity of grey and black friars alike was remarkable. More than a few became martyrs after 1400 to the belief that divine protection, having enabled Richard to escape, would restore him to the throne.[13]

Following the death of Queen Anne, the king sought more consistently the companionship of monks and students of theology rather than administrators or lawyers. Several clergymen, including such an old-timer as his kinsman, Bishop Braybrook of London, accompanied him on the Irish expedition of 1399.[14] Among his intimates were Tydeman of Winchcombe, John Burghill, Roger Walden, the former favourite secretary Richard Medford, Richard Maudeleyn and, above all, Thomas Merke and William Colchester, Abbot of Westminster.[15] Others of the

[12] Bede Jarret, *The English Dominicans* (1937), pp. 15, 110, 9, 124.

[13] Wylie summarizes the movements among the friars in Richard's behalf, *England Under Henry IV*, I, Ch. XVI. The story of the Francisan, derived from *Cont. Eul. Hist.*, III, p. 390, best illustrates the devotion of the friars to the notion of kingship divinely ordained. Cf. Clarke, *Fourteenth Century Studies*, pp. 87, 88.

[14] Tout, *Chapters*, IV, pp. 54, 55. Others were Merke, Burghill, Lincoln, Medford, Mone, William of Colchester and Henry Beaufort.

[15] Many of these clerics received ecclesiastical preferment. Tydeman, translated over the opposition of the Worcester Chapter at Richard's request from Llandaff to Worcester, was especially close to the king. His successor in 1401 was Richard Clifford, elected by the monks. *Victoria County History of Worcester*, II, p. 37. Tydeman was one of Hereford's attorneys during his banishment. *Foedera*, VII, p. 49. Walden succeeded Archbishop Arundel at Canterbury when Arundel was translated to St. Andrews. He, of course, lost the see when Henry IV secured Arundel's restoration, but the old archbishop, himself, is said to have been responsible not only for his lenient treatment but also for his preferment as Bishop of London in 1404. Walden was noted for his piety; he was, however, unlike many of Richard's later clerical favourites, a man of affairs. Cf. J. Tait, *D.N.B.*, XX, pp. 481-3. Medford was Waltham's successor at Salisbury; Mone was Bishop of Saint David's and Burghill, a former royal confessor, was Bishop of Lichfield.

M

monks of Westminster may have been members of the circle for Merke and the abbot were surely at its centre. Richard's special interest in the abbey began at least as early as 1388.[16] His excessive partiality for the Chapter may be an explanation for the persistent hostility toward him of the St. Albans scriptorium. The houses generated a bitter rivalry in the last decades of the century.[17]

The queen's death strengthened the already firm bonds between the court and the abbey where magnificent memorials were established in her honour. Among the monks designated especially for service to her memory were Oxford scholar Peter Coumbe and John Borewell, who for some years represented the abbot at the Roman curia.[18] Coumbe was one of many sent from the abbey to study at Oxford where they lived at Gloucester College. The curriculum at the Benedictine colleges was generally limited to study of the Bible and patristic texts including Augustine. Their theoretical outlook was conservative, though there was much interest in the forms of writing according to new, that is to say Classical, models. Students were not perceptibly affected by exposure either to canon law or civil law, and even less perhaps to the impact of Aristotelianism.[19]

Among the Westminster monks, only a small minority were in fact broadly learned.[20] Abbot William, himself, who had done a turn at Oxford, possessed some legal competence but he was not conspicuous for his learning. A lover of music and art, his ascendancy among his brethren should probably be attributed more to his character and good judgment than to his qualities of

Another bishop for whom Richard expressed great affection was John Trefnant of Hereford. *C.Ch.R.*, V, p. 349. Both Usk and the Monk of Evesham describe the ascendancy of Tydeman over Richard in unflattering terms. *Chronicon Adae de Usk*, p. 64; *Vita Ricardi*, p. 168. The latter includes Merke among the king's companions in dissipation.

[16] *C.Ch.R.*, V, p. 312.
[17] Williams, *History of the Abbey of St. Alban*, p. 188; cf. *Gestae Abbatum Monasterie Sancti Albani*, III, pp. 435, 436; Introduction, pp. lxxii, lxxiii.
[18] E. H. Pearce, *The Monks of Westminster* (1916), pp. 109, 118.
[19] Ibid., p. 27; H. Rashdall, *The Universities of Europe in the Middle Ages* (ed. Powicke, 1936), III, pp. 184–88. J. K. Floyer, 'The Medieval Library of the Benedictine Priory of St. Mary in Worcester Cathedral Church', *Archaeologia*, LVIII (1903), p. 564.
[20] Richard Cirencester, scholar at Oxford, was the author of *Speculum historiale de gestis regum Anglie*. William of Sudbury was a writer who made a series of tables and indices to the writings of St. Thomas. Pearce, op. cit., pp. 100, 113; R. Widmore, *A History of the Church of St. Peter, Westminster commonly called Westminster Abbey* (1751), p. 112.

intellect. He was the choice of the Chapter to be head of the house over the opposition of the king who preferred John Lakyngheth. The difference of opinion apparently never affected his relationships either with Richard or his candidate.[21] Lakyngheth, a probable author of the Westminster *Chronicle*, was one of Abbot William's closest collaborators.[22] No one was more steadfast in his loyalty to the king than William of Colchester, a central figure in the conspiracy of the *duketti* to reinstate him in 1399. The higher politics of the kingdom may in fact have been reflected in the internal affairs of the abbey. Late in Richard's reign, Abbot William addressed to his fellows a letter containing a prayer for the king and a warning of plots against the peace of the realm. Significantly omitted from the list of those to whom the letter was directed was William Wrattinge, the prior. He was known to be hostile to the abbot and he was alleged to be treasonably involved with the Duke of Gloucester and John Moote, Abbot of St. Albans, William of Colchester's personal enemy.[23]

Outside the abbey, William's closest associations were with men devoted to Richard. He was connected with Nicholas Brembre. Bishop Waltham of Salisbury and Bishop Despenser of Norwich were his intimate friends.[24] The fighting Bishop of Norwich, who was also noted as a good pastor, a builder and a patron of the arts, was one of the few who attempted to rally support for Richard II when Henry of Lancaster returned from exile to seize the throne. His prestige and Henry's politic clemency saved him from serious punishment, but it was his last foray into politics. He died at prayer in his cathedral in 1406. Abbot William, likewise, suffered only a brief imprisonment for the more grave offence of leadership in the conspiracy of the *duketti*. He, too, withdrew from public affairs until 1413 when he emerged to assume a prominent part in the ceremonies for the

[21] E. H. Pearce, *William de Colchester* (1915), pp. 43–46; Pearce, *Monks of Westminster*, p. 104.

[22] J. A. Robinson, 'An Unrecognized Westminster Chronicler', *British Academy Proceedings*, III, pp. 75–77.

[23] Pearce, *William de Colchester*, pp. 70, 71. This may be a further confirmation of anti-Richardian plots in 1397. The details which can hardly be accurate though they may well incorporate a substantial truth are to be found in *Traison et Mort*, p. 3.

[24] Robinson, op. cit., p. 70; *Polychronicon*, IX, p. 167; Pearce, *Monks of Westminster*, p. 105; Pearce, *William de Colchester*, p. 68. Cf. J. Capgrave, *Liber de Illustribus Henricis* (R.S. 1858), pp. 170–4.

coronation of Henry V. He had not even participated in the
obsequies for Henry IV who was buried at Canterbury.[25]

Abbot William inspired widespread affection and respect, but
no one was so close to him as Thomas Merke, the Westminster
monk who for two years was Bishop of Carlisle.[26] Before he
settled at Westminster he was for some time a scholar at Merton
where the influence of Aristotle was dominant but where the
Augustinian tradition was also strongly represented particularly
in the faculty of theology, Merke's course of study. It was
perhaps at Merton that he developed an interest in Ciceronian
rythmical style.[27] Form and ritual were important to him. He
was also, like many other Ricardians, an effective preacher and a
zealous prelate. His brief tenure was enough to establish a
tradition of high regard for him in Carlisle, but his outspoken
challenge to Henry IV in the meeting of the Estates in 1399 cost
him his ecclesiastical preferment.[28] He returned, it may be
suspected not unhappily, to Westminster. Until his death in 1409
he held only minor benefices. The sentiments attributed to him
by contemporaries on the divine sanctions of kingship are faithfully represented by Shakespeare. The ruler apostrophized as 'the
figure of God's majesty, His captain, steward, deputy-elect' is in
very essence the Christological king. It is not unlikely that many
of the brethren, who shared Richard's artistic tastes and his love
of books, shared as well his avid interest in the 'divinity that doth
hedge about a king'. Although secularist writings were available
to them, the emphases of their training and their intellectual
environment were conducive to belief in theocracy.[29]

[25] Pearce, *William de Colchester*, pp. 80, 81. G. E. Morey, who cites persistent
efforts in Richard's behalf in East Anglia by the de Veres and others, suspects that
Bishop Despenser may also have continued to be interested in his cause. 'East
Anglian Society', pp. 414, 415.   [26] Pearce, *Monks of Westminster*, p. 104.
[27] Pearce, *William de Colchester*, p. 88; N. Denholm Young, 'The Cursus in
England', *Oxford Essays in Medieval History Presented to H. E. Salter* (1934), p. 81.
Merke wrote a treatise on the cursus, entitled *De moderno dictamine*. The broad
humanistic interests represented at Merton in the acquisitions to its library in the
later fourteenth century may be attributed to the influence of Thomas Bradwardine
and his circle. Powicke, *The Medieval Books of Merton College*, pp. 20–23, 25.
[28] W. Hutchinson, *The History of the County of Cumberland* (1794), II, p. 625.
Merke may, in fact, have been first arrested not for the speech but for his part in
the 1399 conspiracies against Henry. J. Tait, *D.N.B.*, XIII, pp. 282–5; but cf.
Clarke, *Fourteenth Century Studies*, pp. 86, 87. In October, 1399, Merke was in the
custody of the Abbot of St. Albans, no friend either to him or to his house. *C.C.R.*
1398–1402, p. 28.
[29] The abbey library to which Abbot Colchester was a contributer contained a
copy of Giles of Rome's *De Regimine Principum*. J. A. Robinson and M. R. James,
Manuscripts of Westminster Abbey, p. 9.

Among the servants of the king in these later years one other group would have done little to discourage tendencies toward autocracy. Richard's personal bodyguard was recruited largely from Cheshire. The Earldom, a special honour attached to the king or his eldest son since 1254, was a rough school for fighting men. There Hugh Calveley and Robert Knollys, among many others, had served their apprenticeship and learned to love the life of the soldier of fortune. In an era when disorder was commonplace, Cheshire was notorious for violence. Its reputation, which perhaps reached a climax under Richard II, was not unjustified. As in other border counties the ties between men and their leaders were almost entirely personal. There was little sense of obligation to a larger community. In Cumberland, Westmoreland and Northumberland this singularly devoted allegiance was at the service of the Dacres, the Nevilles and the Percies. In Cheshire it belonged to the king. Richard's bodyguard in 1397 probably included two thousand Cheshire archers. Their numbers gave him a sense of power. To their commanders his word was law.[30]

By 1399, the intellectual defences of Ricardian absolutism were drawn from widely disparate and sometimes incompatible sources. Giles of Rome, for example, had repeated the dictum that the laws were in the king's breast, but for him absolute monarchy was necessary because of what it could accomplish. Neither he nor the civilians, or for that matter the common lawyers, attached great significance to ritual in affairs of state. On the other hand, they would have been as little inclined as Richard's councillors to defend the despotism which met the challenge of opportunity in fourteenth century Italy, even though despots generally sought the justification of service to the community. Such men as Bushy and Scrope were by no means indifferent to the rewards of office or to the advantages of intimacy with a king whose word in effect was law. A careful scrutiny of the record, however, prompts the judgment that contemporary charges of incitement to arbitrary tyranny are careless distortions of the truth. They and their fellows were useful primarily because of their skill in manipulating well-

[30] H. J. Hewitt, *Medieval Chester* (1929), pp. 147–52. Cf. Steel, *Richard II*, p. 233 and n. 5.

established institutions and procedures. They were shrewd pragmatic politicians, not the instruments of despotism.

The value of strong monarchy may have been self evident to Bushy and Scrope. The king, however, became increasingly concerned with ideological justification. In the process he encountered problems which might have disturbed a more systematic thinker, but he made no attempt at system. His theory of kingship was as untidy as his absolutist programme. In action he was neither firm nor prudent. In thought he was sensitive and imaginative, but he had no gift for logical consistency. He grasped at theoretical bucklers for royal power wherever he found them and he was inhibited neither by the implications of ecclesiastical supremacy inherent in theocracy nor by the incompatibility of immutable divine law with ultimate obligation to the needs of the community. After the shock of the Hereford-Norfolk controversy, he became increasingly anxious. His heightened sensitivity to criticism and his intimacy with theologians perhaps combined in the last months of the reign to direct his attention almost exclusively to those defences of his station to which human judgment would not be relevant.

More than two centuries earlier Pierre de Blois swore to aid King Henry II, 'that is to do a holy thing; for the king is holy; he is Christ as Seigneur; for it is not in vain that he has received the sacrament of unction'. In the next generation Pope Innocent III proclaimed John to be immune from trial by his peers because he was an anointed king.[31] Those declarations were far back in the past; the affirmation of Christ-centred kingship by the Anonymous of York was yet more remote by a hundred years. Perhaps there were echoes, nonetheless, to which the ears of monks and clerks as late as the last decade of the fourteenth century might be attuned.

Be that as it may, when Richard was still a minor John Wyclyf, in condemning all resistance to the secular ruler, reiterated the old doctrine of the divine source of power. It had been instituted as a remedy for sin and must be obeyed whether just or unjust. Richard probably had no knowledge of Wyclyf's views, which were an extension of his voluntarist philosophy. Where Wyclyf followed the theoretical consequences of his argument on

31 M. Bloch, Les rois thaumaturges (1924), pp. 41, 127.

dominion, Richard was led by apparent necessity. It would have been comfortable, as it would one day be valid, to rest authority on the requirement of the common good. In the late fourteenth century, however, the principle of the common good could be invoked to check royal supremacy as readily as to assert it. Not everyone was a Bushy or a Scrope. A king who could not rely on the self-interest of his own intimates to ensure loyalty could hardly feel secure in dependence on the rational persuasion of all his subjects. He, therefore, proclaimed by word and ceremony an inherent right immune to terrestrial challenge. The tenet was agreeable to his temperament and soothing to his circumstances. He clung to it with solicitous relish. Yet paradoxically, as his experience with the Lancastrian patrimony demonstrated, the self-sufficient monarchy to which he was committed could only become a reality through the suppression of inherent particular rights.[32]

Absolutism remained for Richard an ideal condition to be supported by sweeping and sometimes contradictory assertions. His exposition wanted consistency both in definition and purpose. Nonetheless, he made his point. His resurrection of emphasis on the sacramental character of kingship impressed contemporaries and successors who were as hard-headed as he was visionary. Henry IV made elaborate use of Thomas à Becket's miraculous balm which Richard claimed to have rediscovered. And Lambert Simnel was supposed to have owed his life to his anointment with holy oil. Even Henry VII preferred to support belief in the salubrious properties of the sacramental.[33]

[32] Cf. De la Garde, *Naissance de l'esprit laique*, IV, p. 190. 'The new principle, which began to be affirmed at the end of the fourteenth century and triumphed after a two hundred year struggle, is that the common good requires in every state an authority which will be the sole judge of its own acts and which is accountable only to God and to history'. The associates of Richard II who had been trained in canon law may, in fact, already have encountered adaptations from theology which were to support Christological conceptions of kingship in later generations. Cf. R. Giesey, 'The French Estates and the Corpus Mysticum Regni', *Album Helen Maude Cam* (1960), pp. 155–171, especially pp. 162–167 and 170; and E. Kantorowicz, 'Mysteries of State, an Absolutist Concept and its Late Medieval Origins', *Harvard Theological Review* (1955), XLVIII, pp. 65–91.

[33] Cf. W. Ullman, 'Thomas Becket's Miraculous Oil', *Journal of Theological Studies*, VIII (1957), pp. 129–33; K. Pickthorn, *Early Tudor Government, Henry VII*, p. 9.

Chapter XIII

CONCLUSION

W HAT Richard actually proposed to do was at once more
and less than what traditional interpretations of his reign
have long ascribed to him. He did not contemplate the destruction of parliament, nor did he project a design of wholesale royal
brigandage which would leave him perpetually free to pursue
his own selfish desires. On the contrary, he inclined to utilize
parliament in what he considered to be its appropriate and
traditional function of assistance to the monarch in his task of
governing the realm, and however much he may have been given
to easy living he took his responsibilities as ruler very seriously.
It is true that he devoted far more attention to the symbols of
absolutism than he did to the development of programmes of
action, but there is no evidence that he sought a universal recognition of the sacred majesty of his station merely in order that he
might enjoy the frivolous pleasure of playing the tyrant. His
historical role was not that of a would-be destroyer of popular
representative institutions which already in their infancy were
giving signs of premature robust toughness. It should hardly be
necessary to argue that his battle was not that of the Stuarts
against an independent national parliament.[1] He did not suffer
deposition and death because in 1397 he chose to cease to rule
'constitutionally and well'.

What he did intend must be understood in its own terms.
Had he succeeded in gaining for monarchy the unqualified
acceptance of his own theoretical position, he would have handed
down to his successors an instrument of government more
potent in its capacity to affect all classes of subjects than any
which had ever existed in England. His Norman and early
Angevin predecessors had developed a royal authority which
could and did override law or custom at its convenience. The
bases of their strength, and of its instrumentation as well, lay,
however, in the manipulation of feudal jurisdiction. They

[1] But cf. Wilkinson, *Constitutional History*, II, pp. 56–77.

affected the community primarily through the feudal structure, not independently of it.[2] Unfettered. control of the manifold agencies developed in the thirteenth and fourteenth centuries to correlate monarchy and community would have constituted power of an entirely different order of magnitude than any they had attained.

The reasons for Richard's failure have already been noted, and they need not be repeated. It is enough to remark that the establishment of political dominion, whatever its nature, requires a more substantial foundation than a theoretical system, however skillfully it may be elaborated, however persistently it may be maintained, and however plausibly it may be linked with historical tradition and precedent. No government can long endure without the support of influential classes within the community, even though the community be trained to think and act in terms of custom. Historical precedents are notably effective, but they are notoriously susceptible of many interpretations. The argument for unqualified divine right where it touched the lives and property of subjects was even less acceptable in the late fourteenth century than it proved to be in the seventeenth. The naked exposition of the theory only frightened many whose adherence was necessary to the stability of the realm. If absolutism were to exist in that time and place, it must be fashioned with other instruments. When something approaching absolutism did for a time become a reality in England, it was based upon the active approval of the powerful groups whose interests in large measure it served. The Tudors knew how to secure consent; they knew, too, what groups must give it if their government was to be maintained. This wisdom was partially a product of the Tudor genius, but it was the product as well of a century of experience with disorder and of social developments which lodged the balance of power in the hands of those who learned to prefer a greater centralization of authority. Controversy about the associations of sixteenth century monarchy and the Middle Classes notwithstanding, there can be little question that the Tudors, and perhaps their predecessors, could discover sub-

---

[2] J. E. A. Jolliffe, *Angevin Kingship* (1953), pp. 344, 345. Cf. Ullman, *Principles of Government and Politics*, pp. 152–168. especially p. 166. But cf. also, J. C. Holt, *King John* (1963), pp. 10–12.

stantial sentiment in behalf of strong monarchy among groups whose opinions carried weight. The Portuguese monarchy has been cited as the unique fourteenth century example of the successful assertion of royal supremacy and Joao I (1385–1433), characterized as 'the first royal leader of the new bourgeoisie'. Even Joao may not initially have been enthusiastic about the role.[3] In any case the social revolution ascribed to Portugal would hardly have been possible in England at that time.

The question of the purposes for which Richard might have utilized his power could he have achieved it becomes, therefore, a profitless inquiry. Historical hindsight prompts the quick judgment that fifteenth century England might have been happier had it been spared the chaos of late feudal violence and dynastic controversy which the removal of the legitimate monarch brought inescapably in its wake. An omnipotent king whose paramount obligation was the preservation of peace and order should have been a sufficient guarantee against civil disorder on any scale, for disorder battened on the decline of royal justice.[4]

Yet the civil unrest of the fourteenth and fifteenth centuries was not a cause unto itself. It had deep roots in the social dis-locations that accompanied the transformation of the old systems of allegiance and tenure. It was not to be curbed by a mere assertion of royal supremacy. Richard may to some extent have been influenced to adopt his position by the predatory behaviour of the greatest of his subjects, but his thought and his action were directed solely toward the preservation of his own rights as he conceived them. A solution of the most serious problems of the day would have called for a more positive programme. His fall would be an even more momentous historical turning-point if it could be demonstrated, for example, that he aimed at a social reformation which would have encompassed the principal demands of the rebels of 1381. There is no evidence of such intent, although a strong, well co-ordinated, central authority might have made social transition less painful. But speculation of this

[3] Cf. *supra*, p. 2; B. W. Diffie, *Prelude to Empire* (1960), p. 74. Cf. Russell, *English Intervention in Spain and Portugal*, pp. 359–64.

[4] E. G. Kimball, whose intimate acquaintance with Peace Rolls of the late fourteenth and early fifteenth centuries is surely unrivalled, produces evidence 'that the lack of law enforcement and the general disregard for the law generally associated with the middle of the fifteenth century existed at least as early as the beginning of the century and perhaps earlier'. *The Shropshire Peace Roll*, p. 42.

sort knows no terminal limits. Perhaps the pain of the fifteenth century was a necessary antecedent to the glories of the sixteenth, or even, in a way quite antithetical to that enshrined in the traditional Whig myth, to the constitutional triumphs of the seventeenth.

Richard's conduct is indicative of his conventional respect for traditional social order. Noble rank and ecclesiastical preferment were the common rewards of his favourites. Those who wore his livery enjoyed special privileges. All of the pomp and ceremony of late medieval chivalry were apparently as dear to him as ever they had been to his father or his grandfather. He made no attempt to institute social changes on his own estates. He was inspired by no revolutionary project for relieving the miseries of the least fortunate of his subjects. To suggest that he should have been so motivated would be to judge him by the standards of another era than his own.

Richard's thinking did not extend beyond the matter of the nature and limits of royal power. It is obvious that English institutions would have been conditioned much differently in the fifteenth century if his constitutional experiments had triumphed. His purposes, however, must not be misconstrued. He himself had no novel plans for the future. He visualized the royal power as operating to preserve peace and justice. If the magnates interfered with the execution of justice they should be brought to heel. If they encroached upon the privileges of monarchy they should be punished. This did not imply in any way the under-mining of the nobility as an estate. If the king's advisers exceeded their authority they should be reduced to their proper station, but that would not involve the destruction of parliament or of the councils. If special privilege thwarted local justice, royal officers should supply remedy. If the king had cause to fear the disloyalty of certain of his subjects, measures should be taken to ensure a restoration of allegiance, but nothing in this suggests the reduc-tion of the realm to unlawful servitude. Richard was, when all is said, essentially a medieval king. To rule wisely and well meant to him to rule with the advice but not the hindrance of others; it also meant to rule within the framework of established traditions and through the operation at his own behest of established institutions.

He was, above all, insistent on the right to select his own advisers and to act upon their advice as he chose. He knew, too, that his councillors must include the great officers of state. He designed no innovations in administrative practice. Although the royal policy originated with the members of the household who, as skilled administrators, understood the ways in which the chamber could be used to advantage, they, nonetheless, recognized the paramount importance of the chancery and the treasury. Both of Richard's attempts at supremacy, and their reversals as well, depended largely upon the co-operation of the chancellors and the great officers of the realm. He demanded advisers who were at once responsive and responsible, not pliant household servants.[5]

Neither Richard's theory of monarchy nor his programme in action, then, was in any sense conceived by him to be revolutionary. He thought rather in terms of restoration and perfection than of novelty. There is no evidence that his opinions were either based upon, or governed by, any concrete historical analysis marking a fixed point in the past which he would have viewed as a time when monarchy had existed in its ideal form. Yet he clearly believed that, during the reign of his grandfather and in the early years of his own minority, the divinely ordained foundations of the institution had been undermined. He was even more acutely disturbed about the deposition of Edward II and the ominous precedents created by the successful assaults on the intimate advisers of that most unfortunate of his ancestors. The English king, therefore, could hardly resume his designated place in the divine scheme until all of the errors of the preceding century had been publicly acknowledged and corrected. This was second in importance only to the complete reversal of actions taken in the parliaments of 1386 and 1388.

In defining his position and in carrying out his programme, he articulated more extreme claims for royal absolutism and developed a more highly centralized organization than any of his

---

[5] Other contemporary attitudes toward council are discussed by A. L. Brown, 'The Commons and their Council in the Reign of Henry IV', *E.H.R.* LXXIX (1964), pp. 1–30. and J. L. Kirby, 'Councils and Councillors of Henry IV, 1399–1413'. *T.R.H.S.* Fifth Series, XIV (1964), pp. 35–66. A classic fifteenth century formulation of personnel which incidentally corresponds roughly to the actual make-up of the councils of Richard's minority and the commission of 1386 is that of Fortescue, *The Governance of England*, ed. Plummer (1885), Ch. XV.

predecessors had done. To some extent this may have resulted from the belief of his advisers that at the outset of the reign monarchical power was on the defensive. It may, also, have been conditioned by tendencies in the late fourteenth century to magnify the importance of symbols and ceremonies as a means of retaining prestige which had formerly been based upon tacit recognition of function. Circumstances, too, seemed to invite increased exercise of the power of the crown. And there can be no question about the identification by the courtiers of good governance, whatever might have been subsumed under that rubric, and strong monarchy. Richard, as indeed did his opponents, looked backward for the justification of his policy. He aimed no more at despotism, either beneficent or otherwise, than they at chaos. His brief triumph, however, was to many of his subjects indistinguishable from despotism, while his overthrow engendered conditions in which chaos was an omnipresent threat.

Yet the legacy of the reign was not entirely sterile. It did make its own positive contribution to the development of the Whig tradition. For, despite precautionary prohibitions, the events of the period were employed as precedents again and again in the ensuing century; and practice, if repeated often enough, would necessarily modify attitudes. The utilization of parliament as a whole, or the commons in particular, as the instrument for inflicting political persecution created an impression of inherent possession of a kind of independent power over royal servants which almost no one would have conceived of in 1400. Such impressions remained for the most part without definite formulation throughout the Lancastrian and Yorkist reigns though the precedents were extended. If parliament would not, or could not, make and unmake kings it would again ratify their removal by armed force and it would again be the instrument of attack on authority by demanding a capital sentence on a favoured minister. The precedents for government by council which responded to other forces than the will of the king and which failed to observe the distinction between the making and the administration of policy would also be strengthened by repetition. This is what makes the definition of the English constitution in the fifteenth century so confusing and perplexing a problem. The confusion was born in the great political crises of the reign of Richard II, for which the policies of the king and his court were immediately responsible.

By the end of the thirteenth century strong monarchies had emerged in France and the Iberian peninsula as well as in England. Kings and their servants employed every resource at their command, including new notions of law, to perfect a *status regis* competent to provide for the *necessitas regni*; that is to say, kingship powerful enough to act as need might require for the common good of the realm. To add that the *necessitas regni* as pursued by an Edward I or a Philip IV might often seem to be indistinguishable from the personal interest of the monarch is in no way to diminish their understanding of the concept or their success in upholding it.

The kings of the fourteenth century were conspicuously less successful. The vigorous particularist assault against royal authority in the Western kingdoms in the fourteenth century is no more a matter of coincidence than their common accretion of strength in the thirteenth. Kings everywhere gave ground grudgingly and violence could extend to regicide.[6] It was in England alone that a ruler combined theory and policy, not merely to stem the particularist tide, but to attempt an unprecedented exaltation of the crown. The attempt and its failure exacerbated the confusions of English political life in the next hundred years. Its results, however, are far less significant than its design. Since no other king of that era projected such a design, what Richard wrought is of less historical importance than what he proposed. He sought to free the royal prerogative from restraint or interference by anyone either in the realm or outside it.

To repeat that he did not aim at despotism or tyranny may seem superfluous; the distinction in his terms, however, between prerogative absolutism and despotism cannot be over-emphasized. The suggestion has been made in an earlier chapter that the Tudors succeeded where Richard failed. It may quite properly be

---

[6]As in the instances of Pedro I of Castille and Albert I of Austria. I agree with Professor Wilkinson about the significance of the observance of the forms of law in English depositions. *Constitutional History* II, p. 162. Even in England, however, they did not hold indefinitely. The verdict of the field of battle would make Richard III a usurper, just as a different outcome at Stoke would have made Henry VII a usurper.

objected that Tudor rule was never really absolute and that, in any case, what the Tudors achieved either in 1500 or 1500, was something vastly different from anything Richard II sought. Be that as it may, there is little question about relative power *vis-a-vis* the aristocracy. Richard invited revolution by his attempt in 1399 to deprive Henry of Lancaster of an inheritance. Henry had once been involved in armed rebellion and recently had been formally exiled as an aftermath to a serious accusation of treason. Richard had every reason to fear him, but he did not proceed with arbitrary indictments or sentences. It is unlikely that he would have believed he possessed the sanctions so to proceed even if it had been politically feasible. The precedents of 1397 would have required nothing less publicly impressive than condemnation in full parliament. Henry VIII destroyed the Duke of Buckingham in 1521 on the flimsiest of trumped-up charges. Buckingham's only crimes were patently his royal ancestry and his popularity. He was tried, not in parliament, but before the lord high steward. His judges were all aristocrats, some of whom wept as the sentence was pronounced. But they accepted the will of the king without protest either then or later, and the king, of course, had no qualms of conscience whatever.[7]

The ascendancy, if not the absolute sovereignty of the early Tudor monarchy, is nowhere exhibited so clearly as in the contrast of Henry VIII's assertive stroke of state with Richard II's cautious provocation to disaster.

The crux of the problem lies in the inadequacy of the term 'absolutism' to describe with equal precision Richard's ambitions and Tudor practice. Perhaps it might be well for these purposes to turn from absolutism and speak instead of statecraft, a word all too often interpreted as though its entire meaning were concentrated in the final syllable. In terms of craft it is true that Edward I or Philip IV, for example, would have had little to learn from anyone in the sixteenth century. Their conception of state, however, was neither dynastic nor territorial. It was suffused with moral content. In the thirteenth century the word *status* was 'charged with the significance of our word 'condition', with a

---

[7] Pickthorn, *Early Tudor Government, Henry VIII*, pp. 45–49. For greater detail, see J. S. Brewer, *The Reign of Henry VIII* (1884), I, Ch. XIII.

sense of value.'[8] Law, whether founded on custom, scripture or Roman jurisprudence, articulated moral content and special sense of value alike. In the sixteenth century, on the other hand, while kingdom, monarchy and state were terms not yet entirely identified with nation, they all had begun to have territorial and dynastic possessive connotations. They had lost their medieval moral content and were only in the first stages of the process of acquiring a new set of principles of definition. Thus 'absolute' as applied to them would have a very different frame of reference than that of the thirteenth century.

Richard II was no rival in statecraft to the great kings of the Middle Ages. Indeed, he was no match for his cousin of Lancaster. But no medieval king had been more concerned than he about the nature of his estate. His intellectual outlook, his concept of *status* and of *regis*, and his sense of prerogative were those of his ancestors and to them he stubbornly adhered. He is the only king of his time who spoke vigorously for kingship. If his voice is sometimes strident, sometimes frightening, if it lacks the firm tone derived from assurance that law and will are one, it is still the voice of the Middle Ages, as remote from that of Henry VIII as the voice of Edward I. His conception of the necessities of the crown would not have extended beyond action to provide for emergencies. He had not pushed his thinking to the justification of a flagrant breach of law on the ground of necessity unrelated to an immediate crisis. In the performance of his obligation to defend the realm, he might indeed, at some time, be required to abrogate established rights. His judgment, on the other hand, that his personal security, the security of the dynasty, or even the security of the institution of monarchy might in an indefinite way be threatened, could not authorize an arbitrary interference with life or property.[9] He took pains, for example, to have Henry of

---

[8] F. M. Powicke, 'Reflections on the Medieval State', *Ways of Medieval Life and Thought* (1949), p. 139. An earlier version of the essay appears in *T.R.H.S.*, 4th series XIX, 1–18. For an examination of Philip IV's view of kingship, which supports Powicke's position, see J. R. Strayer, 'Philip the Fair—a "Constitutional" King'. *A.H.R.* LXII (1956), pp. 18–32; also, Pegues, *The Lawyers of the Last Capetians*, pp. 226, 227. Cf. *supra*, p. 99.

[9] Beaumanoir explains the unusual power which monarchy could assume in time of war or threat of war in terms quite consistent with the views of Richard II. *Coutumes de Beauvaisis*, II, p. 262. This was the reason of State of the Middle Ages related to specific emergency as contrasted with the more sophisticated and more all-inclusive concept of the sixteenth century.

Lancaster declared to be ineligible legally to inherit as a consequence of the sentence at Coventry. His consistent efforts to mask the sequestration, some of them unpublicized, have the appearance rather of rationalization to soothe his own conscience than explanation to prevent alarm among the feudality.[10] The medieval monarchy in decline was yet in its ideals and aspirations, no matter how strained by controversy, the medieval monarchy.

The history of the reign of Richard II is not the history of constitutional victories over rampant tyranny. It is a history which exhibits both in the claims of the king and the behaviour of his opponents irreparable breaches in the fabric of the community; it demonstrates the impossibility in traditional terms of making *status regis* correspond to *necessitas regni* in the later fourteenth century.[11] Richard's disaster both explains the rift and is explained by it. In the final analysis his blunders in statecraft were of less significance as causes of his fall than was the incapacity of kingship in his generation at once to command and to serve community.

[10] Cf., *supra*, p. 99, n. 22; *Rot. Parl.*, III, p. 372. As to efforts to placate the magnates, it is interesting to note, particularly in view of their later behaviour, that York and Northumberland were among the councillors who subscribed to the judgment that the sentence at Coventry made Henry ineligible to inherit.

[11] Post comments on the elements of change and continuity in conceptions of 'reasons of state' and 'necessitas' between the thirteenth century which enjoyed the security of one 'kind of science or art of the State' and the sixteenth which emphasized another. *Studies in Medieval Legal Thought*, pp. 301-9.

N

APPENDIX A

THE 'LANCASTRIAN PARTY'

The persistent reappearance of the notion that an identifiable Lancastrian party was a factor in English politics in the seventh and eighth decades of the fourteenth century requires attention. The case rests upon the assumption that after the Good Parliament of 1376, if not earlier, an organized Lancastrian faction was a permanent feature of every session of the lords and commons. Its principal constituent elements are held to have been members of the great families of Percy, Neville, Mowbray, Stafford, Scrope and Latimer among the nobility and clergy, together with Lancaster's younger brothers, the Earls of Cambridge and Buckingham, and his son, the Earl of Derby. To these were added important officials like Michael de la Pole, a faction in the city of London headed by John of Northampton, and the followers of John Wyclyf.[1]

The policy of the faction is supposed to have been founded upon four cardinal principles. Of these the first was an exalted sense of the royal prerogative which Richard borrowed to develop into a theory of regal absolutism. The second was a half-hearted opposition to extravagance and to clerical intervention in government. The third was hostility to trade monopolies, both local and foreign, and the fourth was the establishment of a permanent peace with France by means of the systematic detachment of all the important French allies. Other factions or parties tended to coalesce in order to check these schemes. One was headed by the personal associates of the young king who were merely jealous of Lancaster's influence and power. Another was led by the great nobles and clergy who saw profit for themselves in the continuation of the war and the curtailment of royal authority. In the long run, these two groups came to represent the old extremes of the royalist party and the baronial party with the Lancastrians enjoying a middle position to which both were hostile.

[1] J. H. Dahmus says that Gaunt's interest in Wyclyf was personal, not political. *The Prosecution of John Wyclyf* (1952), p. 155.

If there were conclusive evidence to support this point of view, historians, despite the tone of contemporary writing, would be forced to deal with the reality of a fourteenth century political group, possessing most of the important distinctive attributes of later political parties. The evidence, however, either for the permanent organization or the national programme is extremely scanty. It rests primarily upon the identification of Michael de la Pole with the Lancastrian design, upon a simplifying of the tangled commercial rivalries of the city guilds, upon a particular interpretation of Lancaster's interests in foreign affairs, and upon the assumption that isolated instances of common action may be construed as indicative of long-term partisan allegiance. The case is strained at best, and each of the arguments upon which it rests fails to stand the test of close scrutiny.

Michael de la Pole, it is true, had served for a brief period under Lancaster's military command, and had been one of his defenders in the Good Parliament of 1376. His record of military service under Richard II's father had been longer. There is nothing in the records to indicate that as chancellor he was in any way identified with any special interest group outside the court. Toward Lancaster's affairs he maintained, insofar as can be ascertained, an impartial attitude. The over-wealthy duke was an object of suspicion to Richard's intimate advisers from 1382 until his departure for Spain four years later. De la Pole is never recorded as having intervened on Lancaster's behalf in any of the open breaches between uncle and nephew which were the results of that suspicion. These occasionally went so far as to involve accusations and counter-accusations of assassination, yet de la Pole continued to be a cordial partisan of the men who are alleged to have accused the duke of high treason, and who were, in turn, accused by him of conspiracy to murder. Never by known word or deed did the chancellor betray any sign of other loyalty than that to the king whom he served. At no time did he demonstrate sympathy for the followers of Lancaster's protege, Wyclyf, nor did he ever act to secure the favour of the court for the London Mayor, John of Northampton.[2] Indeed, de la Pole was closely

[2] Steel says that Pole was in close alliance with Northampton but cites no evidence. *Richard II*, p. 104. An entry in the *Calendar of Letter Books H*, p. 200,

associated from 1384 until 1388 with the successor of John of Northampton in municipal office, Nicholas Brembre, who secured the exile and the imprisonment of his rival.[3]

On foreign policy the duke and the chancellor were in frequent disagreement. Lancaster was a consistent advocate of attack on France by way of Spain. De la Pole favoured a direct assault on France in 1383 and a peace programme in 1384 and 1385. He only came around to the support of the Lancastrian position prior to the expedition of 1386. In all instances he was the spokesman of the court, while Lancaster was on more than one occasion a public critic of the government's behaviour. Finally, when in the parliament of 1386 an attack was made upon the ministers of the crown, de la Pole was its target. This was as it should have been, for he was, if not the chief creator, at least the major executor of royal policy. Among his attackers were the majority of the men who are supposed to have constituted the solid Lancastrian phalanx. It may be concluded that de la Pole's programme was the programme of the king's advisers and not that of a Lancastrian party.

In the politics of the city Lancaster did extend his protection to John of Northampton. He was, however, in no way directly associated with the mayor's anti-monopolist campaign against the grocers and the fishmongers. On the other hand, he was the object of the bitter hatred of the very classes among the London citizenry with whom John of Northampton's programme was most popular. By 1385 he had become reconciled to John's enemy, Nicholas Brembre, who was a member of the king's intimate circle of advisers and whose influence might have been useful in urging the Spanish campaign.

The Spanish démarche provides a probable key to Lancaster's course of action in the years following Richard's accession to the throne. In the words of Edouard Perroy 'the English intervention in Spain was above all else a pretext to mask the dynastic ambitions

indicates that the king had suggested to the city officials reelection of John of Northampton as mayor in October of 1382. Pole did not become chancellor until the following year. I know of no reason for attributing responsibility for such a move to him.

[3] A statement of Pole's intent in 1379 to found a monastery endowed for prayers for relatives, friends and patrons contains no mention of John of Gaunt. *C.C.R.* 1377–1381, p. 228.

of the house of Lancaster.'[4] It was this for which the duke consistently had laboured. There is no valid basis for identifying either him or members of his supposed following as sponsors of ultra-royalist views.

The Lancastrian policy, then, if thus distinguished from the programme of de la Pole and the municipal reforms of John of Northampton is reduced to nothing more than the aggregate of the special interests of a particular great nobleman. The stable party likewise disappears under examination. A few examples will suffice. Henry Percy, Earl of Northumberland, was an opponent of Lancaster in 1376. The two became close associates, to their mutual profit, in 1377. By 1381 they were quarrelling in public and in the ensuing years their animosity became so intense as to threaten to bring disorder to the entire realm. Thomas Mowbray, Earl of Nottingham, was among the group of courtiers specifically accused by Lancaster in 1384 of plotting his assassination. In 1386 Nottingham was a defender of de la Pole against the parliamentary attack, but in 1388 he was one of the five Lords Appellant who demanded the chancellor's death. Thomas, Earl of Buckingham, later Duke of Gloucester, was the acknowledged head of the group who carried on the attack against de la Pole and other courtiers in 1386 and 1388. None of these men supported Lancaster's foreign aspirations prior to 1385. None of them was associated with the duke in any well defined programme of domestic politics. The examples might be multiplied indefinitely until the whole list of the supposed Lancastrians had been tabulated without producing a single name to support the thesis of a permanent organization. Each member of the group, however, at one time or another did act in a common cause with Lancaster. The Lancastrian record, therefore, documents the point that any nobleman could count upon the allegiance of his own retainers and that from time to time mutual self-interest would bring him into close alliance with one or more of the other great magnates. John of Gaunt was the head of no permanent party.

4 *L'Angleterre et le Grand Schisme*, p. 211.

APPENDIX B

The fifteenth century has been the subject of much recent discussion leading to revisions of traditional views. This is not the place to attempt a review of the literature. It is obvious that I tend toward a relatively conventional interpretation of the reigns of the houses of Lancaster and York, and for that matter of the early Tudors as well. Such an interpretation not only lends support to my case for Richard II but is consistent with the facts as we know them. Disorder and violence were common in medieval England. But I am not convinced that the testimony of contemporaries and near contemporaries pointing to an increase through the fifteenth century which seemed to them to be so great as to create qualitatively different conditions should be rejected. A crucial factor was that the crown could offer no hope of redress. I think the best recent work on the period is R. L. Storey's *The End of the House of Lancaster*. Because Mr. Storey's analysis is so judicious, it is necessary to address attention to one of his principal theses which is antithetical to the main lines of my argument concerning Richard II.

The problems of England in the late fourteenth and early fifteenth centuries were too complex to be solved simply by the good fortune of the accession of a strong king. The significance of the character and qualities of the ruler at any time in the Middle Ages should never be underestimated. But it is crucial to the case I have been presenting concerning Richard II that although men of different ambitions and capacities on the throne might substantially have altered the details of the history of the era— and indeed the lives and fortunes of many of their subjects—the obstacles to the establishment of essential good governance would continue to be staggering until sweeping changes in outlook and social structure had taken place.

Richard might personally have come to a happier end if he had been a great warrior like his father or Henry V. But that military prowess alone would have checked the progress of disorder is hard to imagine. Edward III had been a conquering king who ruled in his own right for forty-seven years without having to face either rebellion or serious conspiracy. Yet the tide which Richard's advisers attempted to stem had run strongly against monarchical power throughout his reign. Finally it was not a heroic knight who brought England some semblance of order at the end of the fifteenth century. The conduct of Henry Tudor at Bosworth field can most charitably be described as prudent, and he led Englishmen to no spectacular victories abroad. By the time he bequeathed his throne to a son who aspired to chivalric distinction the prowess of the king on the battlefield was irrelevant. The decisive change was not in the military prowess of the ruler but in his capacity to command the cooperation of his subjects. As events proved the one was not a pre-requisite to the other.

INDEX

Abberbury, Richard, 134, 136, 146
Albemarle, Duke of, *see* Edward of York
d'Angle, Guichard, 12, 146
Anne of Bohemia, 13, 21, 55, 67, 69, 76, 138 n., 144, 169, 170
Anonymous of York, The, 174
Appellants, 44, 45, 46, 49, 51 n., 52, 53, 54, 55, 56, 57, 58, 59, 60, 61, 64, 65, 66, 88, 92, 108, 114, 117, 121, 125, 127, 138, 139, 140, 144
Aquinas, St. Thomas, 153, 154, 159, 160, 162 n.
Aristotle, 150, 152 n., 153, 155, 158, 159, 160, 162, 170, 172
Arundel, *see* Fitz-Alan, Richard; Fitz-Alan, Thomas
Augustine, Saint, 150, 159, 160, 170, 172

Bacon, John, 137
Bagot, William, 94, 135, 166
Baker, W., 114
Baldwin, J. F., 122
Bealknap, Robert, 39, 66 n.
Beauchamp, John of Holt, 34, 36, 45, 54, 136 n.
Beauchamp, Thomas, Earl of Warwick, 24, 43, 61, 65, 66, 74, 77, 81, 83, 85, 98, 119
Beaufort, Henry, Bishop of Lincoln, 96, 169 n.
Beaufort, John, Earl of Somerset, Marquis of Dorset, 77, 84, 96, 101 n., 130
Beaumanoir, Philip, 184 n.
à Becket, Thomas, 175
Berners, James, 45, 54

Blake, John, 40 n., 52, 53, 145
Blake, Nicholas, 54
Blount, Thomas, 132, 133
Boniface VIII, Pope, 151
Bracton or Bratton, Henry of, 158
Bradwardine, Thomas, Archbishop of Canterbury, 159, 160
Brantingham, Thomas, Bishop of Exeter, 65, 66
Braybrook, Robert, Bishop of London, 14, 34, 56 n., 61, 138, 140, 145, 169
Brembre, Nicholas, 23, 42, 44, 48, 51, 52, 59, 62, 81, 144, 145, 171, 188
Bretigny, Peace of (1360), 9
Brinton, Thomas, Bishop of Rochester, 140, 142, 143, 145
Burghill, John, 169
Burgh, William, 39
Burley, Simon, 12, 13, 14, 33, 45, 54, 55, 81, 82, 83, 85, 89 n., 98, 116, 134 n., 136, 143, 146, 155 n., 160, 161, 166 n.
Burley, Walter, 159, 160, 161, 162 n.
Burley, W., 166 n.
Bushy, John, 78, 80, 94, 102, 135, 166, 173, 174, 175

Calveley, Hugh, 133, 143, 173
Capgrave, John, 121, 162 n.
Carey, John, 39 n.
Charles I, 114, 115
Charles II, 115
Charles V, King of France, 118, 159 n.

Charles VI, King of France, 2, 28, 45, 67, 68, 118
Charles VII, King of France, 118
Chaucer, Geoffrey, 134 n., 145, 146, 147
Chaucer, Thomas, 99 n.
Cheshire Guards, 78, 92, 102, 110, 173
Clifford, Richard, 45, 54, 94, 138, 139
Clovis, 168
Cobham, John, Lord, 34, 55, 61, 89, 98
Colchester, William of, Abbot of Westminster, 169, 170, 171, 172
Commission of 1386, 34, 39, 57, 65, 116, 117, 126, 136
Courtenay, William, Bishop of London, Archbishop of Canterbury, 11, 17 n., 24, 25, 34, 47, 62, 68, 130, 164
Creton, Jehan, 121

Dagworth, Nicholas, 45, 54, 134, 135, 136 n., 166
Dalyngrigge, Edward, 133 n., 134, 135, 136 n.
Dalyngrigge, John, 136 n.
Derby, Earl of, *see* Henry IV
Despenser, Henry, Bishop of Norwich, 19, 126, 132 n., 133, 166 n., 171, 172 n.
Despenser, Hugh, and Hugh *fils.*, 3, 36, 44, 86, 97
Despenser, Thomas, Earl of Gloucester, 77, 84, 89, 130
Devereux, John, 17 n., 34, 136 n.

Edmund, Duke of York, 34, 47, 55, 62, 81, 93, 97, 99 n., 101, 102, 106 n., 118, 128, 130, 144, 185 n., 186

Edward, the Confessor, 14
Edward I, 14, 145, 162, 165, 182, 183, 184
Edward II, 3, 4, 14, 30, 35, 39, 41, 69, 75, 86, 97, 115, 125, 127, 128, 180
Edward III, 2, 3, 4, 5, 6, 9, 14, 51 n., 94, 110 n., 116, 118, 125, 128, 129, 131, 141, 145, 158, 162, 164, 190
Edward, Prince of Wales, 12, 13, 14, 17, 55, 128, 130, 131, 132, 133, 134 n., 136 n., 137, 140, 141, 142, 143, 144, 160, 161, 166, 187, 190
Edward, Duke of Albemarle (or Aumale), 77, 84, 99 n., 102, 106 n., 119, 130
Elmham, William, 45, 54, 132, 133, 134, 136 n., 166
Erghum, John, 141, 142, 143
Evesham, Monk of, 120, 121, 170 n.
Exeter, Duke of, *see* Holland, John

Favent, Thomas, 115, 120
Fitz-Alan, Richard, Earl of Arundel, 21, 24, 27, 34, 43, 45, 47, 52, 53, 56 n., 57, 61, 65, 66, 69, 70, 71, 74, 76, 77, 80, 81, 82, 84, 85, 89, 98, 108, 133 n., 136 n., 144
Fitz-Alan, Thomas, Bishop of Ely, Archbishop of York, Archbishop of Canterbury, 24, 27, 30, 34, 36, 57, 58, 65, 66, 68, 70, 72, 77, 78, 80, 83, 84, 85, 101, 103, 105, 106, 108, 119, 169 n.
Fitz-Ralph, Richard, Archbishop of Armagh, 140, 141
Flete, William, 142

Fordham, John, Bishop of Durham, Bishop of Ely, 14, 57, 137, 138, 140, 145
Froissart, John, 121, 135, 136
Fulthorp, Roger, 39

Gaveston, Piers, 36, 44
Gilbert, John, Bishop of Hereford, 56 n., 65
Giles of Rome, 144, 154, 155, 156, 157, 158, 161, 162 n., 163, 172 n., 173
Gloucester, Duke of, see Thomas of Woodstock; Earl of, see Despenser, Thomas
'Good' Parliament of 1376, 2, 9, 10, 16, 18, 23, 31, 186, 187
Gournay, Matthew, 132, 133, 135
Gower, John, 147, 148, 149
Great Revolt of 1381, 16, 17, 18, 20, 22, 27, 55, 126
Greene, Henry, 94, 102, 135, 166
Grosseteste, Robert, 159

Hales, John, 19
Hallam, Henry, 117, 118
Hardyng, John, 120
Harewell, John, Bishop of Bath and Wells, 137
Hawkwood, John, 132, 133, 134 n., 136, 143
Haxey, Thomas, 71, 72, 73, 74, 79, 80, 97, 119, 166
Henry II, 174
Henry III, 162
Henry IV, 1, 8, 45, 46, 54, 61, 66, 70, 81, 82 n., 84, 85, 88, 89, 90, 91, 93, 94, 95, 98, 99, 100, 101, 102, 103, 104, 105, 106, 107, 108, 109, 110, 111, 113, 117, 118, 119, 122, 123 n., 125, 133 n., 138, 139, 144,

147, 148, 167, 171, 172, 174, 175, 180 n., 183, 184, 185 n., 186
Henry V, 96, 113, 118, 133 n., 137 n., 161 n., 169, 172, 190
Henry VI, 113, 118
Henry VII, 111, 112, 175, 182 n., 191
Henry VIII, 183, 184, 191
Hereford, Duke of, see Henry IV
Hilton, Reginald, 14
Hoccleve, Thomas, 161 n.
Holinshed, Raphael, 160, 161 n.
Holland, John, Earl of Huntingdon, Duke of Exeter, 13, 56, 65, 75, 77, 84, 88, 93, 99 n., 103, 107, 128, 130
Holland, Thomas, Earl of Kent, 13, 39 n., 62, 128, 130
Holland, Thomas, the younger, Earl of Kent, Duke of Surrey, 77, 84, 89, 99 n., 103, 107, 130
Holt, John, 39
Hostiensis, 152
Howard, R., 115
Hume, David, 116, 117, 118
Hundred Years' War, 9, 131
Huntingdon, Earl of, see Holland, John

Innocent III, Pope, 174
Innocent IV, Pope, 152
Ireland, Duke of, see DeVere, Robert
Isabella of France, 67, 68

James II, 115
James of Viterbo, 157 n.
Joan of Kent, Princess of Wales, 11, 12, 16, 128, 134 n., 137, 138
Joao I, King of Portugal, 1, 178

John, King, 113, 163 n., 174
John, King of France, 118
John of Gaunt, Duke of Lancaster, 3, 9, 10, 11, 12, 16, 17, 18, 20, 22, 23, 24, 25, 27, 28, 53, 56, 65, 66, 72, 74, 81, 82, 91, 93, 95, 96 n., 98, 118, 123 n., 127, 130, 131, 132 n., 134 n., 164, 175, 186, 187, 188, 189
John of Northampton, 23, 42, 43, 66, 186, 187, 188, 189
John of Paris, 154, 155
Judicial Opinions of 1387 at Shrewsbury and Nottingham, 38, 46, 49, 53, 54, 74, 80, 86, 87, 139, 145

Kent, Earls of, see Holland, Thomas
Kilwardby, Robert, Archbishop of Canterbury, 159
Knighton, Henry of, 120, 121
Knollys, Robert, 131, 133, 173

Lakyngheth, John, 120, 121, 171
Lancaster, Duke of, see John of Gaunt
Langland, William, 147, 148, 149
Lingard, John, 117, 118, 120
Latimer, William, Lord, 31
Lincoln, John, 45, 54, 139, 166, 169 n.
Lockton, John, 39
Louis IX, King of France, 87 n.
Lucas de Penna, 154 n.
Lyons, Richard, 31

Macaulay, T. B., 118
March, Earls of, see Mortimer, Edmund and Mortimer, Roger

de la Mare, Thomas, Abbot of St. Albans, 141, 142
Marsilio of Padua, 153, 158
Martin, Godfrey, 47
Maudeleyn, Richard, 169
Medford, Richard, Bishop of Chichester, Bishop of Salisbury, 45, 54, 139, 169
'Merciless' Parliament (1388), 47, 57, 61, 63, 64, 65, 66, 81, 84, 86, 97, 115, 138, 139, 144, 159
Merke, Thomas, Bishop of Carlisle, 107, 110, 116, 169, 170, 172
Modus Tenendi Parliamentum, 122 n.
Mone, Guy, Bishop of St. Davids, 94, 169 n.
Montagu, John, 14, 130, 136
Montagu, John, Earl of Salisbury, 77, 89, 93, 99 n., 102, 107, 130, 136 n., 166
Moote, John, 171, 172 n.
Mortimer, Edmund, Earl of March, 96
Mortimer, Roger, Earl of March, 51 n., 96, 100
Mortimer, Thomas, 56 n., 81, 84, 86
Mowbray, Thomas, Earl of Nottingham, Duke of Norfolk, 13, 45, 56 n., 61, 66, 70, 75, 77, 81, 82, 84, 85, 88, 89, 90, 91, 93, 95, 98, 100, 119, 130, 134 n., 144, 174, 189
Mowbray, John, 13

Neville, Alexander, Archbishop of York, 23, 34, 36, 44, 48, 51, 53, 57, 67, 81, 84, 130, 145
Neville, Ralph, Earl of Westmoreland, 62, 84, 101, 145, 173
Neville, William, 130, 145

Norfolk, Duke of, *see* Mowbray, Thomas
Northumberland, Earl of, *see* Percy, Henry
Nottingham, Earl of, *see* Mowbray, Thomas

Ockham, William of, 153, 158, 159, 160, 162
Oman, C. W. C., 120
Oxford, Earls of, *see* De Vere, Aubrey and Robert

Pakington, William, 14, 137
Parliament of Cambridge (1388), 57, 58, 59
Peckham, John, Archbishop of Canterbury, 159
Pedro I, King of Castille, 2, 161 n., 182 n.
Percy, Henry, Earl of Northumberland, 43, 62, 66, 101, 103, 104, 110 n., 133 n., 164, 173, 185, 189
Percy, Henry, *fils.*, 56 n., 110 n.
Percy, Thomas, Earl of Worcester 78, 84, 93, 94, 102, 110 n., 130
Philip IV, King of France, 154, 161 n., 182, 183, 184 n.
Pierre de Blois, 174
Plucknett, T. F. T., 122
de la Pole, Michael, Earl of Suffolk, 13, 21, 25, 26, 28, 29, 30, 31, 32, 35, 36, 39, 44, 48, 51, 53, 60, 61, 67, 73, 81, 85, 116, 127, 134 n., 138, 140, 145, 186, 187, 188, 189
Radcot Bridge, Battle of (1387), 45, 47, 58, 61, 125, 164
Raddington, Baldwin, 13, 136
Raleigh, Walter, 114, 115, 120

Richard II, 1, 2, 3, 5, 6, 7, 8, 10, 11, 12, 13, 14, 15, 17, 18, 19, 20, 21, 22, 24, 25, 26, 28, 29, 30, 31, 32, 33, 34, 36, 37, 38, 39, 40, 41, 42, 43, 44, 45, 46, 47, 48, 49, 50, 51, 52, 55, 56, 57, 60, 63, 64, 65, 66, 67, 68, 69, 70, 71, 72, 73, 74, 75, 76, 77, 78, 79, 80, 81, 82, 83, 84, 85, 86, 87, 88, 89, 90, 91, 92, 93, 94, 95, 96, 97, 98, 99, 100, 101, 102, 103, 104, 105, 106, 107, 108, 109, 110, 111, 112, 113, 114, 115, 116, 117, 118, 119, 120, 121, 122, 123, 124, 125, 126, 127, 128, 129, 130, 131, 132, 133, 135, 136, 137, 138, 139, 140, 141, 142, 143, 144, 145, 146, 147, 148, 158, 161, 162, 164, 165, 166, 167, 168, 169, 170, 171, 172, 173, 174, 175, 176, 177, 178, 179, 180, 181, 182, 183, 184, 185, 186, 187, 188, 190, 191
Richard III, 182 n.
Rickhill, William, 83
Rushook, Thomas, Bishop of Chichester, 53, 57, 138, 139, 169
Russell, John, 94, 135

St. John, Henry, Viscount Bolingbroke, 116
Salisbury, John, 45, 54
Salisbury, Earl of, *see* Montagu, John
Salutati, Coluccio, 156 n.
Scrope, Richard, 22, 32, 34, 45, 47, 61, 145
Scrope, William, Earl of Wiltshire, 77, 84, 89, 93, 94, 99 n., 102, 130, 166, 173, 174, 175

Segrave, Hugh, 17 n., 136
Shakespeare, William, 8, 107, 113, 114, 115, 118, 124, 172
Simnel, Lambert, 175
Simon of Sudbury, Archbishop of Canterbury, 14, 15, 16, 19, 143, 145, 167
Skirlaw, Walter, Bishop of Lichfield, Bishop of Durham, 56 n., 138, 140, 142, 145
Stafford, Edmund, Bishop of Exeter, 65, 68, 79, 86, 94, 108 n., 130, 166, 167
Stafford, Edward, 183
Stafford, Sir Richard, 14
Statute of Treason, (1352), 41, 42, 44
Steel, Anthony, 122
Stokes, Alan, 137
Stubbs, W., 119, 120
Stury, Richard, 134, 135, 136 n.
Suffolk, Earl of, see de la Pole, Michael
Surrey, Duke of, see Holland, Thomas
Swaffham, John, Bishop of Bangor, 138, 139
Swynford, Katherine, 67, 74, 95, 99 n.

Tait, James, 120
Thomas of Woodstock, Earl of Buckingham, Duke of Gloucester, 24, 26, 27, 30, 33, 34, 38, 43, 45, 46, 47, 50, 52, 53, 54, 55, 56, 57, 60, 61, 64, 65, 66, 69, 70, 71, 73, 74, 76, 77, 78, 80, 81, 82, 83, 84, 85, 89, 91, 97, 98, 108, 116, 118, 119, 120, 128, 136 n., 144, 161 n., 171, 186, 189
Tout, T. F., 122, 123

Trefnant, John, Bishop of Hereford, 170 n.
Tresilian, Robert, 39, 44, 48, 51, 52, 53, 89 n., 144, 145
Trevor, John, Bishop of St. Asaph, 121 n.
Trussell, J., 114
Tryvet, Thomas, 45, 54, 132, 133, 134 n., 135
Tydeman of Winchcombe, Bishop of Worcester, 169, 170 n.
Tyler, Wat, 19, 126

Urban, VI, Pope, 25, 57, 59, 62, 83, 109
Usk, Adam of, 120, 170 n.
Usk, Thomas, 53

Vache, Philip, 134 n., 146, 166
de Vere, Aubrey, Earl of Oxford, 14, 130, 134 n., 136, 166, 172 n.
de Vere, Robert, Earl of Oxford, Marquis of Dublin, Duke of Ireland, 13, 25, 29, 33, 37, 44, 45, 48, 51, 54, 67, 116, 125, 130
Villiers, George, Duke of Buckingham, 116
Visconti, Giangaleazzo, 135

Waldby, John, 140, 141
Waldby, Robert, Archbishop of Dublin, Bishop of Chichester, Archbishop of York, 68, 133 n., 137, 139, 140, 142, 169
Walden, Roger, Archbishop of Canterbury, 169
Wallon, Henri, 118, 119, 120
Walsingham, Thomas, 120, 121, 127, 141

Waltham, John, Bishop of Salisbury, 138, 139, 140, 169 n., 171
Walworth, William, 19, 20
Warwick, *see* Beauchamp, Thomas, Earl of
Wenceslas, King of Bohemia, 75
Wiltshire, Earl of, *see* Scrope, William

Worcester, Earl of, *see* Percy, Thomas
Wrattinge, William, 171
Wyclyf, John, 6, 11, 167 n., 174, 186, 187
Wykeham, William of, Bishop of Winchester, 34, 56 n., 62, 65, 66, 81, 101 n.